The Uncertain Superpower

Berliner Schriften zur Internationalen Politik

Herausgegeben vom Forschungsinstitut der
Deutschen Gesellschaft für Auswärtige Politik, Berlin

Diese Studie wurde ermöglicht
durch die großzügige Unterstützung
der Fritz Thyssen Stiftung

The Uncertain Superpower

Domestic Dimensions of U.S. Foreign Policy after the Cold War

Bernhard May · Michaela Hönicke Moore
(Hrsg.)

Leske + Budrich, Opladen 2003

Deutsche Gesellschaft für Auswärtige Politik e.V. D-10787 Berlin, Rauchstr. 18, Telefon (030) 25 42 31-0 / Fax: (030) 25 42 31-16; Internet: http://www.dgap.org

Die Deutsche Gesellschaft für Auswärtige Politik hat nach ihrer Satzung die Aufgabe, die Probleme der internationalen, besonders der europäischen Politik, Sicherheit und Wirtschaft zu erörtern und ihre wissenschaftliche Untersuchung zu fördern, die Dokumentation über diese Forschungsfragen zu sammeln und das Verständnis für internationale Fragen durch Vorträge, Studiengruppen und Veröffentlichungen anzuregen und zu vertiefen. Sie unterhält zu diesem Zweck ein Forschungsinstitut, eine Bibliothek und Dokumentationsstelle sowie die Zeitschrift »Internationale Politik«. Die Deutsche Gesellschaft für Auswärtige Politik bezieht als solche aufgrund ihrer Satzung keine eigene Stellung zu internationalen Problemen. Die in den Veröffentlichungen geäußerten Meinungen sind die der Autoren.

Gedruckt auf alterungsbeständigem und säurefreiem Papier

Die Deutsche Bibliothek – CIP-Einheitsaufnahme
Ein Titeldatensatz für diese Publikation ist bei
Der Deutschen Bibliothek erhältlich.

ISBN: 3-8100-3437-1

Satz: Leske + Budrich, Opladen
Druck: DruckPartner Rübelmann, Hemsbach
Printed in Germany

Contents

Notes on the Contributors

Thomas E. Graham, Jr. is associate director of the policy planning staff, Department of State, Washington, DC. He was formerly senior associate, Carnegie Endowment for International Peace, Washington, DC.

Petra Holtrup is research fellow at the German Council on Foreign Relations (DGAP), Berlin, Germany

Michaela Hönicke Moore, is a DAAD Visiting Assistant Professor in European History and Transatlantic Relations at the University of North Carolina at Chapel Hill. She was formerly a research fellow at the German Council on Foreign Relations (DGAP), Berlin, Germany

Charles A. Kupchan is a senior fellow and director for Europe studies at the Council on Foreign Relations and Associate Professor of International Relations, School of Foreign Service and Department of Government, Georgetown University, Washington DC.

James M. Lindsay is senior research fellow in the Foreign Policy Studies Program at the Brookings Institution, Washington, DC.

Edward C. Luck is director and professor at the Center on International Organization, School of International and Public Affairs, Columbia University, New York

Bernhard May is deputy director of the Research Institute at the German Council on Foreign Relations (DGAP), Berlin, Germany

Peter W. Rodman has served as Assistant Secretary of Defense for International Security Affairs since July 16, 2001. He was formerly Director of National Security Programs, The Nixon Center, Washington DC.

Peter Rudolf is senior research fellow at the Research Institute for International Affairs (SWP), Berlin, Germany

David Ryan is principal lecturer in History at De Montfort University, Leicester, United Kingdom

Gebhard Schweigler is professor of international relations and national security at the National War College, Washington, DC

Susan L. Shirk is research director at the Institute on Global Conflict and Cooperation, University of California, San Diego.

Paul S. Shoup is professor emeritus, Department of Government and Foreign Affairs, University of Virginia

Stanley R. Sloan is President, Vienna International Consultants. He was formerly senior analyst at Congressional Research Service, Washington, DC

Bernhard May

Introduction: The Uncertain Superpower 'After September 11th'

"For the United States, September 11, 2001,
cut a deep dividing line in our history –
a change of eras as sharp and clear as
Pearl Harbor or the first day of the Berlin Blockade.
There can be no lasting security in a world
at the mercy of terrorists – for my nation or for any nation."
President George W. Bush

Speech at the German Bundestag,
Berlin, May 23, 2002.

The terrorist attacks of September 11, 2001 ushered in a period of profound change in global politics, revealing new threats and creating fresh opportunities for international cooperation. The priorities and preoccupations of US leaders and the US public shifted dramatically in the ensuing months. The Bush administration's attention shifted fundamentally and understandably focused primarily on the global campaign against terrorism, necessarily relegating other issues, including the future of Sino-American relations, to the sidelines. While the impact of September 11 has been less dramatic in Europe and Asia, the reorientation of US policy has had worldwide repercussions, prompting a strategic realignment between Russia and the West and concerted cooperation to thwart future terrorist attacks.

The challenges associated with managing this global transformation are all the more daunting because they come at a time of fundamental change in Europe and the transatlantic relationship. With the increasing economic, political and security integration of the member states of the European Union (EU) and prospective expansion of the EU's borders to embrace the states of eastern and central Europe, the United States will be faced with a Europe that is more united, yet more complex and fractured. The United States and Europe will continue to cooperate in Europe through the North Atlantic Treaty Organization. But the transatlantic agenda is expanding to include transnational and regional problems that extend far beyond Europe's borders.

These developments coincide with a period of increasing friction in US-European relations and a growing perception on both sides of the Atlantic that cooperation between the United States and Europe has become less important in a post Cold War world of fluid coalitions and alignments. Whether the transatlantic partnership will prove equal to these challenges depends, in part, on the ability and willingness of both partners to adapt to changes in the world and in their respective positions to one another. Likewise they must redefine the parameters and expectations of their mutual cooperation.

The terror attacks of September 11, 2001 in New York, Washington, DC, and Pennsylvania killed more than 3,000 people from more than 60 countries. "9/11" – as it is called in the States – was not only a terror attack on the United States, it was felt by many people as a terror attack on all civilized countries. The French newspaper *Le Monde* put it succinctly in its headline the day after September 11: "We are all Americans".

Romano Prodi, President of the European Commission, spoke for Europe when he declared the day after the terror attacks: "This barbaric attack was directed against the free world and our common values. It is a watershed event and life will never be quite the same again. European institutions and governments will work closely together with our American friends and partners in the defense of freedom. (...) In the darkest hours of European history, the Americans stood by us. We stand by them now."

Immediately after the dramatic events of September 11, 2001, Europe showed itself to be a loyal ally of the United States. Forgotten were the transatlantic quarrels over issues like the Kyoto Protocol, the future of the Anti-Ballistic Missile (ABM) Treaty, and the role of the International Criminal Court (ICC). For a moment, all attention was focused on the fight against a common enemy challenging the fundamentals of western civilization.

Since President George W. Bush moved into the White House in January of 2001, transatlantic relations have been on a roller-coaster ride. During the election campaign, the Bush team favored a more unilateralist and isolationist approach in foreign policy. This was seen as an effort to formulate a post Cold War US foreign policy. When President Bush told the world in the first half of 2001 that the United States would withdraw from the Kyoto Protocol, would cancel the ABM Treaty, would fight instead of support the International Criminal Court, and would no longer play the role of peacemaker in regional conflicts from the Korean Peninsula to the Middle East, many analysts argued that this would be the beginning of a new phase of American isolationist and unilateralist foreign policy.

There were two strong elements pushing towards a new isolationism and even a nationalistic unilateralism in American foreign policy. First, domestic issues were given top priority – Bush promised the voters to be a "domestic President". This was, however, nothing new. After all it was President Clinton who won the presidential elections in 1992 with his campaign mantra "It's the economy, stupid!" Second, there was a growing unilateralism within the republican party, especially within those groups that supported President Bush.

There was a strong backlash in Europe against this more unilateralist and more isolationist foreign policy of the Bush administration. Transatlantic relations went through a difficult phase in the Spring of 2001, each side criticizing the other for doing the wrong thing and for damaging transatlantic relations. In Europe, President Bush was not seen as a world leader, but rather as the governor from Texas. Europeans criticized the Bush administration for not accepting the role as the only remaining superpower and for not accepting the global responsibility linked to being a global power. Transatlantic relations were at a low point in June of 2001 when President Bush came to Europe the first time.

All of that changed overnight with the terror attacks of September 11, 2001. Millions of Europeans demonstrated their solidarity with the American people. In Berlin, for example, approximately 200,000 people took part in a demonstration in front of the Brandenburg Gate on September 14 to show their solidarity with the American people. International terrorism was the new common challenge. For several months it seemed like the old transatlantic quarrels would be forgotten. There was a new spirit in transatlantic relations, a new commitment to fight common enemies and protect common values. The question was, how long would it last.

The change came at the beginning of 2002. The old and unsolved problems were put on the agenda again. And worse, it became obvious that Europe and the United States had profound differences about how to respond to the longer-term challenge of international terrorism. This was not the case fighting the Taliban regime in Afghanistan. But when the Bush administration began pushing for an alliance to change the regime in Iraq, most European countries supported neither a military action in Iraq, nor a unilateral action without a resolution from the United Nations Security Council (UNSC).

The struggle went on for months and created a transatlantic crisis in August 2002 when Vice President Cheney argued in a speech that unilateral military action would be needed to change the regime in Iraq and to wait any longer would be too dangerous. European governments and especially the German Chancellor, Gerhard Schröder, rejected such an approach. Any action in Iraq would need UNSC approval – and regime change would not be a legitimate goal for any UNSC resolution. So one year after "9/11", transatlantic relations were in a state of crisis – no more demonstrations to show solidarity with the American people, but instead demonstrations against President Bush and against a war with Iraq.

The terror attacks of September 11, 2001 changed the world but "9/11" changed the way Americans look at the world even more. Many Americans view "9/11" in the same way as the attack on Pearl Harbor in 1941. Yet, with "9/11", came a new sensitivity – the loss of the feeling of invulnerability. These views led the public to support strong measures to get the people who were responsible for "9/11" and to punish those supporting international terrorism. Furthermore, new security threats, especially the spread of weapons of mass destruction, are seen as an imminent threat and there is broad support in the United States for the Bush administration to fight those new security threats.

These new security threats are also linked to globalization. We are living in the age of globalization. And politics is global. "9/11" is a good example of the dark side of a globalizing world. But there are also the threats of the proliferation of weapons of mass destruction, religious fanaticism, climate change, global financial and economic crises, as well as the challenges of a growing digital divide and a grotesque global inequality. We are witnessing the beginning of a new era with new opportunities and new challenges. The international community will have to find answers to these daunting questions. In this globalizing world, what role should America play? What are the key challenges in the 21st century? How can national interests be defined and protected in a globalizing world?

After the end of the Cold War, the United States is the only remaining superpower, some even call it a hyperpower pointing to the fact that there is no challenger in terms of economic, military and political power. Nevertheless, in a globalizing world, not even the most powerful country can solve global problems like terrorism, environmental degradation, and the proliferation of weapons of mass destruction alone without involving other nations. In his new book, *The Paradox of American Power*, Joseph S. Nye argues that the threat of terrorism is merely the most alarming example of why the United States must seek constructive relations with nations weak and strong. As technology spreads and non-governmental organizations ranging from transnational corporations to terrorists increase their power, American leadership must reorient itself toward the global community. In a globalizing world, Nye points out, hard power is no longer sufficient; what is needed is more "soft power", i.e. power that derives from the appeal of culture, values, and institutions.

Reading Nye's analysis and comparing it with the foreign policy of President Bush, it looks like the two are living in different worlds. Obviously, Joseph Nye does not have many supporters in the Bush administration. It will be a difficult learning process for the Bush administration to understand that in a globalizing world many global challenges cannot be solved with military power, or at least cannot be solved with military power alone.

In this book we have published selected papers that were first presented at a conference at the German Council on Foreign Relations in Berlin in the Fall of 2000. The fundamental questions we wanted to discuss at this conference were: What role should America play in the world? What kind of foreign policy would the United States pursue in a post Cold War world? How would domestic issues influence US foreign policy after the end of the Cold War? And would America, after the threat from the Cold War was gone, move towards a more isolationist and unilateral foreign policy?

Most of the papers were updated and rewritten in Spring 2001. Just when we wanted to publish them, the terrorist attacks of September 11, 2001 occurred. At that time we decided to postpone the publication to see if "9/11" might have outdated some of the papers. Some of the papers have been rewritten after September 11, 2001, but not all. One year after "9/11", the discussion on American foreign policy has again focused on some of the old issues, while also integrating some new themes.

We have an excellent group of experts presenting their views on various issues of American foreign policy in this book. In the first part, there are four papers on constitutional and institutional dimensions. Stanley Sloan focuses on the relations between the White House and Congress. Michaela Hönicke Moore discusses the democratic dilemma of US foreign policy making. James Lindsay analyzes the apathetic internationalism and the changed politics of American foreign policy. Gebhard Schweigler examines the Jeffersonian and Jacksonian traditions in American foreign policy.

In the second part of the book, three papers cover US leadership and the reform of Western security institutions. Peter Rodman focuses on the domestic factors in the US reaction to ESDP and NATO enlargement. Charles Kupchan analyzes American views on the rise of Europe. Peter Rudolf discusses US leadership and NATO enlargement.

In the third part, four authors discuss US leadership in crisis. David Ryan discusses the interventions in the Persian Gulf and Kosovo and especially the role of Congress and the media. Paul Shoup explores the role of domestic factors in crisis management for the Balkans during the 1990s. Thomas E. Graham, Jr. focuses on US leadership and domestic factors in dealing with Russia. And Susan Shirk analyzes how domestic politics have shaped the US approach to China.

In the final part, Edward C. Luck focuses on American exceptionalism and leadership in international organizations. And Petra Holtrup analyzes the lack of US leadership in climate change diplomacy.

Furthermore, we have included a list of selected books for further reading as well as some information about the authors.

We are very grateful to the Fritz Thyssen Foundation for the generous support of this project. We owe particular thanks to Scott Brunstetter for editing the papers.

[illegible] the papers were updated and [illegible] in spring 2002, [illegible] the terrorist attacks of September 11, 2001 [illegible]. At that time, we decided [illegible] the public [illegible] might have [illegible] some of the papers. [illegible] September 11, 2001, [illegible]

[illegible] issues of American [illegible] papers [illegible]

[illegible]

[illegible] Congress [illegible]

[illegible]

[illegible]

[illegible]

Part I
Constitutional and Institutional Dimensions: Executive, Legislative, Public Opinion and the Media

Stanley R. Sloan

Constitutional and Institutional Dimensions: White House-Congress Relations After the End of the 'Imperial Presidency'

The Congressional-Executive "Balance"

As we discovered in the controversy over the outcome of the November 2000 U.S. presidential election, constitutional law is open for political as well as legal interpretation. I am not a constitutional law expert, and I address this topic simply as someone who has spent most of his professional life in and around the institutions that make and implement U.S. foreign policy. For almost 25 years, I observed and participated in the role of the Congress in foreign policy. I start my discussion of this topic from the following premise: There is no other deliberative body in the world that is as powerful and independent as the United States Congress. The leading role of the President in U.S. foreign policy is carefully balanced by powers the Constitution allocated to the Congress, but the main responsibility – including credit and blame – continues to rest with the President.

We have just experienced a period, in the wake of the September 11, 2001 terrorist attacks on the United States, in which a "wartime" atmosphere distorted the normal relationship between the President, Congress, and the American people. All rallied around the President as the nation came under attack and organized a response. That period, however, is ending, and more normal patterns of behavior will assert themselves, at least until the next crisis.

Our "founding fathers," who fought to escape from British colonial rule, established a democratic system to ensure that no "King" – domestic or foreign – would ever again rule over the American people. The system was carefully designed to mitigate against an "imperial presidency," even if it allowed for strong presidential leadership in times of crisis.

The U.S. Constitution established a careful set of checks and balances to ensure that outcome. Part of that system was designed to give the Congress sufficient influence over both domestic and foreign policy to keep any President from acting in an authoritarian manner. The Constitution ensured that power over foreign and defense policy would be shared between the President and the Congress.

Today, some experts argue that the balance of power has shifted too far toward the Congress. Others argue that the Congress has in recent decades allowed the President to usurp most of the Congressional war powers, for example, by engaging U.S. forces in what is perhaps euphemistically called "operations other than war." The current debate after the events of September 11 has focused mainly on the second tendency. The main concern has been that actions by the executive branch to respond to the threat of future terrorist actions could undermine constitutionally guaranteed individual rights.

It is first and foremost the responsibility of the President to lead on foreign and defense policy. The Congress can – and should – critique and offer alternatives to the President's approach. The power of the Congress, however, rests primarily in its constitutional responsibility to provide the resources for government programs. Its responsibility therefore includes judging whether or not to support programs proposed by the President with the resources requested by the President.

From time to time, the Congress uses this role to change or defeat Administration proposals. The bottom line is that the system works best when the final outcome is based on a bipartisan (and bi-branch) consensus or on a compromise with which both the President and Congress can live.

The Constitution created a permanent tension between Congress and the President in the area of foreign and defense policy. The founding fathers clearly intended that the Congress be an important contributor to the shaping of U.S. national security policy. They made the President the "Commander in Chief," but they gave the Congress the responsibility for raising (and financing) military forces, declaring war, and approving treaties – through the Senate's responsibility to give its "advice and consent" to international treaties.

In addition, Congress, in Article 1/8, was given the power to "regulate commerce with foreign nations." Most importantly, for all foreign and defense needs, the Congress had to raise and allocate the money required for those programs. The "power of the purse" is in the hands of the Congress, not the President.

Evolving Congressional/Executive Relations

Discussion of the role of Congress is framed by two classic and sharply-contrasting cases of Congressional-Executive relations in foreign policy. The first case occurred at the end of the First World War when President Woodrow Wilson played such an important role internationally in organizing the post-war peace around the League of Nations. But Wilson did not do what was necessary to bring the Congress along with this plan. Wilson's failure to get the Congress on board contributed to the failure of that organization and, ultimately, of the peace.

The counter-case followed the Second World War. The Roosevelt Administration involved influential U.S. Senators in the San Francisco conference that shaped the United Nations and U.S. participation in the UN. The Truman Administration, following that example, involved the Senate in preparation of the Treaty of Washington that established the transatlantic Alliance. The Administration's careful courting of the Senate also helped ensure a successful outcome in the 1951 "Great Debate" in the United States which concluded with Senate approval of the Administration's decision to deploy significant military forces to Europe in response to the Soviet threat.

These two cases establish the broad lessons about how a U.S. Administration should, and how an Administration should not, handle foreign and defense policy with the Congress. A President ignores the power of Congress at his peril. Successful policy requires thorough consultations, co-decision making or co-option, and, usually, compromise.

During the 1950s and into the 1960s, the Soviet threat and the policy of containment helped preserve a broad bipartisan consensus on foreign and defense policy. But the war in Vietnam disrupted that consensus, creating new mistrust between Congress and the President. The war led to the "War Powers" legislation, which was supposed to force future Administrations to pay attention to the Congress regarding overseas military commitments.

In spite of the broad containment consensus, the tension remained. Henry Kissinger, who served as President Nixon's National Security Advisor and then as Secretary of State, had no tolerance for the Congressional role in foreign policy. (I personally think this attitude clearly exposed his European roots and preference for Machiavellian policy making methodology.) Harvard historian Ernest May tells the story of Kissinger proclaiming to a small group of academics that "The Senate doesn't understand foreign policy." According to May's story, when he related this to some Hill staffers, one of them responded, "Kissinger does not understand America."

Kissinger may already have been reacting with frustration to some of the trends that, since his time as Secretary of State, have made it more difficult to contain foreign policy decisionmaking inside an executive branch box.

Several factors have tended to make the U.S. foreign policy decision-making process more chaotic. They include:

- Global interdependence, which makes many aspects of U.S. daily life and national security more dependent on international developments. This has led to what some people call:
- The phenomenon of "intermestics," a term coined to describe the increasing interrelationship between domestic and international issues. Tip O'Neil, former Speaker of the U.S. House of Representatives, used to say that "all politics are local." Now, it could be said that the dynamic is a two-way street and that "all local politics are global," as Congressional Research Service expert Walter Oleszak is fond of observing.
- another factor is the communications explosion, both in timeliness and breadth of coverage. Any citizen (and any Member of Congress) can be

as well informed on many issues as the President simply by watching CNN and other news services. Much of diplomacy is conducted in public, as is much of the work of the Congress.

- The consequences include: many more players in foreign policy in the executive branch and in Congress. Most U.S. government agencies have some vested interest in, or responsibility for, some aspect of foreign and defense policy.
- In Congress, virtually all committees have an interest; virtually all Members have some perspective; plus, the communications explosion and other factors have dispersed power in the Congress. Congressional leaders do not dominate the process; they have to work hard to try to build consensus even within their own party.

The Foreign Policy Struggle

Against this backdrop, I will address some of the issues that my colleagues and I explored in the Georgetown University survey entitled *The Foreign Policy Struggle: Congress and the President in the 1990s and Beyond.*[1] That study observed that, in recent years, relations between the executive and legislative branches of government over the direction and content of U.S. foreign policy have been marked by partisanship, disputes, deadlock and ill-feelings.

Some disagreement, of course, is inevitable in our system of Constitutionally shared power, especially at a time of politically divided government when, as during the Clinton Administration, Democrats controlled the White House and Republicans controlled both houses of Congress. But a number of factors suggest that a deteriorating Congressional-executive relationship increasingly affects the U.S. ability to advance its interests internationally.

This apparent decline in common purpose came at a time when the United States found itself as the only remaining global power. Its world role may be described as "indispensable," as the Clinton Administration claimed, and it may often be able to act alone, as the George W. Bush Administration clearly believes. But, at the same time, growing interdependence, or globalization, has made U.S. interests more dependent on economic, political and military developments around the world.

The contemporary security environment is much less predictable than it was during the Cold War: threats of terrorist groups armed with weapons of

1 Stanley Sloan, Mary Locke, Casimir A. Yost, *The Foreign Policy Struggle, Congress and the President in the 1990s and Beyond*, Institute for the Study of Diplomacy, Georgetown University, 2000.

mass destruction; the financial crisis in Asia, and Russia's political and economic weakness already have posed unique challenges to stability. Conflicts in the Balkans, the Middle East and elsewhere continue to raise issues about the appropriate role of force in international relations and U.S. foreign policy. Coherent international responses to such issues require effective U.S. leadership, and failure to respond in a timely and decisive manner could seriously undermine U.S. economic, political, and security interests.

New factors at work

Constitutional scholar E.S. Corwin has observed that the Constitution provides an "invitation to struggle" for the privilege of directing American foreign policy. The question is whether this struggle between the branches is exhibiting some new features or is merely a continuation of past competition. In my judgment, *there are new factors at work*, which make the struggle between the branches more intense than in the recent past, with potential consequences for American foreign policy.

Over the last decade, the Congress ultimately supported, or at least did not block, many major foreign policy initiatives of Presidents Bush (1989-1992) and Clinton (1993-2000). These included: the Gulf War, North American Free Trade Area, aid to Russia, sending peacekeeping troops to Haiti and Bosnia, and NATO enlargement. The Congress, with the Senate controlled by the opposition Democrats, almost unanimously supported the decision of President George W. Bush (2001-) to attack the Taliban regime in Afghanistan for hosting the al Qaeda terrorist organization. The Congress has continued to support the positioning of 100,000 U.S. troops forward deployed both in Asia and in Europe.

However, Congressional opposition to Clinton Administration foreign policy initiatives increased perceptibly in the late 1990s. The Congress resisted Administration policy approaches on funding for Mexico, the United Nations, and the International Monetary Fund. Congress was unwilling to provide "fast track" trade negotiating authority to the President. Congressional action produced deep cuts in budgets for foreign affairs agencies and programs. The Congress was resistant to executive branch policies with respect to North Korea and frequently differed with the Administration on U.N. peacekeeping.

The Congress has been particularly energetic in passing sanctions against other countries – frequently despite executive branch objections, although more often than not acceded to by the President. The United States according to one count, has imposed sanctions 104 times since World War II, 61 of them during President Clinton's term of office. This resort to sanctions seems to reflect a Congressional preference for unilateral American foreign policies over cooperative or multilateral approaches.

These examples hardly exhaust the list of Congressional actions in the post-Cold War era. Taken together, they seemed to indicate a substantial shift of initiative in foreign affairs from the executive to the legislative branch, changing the relative relationship between the foreign policy authority of the two branches of government, at least in normal, non-crisis periods.

Many reasons can be offered for this shift of initiative and, consequently, authority, including the fact that the American people appear broadly to support an internationalist U.S. role in the world but, since the end of the Cold War, there has been no defining and unifying international threat to focus the attention of the American electorate and their elected representatives. In this circumstance, Americans have not generally felt intensely about foreign policy questions.

This lack of intensity has had two consequences: it enhanced the influence of special interest groups which have money and intensity, and it diminished the need for Members of Congress to concern themselves with broad public opinion on foreign policy issues. Whether or not the war on terrorism will change all of this remains to be seen.

Furthermore, there has been no national consensus as to America's role in a post-Cold War world. According to Jeremy Rosner, in his book the *New Tug of War*, "As long as it continues, today's general lack of a consensus on America's security threats will tend to strengthen the hand of Congress in national security relative to the executive." The argument here is that domestic priorities and constituencies more easily influence national security policy decisions when there is no overriding sense of threat or national purpose. The September 11 attacks made the war on terrorism the number one concern of the American people. However, four months later, worries about the economy had re-taken first place in public opinion polls.[2]

In addition, the dramatically changed composition of the Congress, in the judgment of some, has made it more difficult to build a consensus with respect to foreign policy means and ends. More than 50 percent of both the Senate and the House of Representatives were first elected in the last decade. There is the obvious point that there have been more Republicans than Democrats in both bodies, but *Washington Post* columnist, David Broder argues that, in addition, "the differences in policy and even philosophy between Democrats and Republicans are as large as they have been at any time since the New Deal."

---

2 "A December survey by Public Opinion Strategies, a Republican polling firm, found that the economy and terrorism dominate the issue agenda but that concerns about the economy were rising and fears of new terrorist attacks were falling at the end of the year. Forced to choose one or the other, 53 percent said they were more concerned about the slowdown in the economy, and 43 percent said the threat of terrorism." Don Balz and David S. Broder, "Uncertainty Marks Campaign 2002, With Balance of Power at Stake, Both Parties Unsure How to Reach Voters" *Washington Post,* January 6, 2002, A01.

More troubling, however, has been the degree to which new members have demonstrated a lack of interest in foreign affairs. There are measurable contrasts between the present generation of members of Congress and preceding ones, which help to explain this lack. For example, according to the *National Journal*, "In the past 25 years, the number of lawmakers with some military training has declined steadily from 77 percent to 34.8 percent." For freshmen members in the 106th Congress the figure is roughly 20 percent. The absence of major military contingencies and the U.S. ability to meet its military needs with a professional military are diminishing the first-person links between America's politicians and its foreign and defense policy commitments.

Let's add a footnote here: the picture may be getting brighter. David Broder observed in 2000 that the new Members of Congress elected in November 2000 – the freshman class of the 107th Congress – look "smart and balanced – just what is needed in this time of power struggles and rancid partisanship." This observation in fact matches up with my own experience of briefing new members of the Congress in 1996 and 1998. Both groups showed a determination to move beyond the partisanship that marked what I have called the "no nothing" 104th Congress that emerged from the 1994 elections. And, I found them interested in and aware of foreign policy issues, even if – as was almost universally the case – such issues played no role in their campaign for seats in the House and Senate. It is still true, however, that Members of Congress travel overseas less than their predecessors and spend more time raising money for more expensive campaigns, leaving less time for dealing with the substance of both foreign and domestic policy issues.

It has become progressively more difficult, for example, to entice members of the Senate to serve on the once prestigious Senate Foreign Relations Committee (SFRC). This is in part because jurisdiction over foreign policy matters has been spread over many committees. Not so long ago it was difficult for a Senator in his first term to get on the Foreign Relations Committee. Today, the Foreign Relations Committee and its counterpart in the House (the House Committee on International Relations) have difficulty attracting quality members.

Moreover, foreign policy decisions are shaped in an increasingly complex environment. The policy issues themselves reflect a broader variety of political, economic and security contours. As a consequence, a greater number of government departments and agencies have stakes and prerogatives on foreign policy issues. In the Congress, power has also been diffused among a wider range of Congressional committees. The most important change is that the appropriations committees in the House and the Senate, whose top priority is allocation of scarce resources, have gained power at the expense of the authorizing committees, where policy issues are supposed to take precedence.

Finally, others point to the absence of presidential leadership to explain the shift in foreign policy power. One must grant that the contemporary American foreign policy agenda is complex and Americans of all persuasions are reluctant to spend money and risk lives abroad, particularly in the absence of a coalescing threat. This said, members of Congress historically have been astute at sensing presidential detachment or weakness when it comes to foreign policy. Even on international economic issues, on which presidential interest is most clear – Mexican bailout, fast track authority, and IMF funding – Congress denied President Clinton his preferences. Although Republican mistrust of the President was a factor, he also struggled for votes from his own party on issues like fast track.

One of the most thoughtful and influential members of Congress, former Representative Lee Hamilton, before retiring from the Congress in 1998, argued that Congress increasingly does not take a "balanced and constructive approach to the serious business of foreign policy." According to Mr. Hamilton, "Congress involves itself erratically. It is often engaged primarily for political reasons, displaying little sophistication about complex and difficult problems."

Summary Observations

Geopolitical environment

The challenges facing the United States around the world are complex and multi-faceted, but have not been perceived to be threatening to American's vital security interests. This fundamental point means that arriving at consensus on foreign policy ends or means is difficult, if not impossible, except in times of crisis. Furthermore, there appears to be no agreed criteria to help judge which national interests are "vital," which are "important," and which are of a lower priority. Early in his term, President George W. Bush asserted that U.S. overseas intervention should be based on an assessment of U.S. "vital interests," among other factors. The war in Afghanistan clearly fell into this category. The problem is that the term could be defined to include most, some, or close to none of the conflict scenarios likely to occur in the years ahead.

The Changing Nature of Congress

The Congress today *is* fundamentally different from the Congress of ten to twenty years ago. Congressional leadership is less interested in and knowledgeable about foreign affairs. New members of Congress have so far been generally less interested in foreign affairs and less willing to devote time to international issues than the people they replaced. Authority over foreign policy issues is more widely dispersed around the Congress with more committees demanding jurisdiction over foreign policy issues. The Congress in recent years has been far more partisan and there have been more intra-party factions, making it difficult for leaders to rally the troops. The extremes of both parties are more capable of influencing decisions and blocking legislative-executive agreement. Further, in a highly charged political atmosphere, statesmanship increasingly takes second place to special interests, constituency issues and partisanship in Congressional actions.

Executive Branch Leadership

The proliferation of agencies with foreign affairs responsibilities makes it difficult for administrations to present a united front to the Congress. Executive branch relations with Congress have deteriorated as a result of mismanagement or inattention. The executive branch is poorly organized to succeed in pressing its foreign policy agenda.

The national security coordinating and decisionmaking system has not been adapted to the fact that foreign policy issues often contain a complex mix of foreign policy, military and, increasingly, domestic and international economic elements. President Clinton, in particular, was more personally interested and involved in domestic issues than in foreign policy issues.

Public Involvement

Waning public interest in foreign affairs has had the practical effect of enhancing the role and influence of special interests. With relatively low election turnout, every vote counts more, and committed or single-issue voters have more say. These special interests, in turn, are pressing their concerns both directly and in election campaigns and are having substantial effects on policies.

The "CNN effect" has reduced the time between international events and the time when politicians feel they must comment and act. In these circumstances, good policy can be sacrificed to good sound bites.

Most importantly, the system designed by the Founding Fathers usually works best when the President takes the initiative and seeks to build bipartisan support for administration positions. This requires a commitment to consultation and to compromise.

When the ball is in the *Congressional* court, the responsibility is to provide constructive criticism and to negotiate adjustments in proposed policies that are consistent with U.S. interests and available resources, including public support.

More Struggles Ahead

The foreign policy road between Capitol Hill and the White House is full of potential potholes, any one of which can block cooperation and produce deadlock. Some of these barriers to cooperation are institutional, based on the constitutionally created tension between Presidential and Congressional prerogatives in foreign policy. Some are partisan, reflecting the constant struggle between the two parties for votes and, ultimately, control of the government and its policies. Others are more idiosyncratic, based on the personalities and performance of the President, the President's top foreign policy lieutenants, and Congressional leaders.

As we enter the 21st century, there is a persistent distrust between the two branches, the origins of which date back to the Vietnam War. That institutional obstacle to cooperation has been exacerbated by the fact that, for most of the last decade, divided government added another competitive layer to the legislative-executive relationship. And, the particularly troubled relationship between President Clinton and the Republican leadership in Congress added several more obstacles to cooperation. Other unique factors helped produce the troubling tendencies of the 1990s, including the end of the Cold War and the U.S. budget deficit.

The Georgetown University study provided evidence of a troubling decline in the quality of executive-legislative communication. The relationship includes substantial continuity with previous decades, but with some new stresses and disturbing discontinuities. This does not necessarily mean that the trends in the 1990s toward reduced focus on and constrained resources for U.S. foreign policy will carry over into the next century. With a decade of experience in coping with challenges to U.S. interests in the post-Cold War world, a public that is for the most part ready to be led in support of U.S. international involvement, and the new focus on U.S. international interests provided by the war on terror, more reassuring trends could well emerge in the early years of the new millennium.

Such an optimistic scenario would require, however, that leaders in both branches and parties seek to remedy problems that have plagued the relationship during the past decade. More and better presidential leadership must be matched by a higher quality of statesmanship among Congressional leaders. The nation needs Members of Congress who are as serious about foreign policy decisions as they are about important domestic policy issues. In the long run, the nation's domestic and foreign policy interests are cut from the same cloth, and a better informed, more aware Congress can help ensure that American democracy remains safe and its interests secure in the 21st century.

Finally, how will the electoral process affect these observations? At least initially, relations between Congressional Republicans and Democrats were soured by the fight for Florida after the 2000 presidential elections. President

Bush and his new Administration lost control of the Senate when Vermont's Republican Senator James Jeffords became an independent and chose to vote with the Democrats on organizing the Senate. The 2002 elections could return control of the Senate to the Republicans or, on the other hand, could put the House as well as the Senate in the hands of the opposition. The odds, therefore, are for continued divided government in one form or other.

Does that mean that the American foreign policy leadership will be unreliable and unpredictable? The President will have to be masterful in both building effective coalitions for his policies and artful in seeking bipartisan support. George W. Bush claims to be an effective coalition-builder and has said that he will pursue a bipartisan approach. But his lack of experience in foreign policy and in the ways of Washington suggests he may find it harder than he expects. The September 11 events gave the president an opportunity to lead a united nation into a war on terrorism, but he may find it more difficult to garner such strong popular and Congressional support during more "normal" times.

It may be reassuring, however, both to overseas friends of the United States and to those who question George W. Bush's leadership capabilities, that he is surrounded by well-known and capable advisors. President Ronald Reagan, also with no prior foreign policy experience, used the "President-above-foreign policy" model in the 1980s.

I well remember the day that I accompanied Senators Sam Nunn and Bill Roth, and Representatives Doug Bereuter and Bill Richardson to deliver to President Reagan a study that I had drafted. Sitting around the Cabinet Room table, the Senators made their formal presentations and President Reagan, sitting across from National Security Advisor Colin Powell, responded in kind. The President congratulated the members for their initiative and noted NATO's continuing importance to the United States. After a Reaganesque pause and smile, he looked across the table and said: "Several of your recommendations have caught the eye of policy makers here in Washington. Isn't that so, General Powell?"

Ronald Reagan was able to get away with not considering himself a "policy maker in Washington." George W. Bush appears to prefer an on-the-job training approach. However, the point is that the presidency is more than the man who occupies the post. It is an institution, vested with considerable power and staffed by a rich mix of officials and advisors. The nation has just survived one President who had the intellect to be a great President but who perhaps lacked the interest and then lost the credibility and political support required to maximize the powers of the presidency. It likely will survive another who is learning as he goes.

We are certainly not entering a new period of imperial presidency, if there ever were such a thing. We must hope, however, that President George W. Bush will make it a high priority to try his best to create the conditions from which an effective, bipartisan U.S. foreign policy can emerge.

Bush and the Republicans [illegible] lost control of the Senate when Vermont Republican [illegible] became an independent and [illegible] with the Democrats [illegible]

[illegible] The President [illegible]

[illegible] Congressional support [illegible]

[illegible] foreign policy [illegible]

[illegible] Richardson [illegible] President [illegible] Colin Powell [illegible] The President [illegible] NATO [illegible] United States [illegible] Washington [illegible]

[illegible] Washington [illegible] George W. Bush [illegible] the President [illegible]

[illegible]

Michaela Hönicke Moore

Divided Government: The Democratic Dilemma of Making U.S. Foreign Policy

Since the mid-1990s the breakdown of an American foreign policy consensus has been widely deplored and held responsible for the more erratic aspects of U.S. engagement in the world. Somewhat nostalgic recollections of "the good old days" of the Cold War have surfaced, when there was agreement on the need for containment and international engagement and when foreign policy had been left to the "real experts." Instead the United States presented, according to this interpretation, a strangely paradoxical image of an unrivaled, at times domineering superpower whose legislature refused to give the president important instruments of foreign policy (fast track authority), declined the ratification of international treaties (Comprehensive Test Ban Treaty, CTBT), and withheld its consent to other key initiatives (sending troops to the Balkans). At the same time the larger public withdrew into "apathy" according to James Lindsay, denying its politicians the necessary support for America's engagement as a world power. This left – even more regrettably – the scene to a "noisy few" whose special interests were not necessarily congruent with the national interest, as witnessed in the case of the Cuban émigré community or the linkage of an anti-abortionist agenda with the payment of UN dues.[1]

A slightly different version of this same interpretation holds that the Republican-dominated Congress of the second half of the 1990s, in particular its conservative leadership, has emerged as the proponent alternatively of obstructionism, neo-isolationism, and unilateralism.[2] This argument on the assertive, though not aggressive, and at the same time internationally incompetent, though not irresponsible, Congress of the late 1990s has clearly raised

1 James M. Lindsay, "The New Apathy: How an Uninterested Public is Reshaping Foreign Policy," in: *Foreign Affairs*, September/October 2000. For background on this article's topic cf. his, *Congress and the Politics of U.S. Foreign Policy* (Baltimore: Johns Hopkins University Press, 1994).

2 Jürgen Wilzewski, "Demokratie und Aussenpolitik: Friktionen zwischen Präsident und Kongress," in: Peter Rudolf and Jürgen Wilzewski, *Weltmacht ohne Gegner: Amerikanische Aussenpolitik zu Beginn des 21. Jahrhunderts* (Baden-Baden: Nomos, 200, 38-61.

alarm. And indeed the problems of divided government (the White House and Congress controlled by different parties) under the second Clinton Administration cannot only be attributed to the fallout from the scandals of the Clinton White House and the peculiar hatred that some conservatives felt for that president. They reflect deeper trends of a self-confident legislature and of underlying opinion shifts in American society regarding their country's role in the world. This becomes apparent, too, between the current Bush Administration and a Senate that the Democrats control by the slightest of margins. Their relationship was at first shaped by a controversial presidential election. But even after September 11th, when there was much talk about a newly found national unity and strong bipartisanship, it soon became apparent that differences would continue.

Clearly the assertiveness of the U.S. Congress in foreign policy making – whose power had increased ever since the end of the "imperial presidency" in the 1970s – has reached a new and unprecedented level with the end of the Cold War.[3] Thus, the worrisome image emerged of a superpower immobilized by domestic factors: the ineffectiveness of divided government, a public that has tuned out international affairs, and special interests that captured the legislature.

Especially among Europeans and American liberal academics, this development was loudly deplored. Their jeremiad reflected, on the one hand, the perspective of foreign policy experts who prefer to keep the uninitiated outside the hallowed halls of statesmanship. On the other hand, this assessment was formed from the vantage point of the late 1990s when proponents of a more liberal internationalist agenda felt overwhelmed by a sense of frustration with an outspoken unilateralist, self-centered, conservative majority in Congress. In the following pages, the lens on this topic will be widened to include other domestic factors that come to bear on foreign policy in the American democratic system and to assess what changes the attacks of September 11, 2001 may have wrought.

"Don't look at the rhetoric, look at the record"

There is a particular democratic dilemma of foreign policy making which Alexis de Tocqueville first pointed out in the case of the United States when he observed that "foreign policy does not require the use of any of the good qualities peculiar to democracy but does demand the cultivation of almost all

3 Ralph Carter, "Congress and Post-Cold War U.S. Foreign Policy," in: *After the End: Making U.S. Foreign Policy in the Post-Cold War World*, ed. James M. Scott, Durham, NC: Duke University Press, 1998), 109-137, here: 129.

those which it lacks."[4] The latter included, in the Frenchman's analysis the formulation of coherent plans, the coordination of the varying parts of an agenda and the need for secrecy as well as persistence, i.e. having control over foreign affairs for long periods. From this perspective the checks and balances and the constitutionally mandated "invitation [to the two branches of government] to struggle for the privilege of directing American foreign policy" appear deficient.[5] While the President is the Commander-in-Chief and is expected to lead the country in international affairs, in particular at times of crises, it is Congress that appropriates funds for his foreign policy agenda, regulates trade, ratifies treaties, approves diplomatic appointments and in the end declares war.

The complaint about societal meddling in foreign affairs targets a phenomenon that lies at the core of American foreign policy conduct: the world policy of the "only remaining superpower" is being devised within the constitutional framework and under the conditions of a democracy.[6] This deserves particular emphasis from a transatlantic perspective. The purpose of democratic institutions and procedures, such as the power sharing between the two branches of government, is not to render the making and execution of foreign policy more effective – as George F. Kennan and Henry Kissinger might have wished and as the European tradition of *Staatsraison* and *Realpolitik* requires – but to represent the voice of the people and to safeguard against executive autocracy in the realm of national security and international affairs.

Significantly, most participants of this cumbersome process express their fundamental acceptance of and tolerance for its frustrations, compromises, and setbacks. Not only representatives of the legislative branch, but also members of the Clinton Administration, bruised in battles with their congressional counterparts over foreign policy initiatives, assert more enthusiastically than most outside commentators the basic soundness of the "invitation to struggle" and express their pride in a fundamentally democratic process.[7] Pointing to the foreign policy achievements of the Clinton Administration, some of which were only achieved after long negotiating sessions

---

4 Alexis de Tocqueville, *Democracy in America* (Garden City, NY: Anchor Books, 1969), 228f. Richard Haass laconically remarks that this judgment that democracy is ill suited for the conduct of foreign policy goes double for world leadership.

5 Edward S. Corwin, *The President: Office and Powers, 1787-1957* (New York: New York University Press, 1957), p. 171.

6 Stanley Hoffmann, *Gulliver's Troubles, or the setting of American foreign policy* (New York: McGraw-Hill for Council on Foreign Relations, 1968), p. 226ff.

7 This assessment is based on interviews, which the author conducted in the fall of 2000 with members of both parties on Capitol Hill and of the Clinton Administration. Michael Haltzel, senior foreign policy adviser to Senator Joseph Biden expressed his fundamental appreciation of the process in a comparison to European institutions and preferences: "We simply have more democracy in our democracy than you do."

and a willingness to compromise, one senior member of Clinton's first National Security Council advised: "don't look at the rhetoric, look at the record."

This recommendation is borne out by a recent study by Rebecca Hersman. Her analyses of different case studies from the 1990s yield a more complex picture than that of continued deadlock and acrimonious partisanship frustrating superpower ambitions. She emphasizes how much gets done – in successful cooperation or through forced compromise. Most of this legislation did not attract the kind of attention that big failures such as CTBT received.[8] Hersman explores in particular the power of the informal universe – of contacts, information exchanges and collaboration – that links Congress with the executive branch and its bureaucracies. She illustrates how – due to the informality and often confidentiality in the current situation of institutional fragmentation and ideological polarization – informal as well as procedural powers enhance the influence and clout of individuals from both ends of Pennsylvania Avenue. Among her three case studies, the struggle for the Chemical Weapons Convention (CWC) provides a perfect illustration of the importance of the informal universe and is full of reversals and suspense.

Her main conclusion, that successful cooperation between the two branches occurs when the Administration begins the process of negotiations with Congress early and then sustains it, is substantiated by Jeremy Rosner. He offers an analysis of the early Clinton Administration's successful plan to provide a substantial package of assistance to Russia and contrasts this with the failed peacekeeping efforts. Through his own experience as Senior Director for Legislative Affairs on Clinton's NSC, he demonstrated the importance of maintaining close ties to Congress during the debate on the first round of NATO enlargement.[9] Furthermore, the congressional hearings on NATO expansion illustrate how interest groups and NGOs constitute a different type of informal universe, provide a network of information and expertise for members of Congress, and help mobilizing public opinion and key constituencies. This indeed highlights the purpose of Congress as a deliberation forum that frames the content and arguments of the public debates on important foreign policy options.

A key figure in most accounts of Congressional "obstructionism" in the 1990s was Jesse Helms (R-NC), then chairman of the Senate's Foreign Relations Committee.[10] The conservative Southerner, who was replaced by Joseph

---

8 Rebecca K. C. Hersman, *How Congress and the President Really Make Foreign Policy* (Washington, DC: Brookings Institution Press, 2000).

9 Jeremy D. Rosner, *The New Tug-of-War: Congress, the Executive Branch, and National Security* (Washington: Carnegie Endowment for International Peace, 1995), here: 101ff.

10 A month after the last presidential elections one of his assistants felt the need for a press release informing "our friends in the media" that contrary to all rumors, Helms was not about to die, that instead "he is absolutely fine and will (God willing) be

Biden Jr. (D-DE) as the Chair of the Foreign Relations Committee in May 2001, was the favorite enemy of all internationalists, multilateralists, liberals, and of most European commentators. His name stands for the mobilization and perpetuation of American resistance against the International Criminal Court, the treaty banning land mines, and the Kyoto Protocol. He was the main architect of the Senate's rejection of the CTBT and the most outspoken and vehement critic of the United Nations. Critics, including fellow congressional leaders from the other side of the aisle, faulted him most sharply for his role in devising the Helms-Burton Act and the Iran-Libya Sanctions Act with their extraterritorial sanctions. Yet in spite of liberal internationalists' intense frustrations with Senator Helms, he represented an important section of popular opinion – conservative, parochial, nationalistic and deeply suspicious of the foreign policy establishment. As a powerful senator, it was he who was in the end capable of striking deals with his political adversaries, as witnessed in his compromise on the payment of American dues to the UN.[11]

Failure of Presidential Leadership and Congressional Timidity

As Stanley Sloan has argued, presidential leadership in this new post Cold War era includes the need to consult, inform and cooperate with Congress.[12] All major examples of both foreign policy successes and failures over the past decade illustrate this point. In this light, the Senate's rejection of CTBT in 1999 should be regarded more as an aberration than as an important piece of evidence in the narrative of the newly assertive Congress. Jürgen Wilzewski sees this event as an "unprecedented act of refusal". But the similarities to the Senate's rejection of Woodrow Wilson's pet project, the League of Nations, are far too striking to be ignored here.[13] The relevant parallel – apart from the role played by Henry Cabot Lodge and Jesse Helm – is executive overconfidence. A former member of the Clinton Administration, suggested: "Don't ask why the senate rejected it, ask why the Administration went ahead with it." It was ill prepared, the previously learned lessons of the CWC were

around to torment you for a long time to come. Relax and accept it." http://www. senate.gov/~foreign/minority/press_template.cfm?rands_id=175490. Senator Helms announced at the end of 2001 that he would not seek reelection.

11 Walter Russell Mead, "Why the World is Better for Jesse Helms," *New York Times*, 22 April 2001.

12 Stanley Sloan, Mary Locke, and Casimir Yost, *The Foreign Policy Struggle: Congress and the President in the 1990's and Beyond* (Washington: Georgetown University, 2000).

13 Wilzewski, p. 38.

ignored, and the conduct of the Administration indicated an arrogance drawn from earlier successes as well as a serious political miscalculation.

More importantly, different and conflicting responses from the White House and Congress to the news about the Balkans and European and UN failure to stop Serb aggression provide a dramatic illustration of the consequences of a breakdown of communication and cooperation between the two branches. A closer look at the arguments on both sides reveals at the same time conflicting positions within the legislature and the Clinton Administration's dilemma of dealing with the disagreement inside the transatlantic alliance. In response to the news of the massacre in the UN safe area of Srebrenica, Congress seemingly took the first initiative and forced the government's hand with the Bosnia Self-Defense Act in 1995, which lifted the arms embargo and demanded air strikes. Clinton vetoed the legislation out of concern of further alienating European allies whose troops on the ground were at risk of becoming targets of Serbian reprisals. In turn, Congress, which by now had embarked on a course of refusing to go along with executive policy, never explicitly supported the troop deployment that followed the Dayton Peace Accords.[14] In no other context were there more complaints from members of Congress about the wide gap between Clinton's rhetoric of consultation and his action of presenting Congress with faits accomplis than in the case of American engagement in Bosnia.[15]

While most of the focus in recent literature is on the rising readiness for conflict, challenge, and assertiveness on the part of Congress, one of its most prominent former members, Lee Hamilton, has strongly criticized his colleagues for the opposite, namely timidity and a lack of readiness to assume the responsibility to "advise and consent." Congress, in Hamilton's view, shirked its constitutional task of authorizing military intervention in the contested cases of Somalia, Haiti, Bosnia and Iraq – and one might add Kosovo. Instead, it left difficult decisions to the President – sometimes even without debating them. Similarly, Hamilton disapproves of the congressional penchant for seemingly simple, but actually ineffective solutions like unilateral sanctions, which he interprets as a combination of posturing and an unwillingness to assume responsibility.[16] He detects in this legislation a kind of

14 Ryan C. Hendrikson, "War Powers, Bosnia and the 104th Congress" *Political Science Quarterly* 113, no. 2 (1998), 241-58; William C. Banks and Jeffrey D. Straussman, "A New Imperial Presidency? Insights from U.S. Involvement in Bosnia," *Political Science Quarterly* 114, no. 2 (1999), 195-217. Cf. also Ivo H. Daalder, *Getting to Dayton: The Making of America's Bosnia Policy* (Washington: Brookings Institution Press, 2000).

15 Dov Zakheim, *Congress and National Security in the Post-Cold War Era* (Washington: Nixon Center, 1998).

16 Lee H. Hamilton, "Congress and U.S. Foreign Policy." Speech delivered to the 1999 annual meeting of the Trilateral Commission in Washington, www.trilateral.org/annmtgs/trialog/trlgtxts/t53/ham.htm.

"leadership on the cheap," which Fareed Zakaria, the former managing editor of *Foreign Affairs,* has similarly criticized as "our hollow hegemony," pointing to the same dilemma between a desire to exert leadership and a lack of will to allocate the resources for it.[17]

Finally, the decline in congressional competence that Sloan and others have noticed has to be somewhat qualified from a transatlantic perspective, which is already saturated with anecdotes of American provincialism and Representatives without passports. It is important for European observers to understand that the level, from which this decline sets in, is still rather high. The average staff of forty people working for a senator, including foreign policy experts with area and linguistic expertise, would still cause envy among many German parliamentarians.[18]

2001: A Turbulent Year

Over the course of 2001 White House-Congress relations continued to undergo dramatic changes – moving from the hopes of a one party government back to a divided government (this one reversed from the later Clinton years) and on to committed, if temporary, bipartisanship when the nation came under attack.[19] The year opened with the arrival of a controversially elected President in the White House who faced an evenly divided Congress with his Vice President as a tiebreaker. The European charge of unilateralism, previously directed against the Republican-dominated Congress, soon broadened to encompass the agenda and politics of the new Administration, too.

By May, the announcement of one Republican Senator that he would become Independent and vote with the Democrats shifted the balance in favor of a Democratic majority. While the process of setting new (mostly domestic) priorities was still in full swing, the attacks of September 11th provoked an overwhelming sense of national emergency and unity. The subsequent show of domestic concord and bipartisanship in Congress was impressive, but even before the year was over, it became clear that the effect of "September 11" was not to be similar to that of the attack on Pearl Harbor with respect to White House-Congress relations. Within weeks of the terrorist strikes, Congress – while offering support and cooperation to President Bush – also

17 Fareed Zakaria, "The New American Consensus: Our Hollow Hegemony," *The New York Times Magazine*, 1. November 1998: 44.

18 Herbert Dittgen, *Amerikanische Demokratie und Weltpolitik; Aussenpolitik in den Vereinigten Staaten* (Paderborn: Schöningh, 1998).

19 "A Year of Power Struggles and Common Purposes," *Congressional Quarterly Weekly*, 22 December 2001, pp. 3018f.

made it clear that it would not relinquish its control of foreign policy making.[20]

Congress rallied behind the Commander-in-Chief in passing a "use-of-force resolution" as early as a week after the attack. The Bush Administration had originally called for a broad authorization for the use of military force not only in retaliation against the terrorists of the September 11th attack and their supporters, but also to "deter and pre-empt any future acts of terrorism or aggression." Many legislators, especially Democrats, rejected such undefined powers with reference to the 1964 Gulf of Tonkin resolution as a carte blanche and asserted, in the words of Senator Biden, their "constitutional right to decide whether force should be used."[21]

There was even more friction between the Administration and Congress over the domestic side of the anti-terrorism campaign and civil liberties as a potential victim of the proposed "USA Patriot Bill."[22] Attorney General John Ashcroft's attempt to cast his critics as lacking in patriotic loyalty was effectively countered by Senators Biden and Patrick Leahy (D-VT), chairman of the Judiciary Committee. Still, the fact that in the end Democrats voted with one exception in favor of the bill, was in large measure due to negotiations in closed-door sessions which included White House representatives from the very beginning, thus further illustrating the importance of close cooperation between representatives from both branches.[23]

Underlying Shifts in Public Opinion and Their Relevance

Finally, trends in Congress have to be placed in a wider societal context. The changing profile and ideological realignment within the parties and their constituencies themselves deserve attention in this regard. Evidence suggests that especially in the second half of the 1990s a kind of culture war occurred, leading to a noticeable differentiation even within the two parties. A divide

---

20 "Congress Fearful of Ceding Too Much Foreign Policy Control," *CQ Weekly*, 29 September, 2001, pp. 2275-2277.

21 In August 1964 President Lyndon submitted a resolution requesting authorization to take "all necessary measures to repel any armed attack against the forces of the United States and to prevent further aggression" after a somewhat murky incident in the Gulf of Tonkin. Congress overwhelmingly approved it. In response to Johnson's and Nixon's use of the resolution for escalating the American war in Vietnam, Congress passed the War Powers Resolution in 1973. For background see Richard F. Grimmett, "The War Powers Resolution: After Twenty-Five Years," CRS Report for Congress, 15 September 1999.

22 "Liberty v security," *Economist*, 8 December 2001 and "Anti-Terrorism," *CQ Weekly*, 22 December 2001, p. 3070.

23 "Anti-Terrorism," *CQ Weekly*, 22 December 2001, p. 3063.

emerged between the two coasts and urban centers on the one hand and the more rural, small town America on the other hand. This conflict has proportions similar to the profound transformation America witnessed a century ago when cultural traditionalism asserted itself in reaction to an industrial revolution.

Foreign economic and trade controversies, for example, arose not out of divided government, but out of clashes between different segments within the parties representing conflicting regional and economic interests. In the case of "fast track authority" (successfully renamed "trade promotion authority" by the Bush Administration) and Permanent Normal Trade Relations (PNTR) with China, splits within both parties became apparent with big business interests, proponents of free trade, and globalization on the one hand aligned against labor, human rights activists, environmentalists, and conservative religious groups on the other hand.[24] Ralph Carter and others have called this phenomenon with respect to executive-legislative relations "intermestics," the merging of domestic and foreign policy issues: "Presidents will call them foreign policy issues, but members of Congress will react to them based on their domestic consequences."[25]

Recent trends in scholarship on foreign policy and public opinion have challenged an earlier "realist" consensus that public opinion is volatile, incoherent and uninformed and therefore *should* have no impact on the conduct of foreign policy.[26] The relevance of public opinion for a democracy's foreign policy has moreover been evident in this country's long tradition of "great debates" in which the national self-image and understanding of one's role in the world have been periodically renegotiated. America's concept of a national self is closely tied to an appreciation of its international position. And rhetoric as well as the reality of American foreign policy express and reinforce concepts of national self. These self-images, however, do not have a Mount-Rushmore-like permanence to them; rather within certain parameters they are subject to public discussions. Three elements in particular are constitutive of American national identity and characterize the ideological foundations of its international engagement: exceptionalism, missionary creed and universalism.[27] These underlying assumptions of the "city upon a hill," as

---

24 During the PNTR debate, the *New York Times* criticized that labor was as protectionist as ever, but had become more sophisticated in its language and tactics – including the mobilization of allies on the Hill – by presenting their concerns as supportive of basic labor, human rights and environmental standards. "America's Labor Pains," *New York Times*, 9 May 2000.

25 Carter, Congress, 131.

26 Ole R. Holsti, *Public Opinion and American Foreign Policy* (Ann Arbor: University of Michigan Press, 1996); Miroslav Nincic, *Democracy and Foreign Policy: The Fallacy of Political Realism* (New York: Columbia University Press, 1992).

27 Amongst a wealth of literature: Knud Krakau, "American Foreign Policy – A National Style?" In: Erich Angermann and Marie-Luise Frings, eds., *Oceans Apart?* (Stuttgart:

John Winthrop called it, have translated into two very different modes of international behavior. In their exemplarist version, emphasizing America's model-character with a focus on domestic self-perfection, the US is to be a leader and inspiration to the world by "conduct and example."[28] On the other hand, the sense of mission has also led to international activism, including intervention and use of force, in order to spread and promote democracy and liberty abroad.[29]

The culmination of the activist-interventionist missionary mode during the period of the Cold War should not cloud our recognition of the regular recurrence of postwar fatigue among the American populace. Popular opinion polls throughout the 1990s reflected this desire for a partial retreat from world responsibility. The same pre-September 11th data that led Lindsay to his argument on the public's apathy can then be read as evidence for contentedness: a sense of living in a basically safe world that does not require constant vigilance and readiness, a preference for according priority to domestic projects, and, of course, a lack of interest in "going abroad in search of monsters to destroy."[30]

This post Cold War weariness of "paying any price and bearing any burden," as John F. Kennedy once promised, should not be misconstrued as evidence for a "new isolationism" as Steve Kull and I.M. Destler have argued.[31] These authors found – using existing surveys, devising new ones and having skeptical members of the policy community in Washington design their own polling questions – that in contrast to widely held assumptions inside the beltway, most Americans support their country's active engagement in the world, but favor a multilateral approach based on cooperation with allies and working through international institutions such as the United Nations. This also squares with the findings of other studies, which interpreted the relatively strong support that the American public voiced for collective security

---

Klett-Cotta, 1981), 121-145. Michael H. Hunt, *Ideology and U.S. Foreign Policy* (New Haven: Yale University Press, 1987).

28 The "conduct and example" quote is from Alexander Hamilton's Federalist No 1. James Madison, Alexander Hamilton and John Jay, *The Federalist Papers*, ed. By Isaac Kramnick (London: Penguin Books, 1987), 88. Bill Clinton showed a greater predilection for this paradigm than his predecessor, cf. for example: "In the end, more than anything else, our world leadership grows out of the power of our example here at home." State of the Union Address, 4 February 1997.

29 H.W. Brands, "Exemplary American versus Interventionist America," in: Robert L. Hutchings, ed., *At the End of the American Century: America's Role in the Post-Cold War World* (Baltimore: Johns Hopkins University Press, 1988), 29-51.

30 The quote is from John Quincy Adams, cited in Brands, *Exemplary*, 34f. For trends in public opinion on U.S. international engagement see John E. Rielly, ed., *American Public Opinion and U.S. Foreign Policy 1999*, (Chicago: Chicago Council on Foreign Relations, 1999) as well as its 1995 precursor.

31 Steven Kull and I.M. Destler, *Misreading the Public: The Myth of a New Isolationism* (Washington, DC: Brookings Institution Press, 1999).

designs as a sign of concern over costs of U.S. international engagement and world leadership. Various surveys note a difference between the public and the elites in this regard. The broader public favors multilateralism and cooperation either as an alternative to US unilateral interventions or at least as a way of sharing the burdens of such activities. "Leaders," on the other hand, a group that in the Rielly report includes members of the Administration, Congress, business, media academia and think tanks, believe that the United States should "go it alone" in international crises, even when it does not have the support of its allies.[32]

The popular desire for retrenchment was at first partially reflected in the new Bush Administration's foreign policy agenda. Presidential candidate George W. Bush's formula of a "strong and humble" America – which some commentators critically translated into "spend, don't send" – addressed at least one aspect of the larger public's preferences: international restraint and greater selectiveness, but it ignored an array of other inclinations. After the terrorist attacks of September 2001, there is no clear evidence that public opinion has shifted to embrace the kind of aggressive and ambitious program outlined in Bush's 2002 State of the Union Address calling for a wider campaign against an "axis of evil".[33]

Conclusion

From the perspective of 2002, the interpretation of a unilateralist, uninformed, yet domineering Congress in the 1990s appears alarmist. What was being criticized was the "interference" of democratically elected, popular representatives in foreign policy matters, but what was meant was their nationalist agenda that differed from liberal internationalism. Today the situation appears almost reverse. Against the hopes of Europeans and some Democrats, that the war against terrorism would make the Bush Administration more amenable to multilateralism, it has withdrawn from two arms-control treaties (as announced before September 11th), from the Anti-Ballistic Missile treaty as well as from the protocol to enforce the Biological Weapons Convention. Moreover, its rhetoric of coalition-building was not even primarily aimed at the Europeans and obviously in no way implied that the Bush Ad-

32 Ole Holsti, "Public Opinion and U.S. Foreign Policy after the Cold War," in Scott, *After the End*, 138-179.

33 George W. Bush, State of the Union Address, http://www.whitehouse.gov/news/ releases/2002/01/print/20020129-11.html. For the Pew Research Center's public opinion polls documenting new developments after September 11, 2001 see http://people-press.org/reports.

ministration would take European concerns or voices any more seriously than before the current war on terrorism.

With respect to the terrorist attacks, the underlying changes bearing on legislative-executive relations may not be apparent at first. The sharp rise in public trust in government, as a result of the state of national emergency, appears to have benefited both branches evenly.[34] The domestic political fallout from the attacks is most likely to strengthen a trend that had been evident for some time, reinforced by the arrival of a Republican in the White House: the decline of the parochial and anti-government wing on the right of the Republican Party. Their agenda of reducing the state does not seem to carry much appeal at a time of national crisis. The current foreign policy consensus – both within conflicting parties in the Administration and in Congress – merges around a more centrist position. Yet, for the most part "politics as usual" has returned to the capital. Caught in campaigns for midterm elections in 2002 and with an eye on a possible 2004 presidential candidacy, Senate Majority Leader Tom Dashle, asserted that Congress was not a rubber-stamp parliament for the current President's global terrorism campaign.

34 "What September 11th really wrought," *Economist*, 10 January 2002.

James M. Lindsay

Apathy, Interest, and the Politics of American Foreign Policy

Who makes foreign policy in the United States? Answers to that question usually point to government institutions. The president is the commander in chief and the one person that Americans look to for foreign affairs leadership. Congress decides how foreign policy funds will be spent, regulates foreign commerce, and shapes the political agenda. The bureaucracy implements presidential and congressional directives, and it frequently plays Congress off against the White House to accomplish its own ends.

Now one doubts that government institutions matter for foreign policy making in the United States. But so too does public opinion. It is not because politicians look to the public for guidance on what to do abroad. They almost never do, for the simple reason that while the public usually knows what it wants to accomplish overseas, it seldom has a precise sense of how to accomplish it. Rather, the public's impact is more subtle and profound. Much as climate shapes the buildings that architects design or terrain shapes how generals fight battles, public opinion shapes the environment in which politicians operate. It affects the attention that the news media pay to foreign affairs, and as a result what appears on the political agenda. Public opinion also determines the risks and benefits that politicians face in courting interest groups. In short, public opinion shapes how politicians address foreign policy issues or whether they address them at all.

It is crucial to understand the American public's influence on how politicians approach foreign policy because its attitudes toward foreign affairs changed in the 1990s. The change was not, as many feared, that Americans embraced isolationism and retreated into Fortress America. The public remained broadly internationalist. What changed was that foreign policy tumbled down its list of priorities. Indeed, at the very moment that the United States had more influence than ever on world affairs, Americans lost much of their interest in the world around them. The news media followed suit, diminishing coverage of foreign stories that they knew would not attract an audience. Interest groups were emboldened; the departure of others from the political fray gave them more influence over policy.

The rise of this apathetic internationalism and the consequences that flowed from it reshaped the politics of American foreign policy. It encouraged politicians to neglect foreign affairs, distorted policy choices to favor the noisy few over the quiet many, and made American foreign policy more capricious and inconsistent. But September 11 made foreign policy a priority once again for Americans. In doing so, it greatly strengthened the White House's say in foreign policy and diminished the role of interest group. The question that remains is how long America's new found interest in events abroad will last.

Public Opinion

To what extent does American public opinion influence American foreign policy? The answer to that question depends on answering two others. First, what do the American people want their government to accomplish abroad? Second, how much do Americans actually care about foreign policy?

What the Public Thinks

With the end of the Cold War, many pundits warned that Americans were destined to go "back to the womb" of isolationism.[1] According to these commentators, Americans naturally wanted to focus their energies on problems at home and turn their backs on the outside world. Some commentators went even farther, arguing that there is a strain in American political life that is deeply suspicious of the outside world and committed to an anti-internationalist, unilateralist approach to foreign policy. With a looming foreign threat no longer forcing Americans to engage abroad, the argument goes, this suspicion of foreign do-gooding was reemerging and intensifying.[2]

Predictions of the death of internationalism were greatly exaggerated, however. Polls showed that Americans overwhelmingly continued to support an internationalist foreign policy.[3] Figure #1 shows the public's responses

1 Arthur M. Schlesinger, Jr., "Back to the Womb? Isolationism's Renewed Threat," *Foreign Affairs* 74 (July/August 1995): 2.

2 Walter Russell Mead, "The Jacksonian Tradition," *National Interest* 58 (Winter 1999/2000): 5-29.

3 For detailed discussions of this point along with supporting data, see Steven Kull and I.M. Destler, *Misreading the Public: The Myth of a New Isolationism* (Washington, D.C.: Brookings Institution Press, 1999); and Steven Kull and Clay Ramsay, "Challenging U.S. Policymakers' Image of an Isolationist Public," *International Studies Perspective* 1 (2000): 105-17.

over a half century to a standard polling question: "Do you think it will be best for the future of this country if we take an active part in world affairs or if we stay out of world affairs?" Throughout the 1990s, a majority of Americans favored taking an active role in world affairs. And while the percentage of Americans saying "take an active part" was slightly lower in the 1990s than in the 1950s, they still outnumbered those saying "stay out" by nearly two-to-one.

Figure 1 Do you think it will be best for the future of the country if we take an active part in world affairs or if we stay out of world affairs?

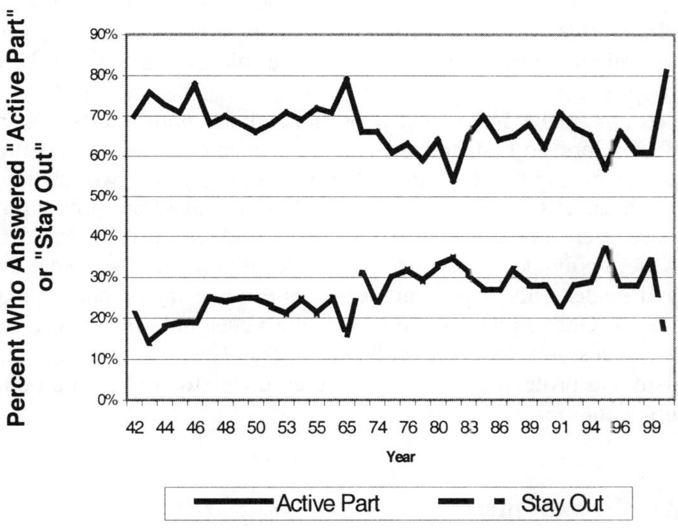

The public's broad internationalist inclinations carried over to questions about activism on specific issues. Gallup found that public support for "U.S. participation in NATO air strikes in Yugoslavia" in 1999 reached as high as 61 percent and never fell below 50 percent, even though the Clinton administration clearly misjudged Serbian President Slobodan Milosevic's resolve and its diplomatic and military strategies attracted widespread criticism.[4] Despite fears that the American public had turned against free trade, the Pew Research Center found in February 2000 that 64 percent of Americans believed that free trade is good for the country and 62 percent said the same about U.S. membership in the World Trade Organization (WTO), the multi-

4 The Gallup Organization, "Kosovo in Crisis: U.S. Role and Clinton Approval," 27 May 1999. Available online at http://www.gallup.com/polls/indicators/indkosovo.asp

lateral body that sets and administers the rules for international trade.[5] These numbers were virtually unchanged from what polls found before an alliance of environmental, human rights, and labor groups disrupted a WTO summit meeting in Seattle in December 1999.[6]

Americans also remained believers in multilateralism. A 1998 poll by the Chicago Council on Foreign Relations found that 72 percent of Americans believed that the United States should not act in international crises if it did not have the support of its allies.[7] No doubt this reflected a desire to share risks as well as costs. The preference for multilateralism extended to support for international organizations. Public opinion polls done in the 1990s repeatedly showed that a substantial majority of Americans preferred to strengthen international institutions such as the United Nations and the WTO. Indeed, one poll found that two-thirds of those surveyed supported creating an International Criminal Court, even after they were told the reasons the U.S. government opposed it.[8]

The results at the ballot box substantiated the poll results. George W. Bush and Al Gore both staked out mainstream internationalist positions on foreign policy during the 2000 presidential campaign. The two leading third-party candidates, Pat Buchanan and Ralph Nader, staked out policy positions with a much more decidedly isolationist and protectionist flavor. Yet when the votes were counted, Bush and Gore took 96 percent of the vote and Buchanan and Nader only 3 percent. And while being major party candidates gave Bush and Gore an advantage in winning votes, both men had every reason to adopt positions popular with the voters. The fact that they shunned isolationism and protectionism suggests they understood what the public did and did not want.

Public Apathy and Interest

Knowing what the public thinks about foreign policy tells only part of the story. Just as important is how intensely it holds its preferences. And here public attitudes changed substantially in the 1990s.

---

5 Pew Research Center for the People & the Press, "Post-Seattle Support for WTO," March 2, 2000.

6 See for example, "Most Americans Don't Show Distrust of Free Trade," *Wall Street Journal*, December 2, 1999; Program on International Policy Attitudes, University of Maryland, "Questionnaire on Globalization," question 61. Available online at http://www.pipa.org/OnlineReports/Globalization/globalq.html.

7 See John E. Reilly, "Americans and the World: A Survey at Century's End," *Foreign Policy* 114 (Spring 1999): 102.

8 Steven Kull, "Americans on Globalization: A Study of US Public Attitudes," Program on International Policy Attitudes, University of Maryland, 16 November 1999, p. 18. Available online at http://www.pipa.org/OnlineReports/Globalization/global_rep.html.

As figure 2 shows, during the first two decades of the Cold War, foreign policy topped the public's list of concerns. When pollsters asked people to name the most important problem facing the country, upward of 50 percent would name a foreign policy issue. That preoccupation with foreign policy diminished after the Vietnam War as international tensions diminished and the Cold War consensus over American foreign policy broke down. Still, in the 1970s and 1980s, 20 to 30 percent of respondents regularly told polling organizations that a foreign policy issue was the most important problem facing the country.

Figure 2 Public Perception of the Most Important Facing the United States, Presidential Election Years

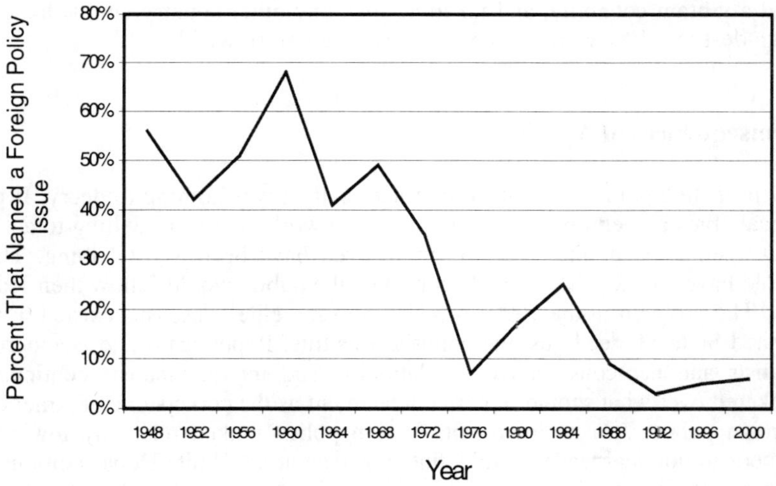

With the end of the Cold War, the disappearance of the Soviet threat, public interest in foreign policy dropped nearly to zero. As figure 2 shows, when pollsters asked people in the 1990s what the most important problem facing the United States was, only about 5 percent named a foreign policy issue. Simply put, with the overriding Soviet threat now gone, Americans were much more worried about what was happening at home than what was happening abroad.

The conclusion that Americans lost interest in the 1990s in events overseas held up even when pollsters focused specifically on foreign policy. Many Americans had trouble identifying *any* foreign policy issues that worried them. One 1998 poll asked people to name "two or three of the biggest foreign-policy problems facing the United States today." The most common response by far, at 21 percent, was "don't know."[9] No doubt swayed by unprecedented peace abroad and prosperity at home, Americans were similarly skeptical that much of what happened overseas would affect their lives. When asked to assess how much impact the rest of the world had on the United States, solid majorities of Americans answered "very little." In one poll, for example, 60 percent said that western Europe – home to most of America's major allies and a market for many U.S. firms – had little or no impact on their lives.[10] Other regions of the world were seen as even less important.

So in the 1990s Americans became apathetic internationalists.[11] They understood in the abstract that the United States had important interests abroad and should be engaged in the world, but they did not see much to worry about. After all, the United States was an unchallenged superpower, it had a vibrant economy, and far more than any other country could shape its own destiny. Why worry when things were going so well?

Consequences of Apathy

By itself, the public's apathetic internationalism was nothing to decry. If political elites agreed on America's role in the world and were willing to act on that vision, the public's apathy might even have been a good thing. They could have enacted their agenda confident the public would follow their lead.

The problem in the 1990s was that no such elite consensus existed in the United States. Indeed, just the opposite was true. Republicans and Democrats, realists and neo-conservatives, isolationists and internationalists continually bickered over what should replace containment as the cornerstone of American foreign policy. Just as important, foreign policy ranked relatively low with American political leaders. Bill Clinton arrived at the White House committed to concentrating on domestic issues. During his two terms in office, he mostly addressed foreign policy issues episodically and reactively. Interest in foreign affairs was, if anything, even lower on Capitol Hill. As a result, political leadership that might have overcome the public's apathy was not to be found.

The political elite's diminished interest in foreign affairs was itself no accident. Public opinion shapes which politicians get elected as well as what they pay attention to and what they do. Politicians naturally gravitate toward issues that voters care about. The reason lies in a basic rule of politics: How many people line up on each side of an issues matters less than how intensely

9 Reilly, "Americans and the World," p. 111.

10 *America's Place in the World II* (Washington, D.C.: Pew Research Center for the People & the Press, October 1997): 103.

11 See James M. Lindsay, "The New Apathy," *Foreign Affairs*," 79 (September/October 2000): 2-8.

each side holds its opinions. Politicians know that opposing impassioned voters may mean looking for a new job. So silent majorities get ignored. In politics, as in the rest of life, the squeaky wheels get the grease.

Thus, the rise of apathetic internationalism encouraged American politicians to neglect foreign affairs. Most foreign policy issues offered no political payoff from the average voter. That was clear during the 2000 presidential campaign. Although Vice President Al Gore presumably had an edge in foreign affairs given his vastly greater experience, both candidates largely avoided the topic. Their pollsters saw the unmistakable message in figure 2 – foreign policy was not on the minds of the voters. And they were right. During the town-hall style format of the third Bush-Gore debate, not one of the citizen-questioners asked a question about foreign policy.

The News Media

The rise of apathetic internationalism affected not just politicians. It also affected news coverage of foreign affairs. There was significantly less of it. Between 1990 and 1997, the portion of airtime that the ABC, CBS, and NBC evening news devoted to international news dropped from 32 percent – with a 50 percent spike during the Gulf War – to 20 percent.[12]

Even these numbers probably overstate things. The quality of international news coverage fell as well. ABC, CBS, and NBC responded to declining audience interest and pressure to maximize profits by cutting staff. In the late 1990s, none had a full-time correspondent stationed in Southeast Asia, Central or South American, or sub-Saharan Africa.[13] In place of their own staff, the news media instead relied on footage and news copy from foreign networks and newspapers, independent news suppliers, and stringers. One result was that expertise and perspective – key ingredients for knowing which stories to tell and how to tell them well – was lost.

Many news outlets also changed how they covered the news in a bid to hold their audiences. Many newspapers began to give more space to so-called "lifestyle" news – stories that emphasized health, finance, fashion, personal improvement, and other "news you can use" to borrow a popular advertising slogan. To make room for these stories, most newspapers, cut back the space devoted to international news. Network television news followed the same

12 Garrick Utley, "The Shrinking of Foreign News: From Broadcast to Narrowcast," *Foreign Affairs* 76 (March/April 1997): 2-10. See also Antony J. Blinken, "Is Anybody Out There Listening: Communicating Foreign Policy in the Post-Cold War Era," in *Economic Strategy and National Security: A Next Generation Approach*, ed. Patrick J. DeSouza (Boulder, CO: Westview Press, 2000), p. 81.

13 Marc Gunther, "The Transformation of Network News," *Nieman Reports* 53 (Summer 1999): 24.

basic trend, shifting to a "softer" approach that emphasized human-interest stories. As a result, when the national broadcast channels did turn to international news they were as likely to focus on events such as the death of Princess Diana as they were to cover traditional news stories such as political change in China.

What about coverage of international news on local news shows, which Americans are twice as likely to watch as the national news?[14] It was (and still is) even more dismal than coverage on the national news. Local news operates on the maxim, "If it bleeds, it leads." Unless an overseas story is especially gripping – an earthquake in India, a plane crash in Colombia, self-immolation in China – it is unlikely to make the newscast. Even then, the report is likely to be too short to provide any background or context. Many local news stations run features called "World News in a Minute," in which coverage usually returns to events within the United States within the first thirty seconds, if it even goes outside the country's borders in the first place.

The declining interest that national and local news shows had in international affairs was accompanied by the public's declining interest in traditional news outlets. (The latter, unfortunately, does not appear to be a consequence of the former.) The percentage of Americans who reported watching the three network television evening newscasts regularly fell by half during the 1990s, though these news shows still drew a combined audience of nearly 30 million people.[15] After growing rapidly in the early 1990s, the audience for cable news networks such as CNN leveled off. In turn, stagnating revenue forced CNN in 2001 to lay off 11 percent of its workforce.[16]

Newspapers experienced similar trends. Regular newspaper reading has fallen more sharply in the United States than in other advanced industrialized democracies; in the 1990s 78 percent of Germans surveyed reported reading a newspaper the day before, only 46 percent of Americans did.[17] Much of the newspaper industry's problem in the United States traces to young adults. In the 1960s, 60 percent of Americans between the ages of eighteen and twenty-nine read a newspaper regularly. In 2000, only 29 percent did.[18]

The one exception to this general trend is the American public's growing use of the Internet as a source for news. In 2000, one-in-three Americans re-

---

14 Pew Research Center for the People & the Press, "Internet Sapping Broadcast News Audience," June 11, 2000, p. 10.

15 John Consoli, "New Context," *Brandweek*, May 29, 2000, p. U10.

16 Lisa de Moraes, "For CNN, No News Isn't Necessarily Good News," *Washington Post*, January 13, 2001.

17 "Hard Numbers," *Columbia Journalism Review*, May/June 1994, 17; and Pew Research Center, "Internet Sapping Broadcast News Audience," p. 3.

18 Richard Harwood, "Rotten News for Everyone," *Washington Post*, September 1, 1991; and Pew Research Center, "Internet Sapping Broadcast News Audience," p. 3.

ported going online for news at least once a week, up from only 20 percent in 1998, with younger Americans being the most likely to turn to the Internet for news.[19] No one knows, however, what types of news people looked for when they went online. There certainly is no reason to believe that people disdained international news on television but actively searched for it on the Internet. Indeed, because the Internet lets individuals serve as their own news editors, it gave them even greater ability to screen out foreign news.

The news media's declining interest in foreign affairs in the 1990s (which reflected apathetic internationalism), coupled with the public's declining interest in news (which reflected broader societal and technological trends), reinforced the public's apathy about events overseas. The news media have never driven American foreign policy making in the way that proponents of the so-called CNN effect have argued.[20] But they do profoundly influence the political agenda in Washington.[21] So when the news media declined to cover international news, it encouraged people to believe that they could afford to ignore events beyond America's borders.

Interest Groups

While apathetic internationalism diminished the news media's interest in foreign affairs in the 1990s, it also empowered interest groups. It did so for two reasons. First, when most people focus on domestic concerns, interest groups constitute a major source of political profit or loss for politicians who do work foreign policy issues. Groups organized around ethnic, commercial, and ideological issues are willing to reward or punish politicians when the broader public is not because they have much to gain by influencing government policy. They are the squeaky wheels, and they get the grease.

Second, interest groups benefited from apathetic internationalism in the 1990s because it lowered the cost of tending to narrow interests. Voters cannot punish behavior they do not notice. And if no one opposes narrow inter-

---

19 Pew Research Center, "Internet Sapping Broadcast News Audience," p. 1.

20 For studies debunking the CNN effect argument, see Daniel C. Hallin. *The "Uncensored War": The Media and Vietnam* (Berkeley: University of California Press, 1986); Jonathan Mermin, "Television News and American Intervention in Somalia: The Myth of a Media-Driven Foreign Policy," *Political Science Quarterly* 112 (Fall 1997): 385-403; Johanna Neuman, *Lights, Camera, War: Is Media Technology Driving International Politics?* (New York: St. Martin's Press, 1996); and Warren P. Strobel, *Late-Breaking Foreign Policy: The News Media's Influence on Peace Operations* (Washington, D.C.: U.S. Institute of Peace Press, 1997).

21 See Bernard C. Cohen, *The Press and Foreign Policy* (Princeton: Princeton University Press, 1963); and Shanto Iyengar and Donald R. Kinder, *News That Matters* (Chicago: University of Chicago Press, 1987).

ests, politicians may come to equate them with the broad public interest. The result is that foreign policy increasingly became – to paraphrase Clausewitz – the continuation of domestic politics by other means. As former Representative Lee H. Hamilton (D-Ind.) put it: "Too many people place constituent interests above national interests. They don't see much difference between lobbying for highway funds and slanting foreign policy toward a particular interest group."[22]

The rising power of interest groups in the 1990s created what former U.S. Ambassador Chas. W. Freeman Jr., called "the franchising of foreign policy."[23] Groups came to dominate specific issues and drive the agenda. Indian-Americans used their growing political clout (membership in the Congressional Indian Caucus in 2000 was nearly double that of the Congressional Study Group on Germany) to block efforts to persuade Congress to condemn Pakistani "aggression" in Kashmir. Human rights activists, labor unions, and environmentalists kept President Clinton from winning "fast-track" negotiating authority in trade. Conservative groups turned U.S. participation in U.N. peacekeeping missions into political poison. Cuban Americans resisted efforts to ease sanctions on Cuba.

Of course, interest group influence on U.S. foreign policy was nothing new. In 1773, a group of Bostonians banded together as the Sons of Liberty and protested the tax policies of the British crown by throwing the Boston Tea Party. In the 1950s, the "China Lobby" pressed for greater support for Nationalist China. In the 1970s, human rights groups pushed for human rights legislation, and in the 1980s steel companies and automobile manufacturers demanded protection against lower-cost foreign imports. Interest groups are so much a part of American politics that the United States is in practice "the interest group society."[24]

What changed in the 1990s was that the countervailing push from broader interests weakened and the grip that interest groups had on their policy issues became firmer. During the Cold War, the consensus that surrounded containment helped keep narrow interests in check. Demands for particular policies had to be and were balanced against broader strategic considerations. At the same time, with the mass public more worried about foreign affairs, politicians were more cautious about indulging interest groups with demands that ran counter to majority preferences. That bulwark eroded with the disappearance of the Soviet threat. Statesmen were in short supply because fewer politicians saw any political payoff in fending off claims by narrow interests in the name of defending a broad and amorphous national

---

22 Quoted in Steven Mufson, "Local Politics Is Global as Hill Turns to Armenia," *Washington Post*, October 9, 2000.

23 Ibid.

24 Jeffrey M. Berry, *The Interest Group Society,* 2d ed. (Glenview, IL.: Scott, Foresman/Little, Brown, 1989).

interest. Interest groups politics moved from being one facet of U.S. policy making to being a defining feature. And with it came a more turbulent and inconsistent foreign policy.

A case in point is the House of Representative's effort in 2000 to pass a non-binding resolution labeling the massacres of Armenians that occurred in the Ottoman Empire from 1915 to 1923 as "genocide." Representative James Rogan (R-Calif.) sponsored the resolution. He made no claim to be a foreign policy expert – none of his committee assignments dealt with foreign policy and he had traveled outside the United States only once in his life – but he was caught in a tight reelection race. And his congressional district happened to have the highest concentration of Armenian Americans of any district in the United States. The resolution offered an easy way to build good will with constituents by promoting a cause they held dear. The Armenian Assembly of America, which routinely grades how members of Congress vote on issues affecting Armenia, had long lobbied for the resolution.

In another time, Rogan's resolution would have languished in committee. In another time, party leaders would have allowed him to introduce the bill – enabling him to gain political credit with his constituents for "fighting the good fight" – but kept the bill from advancing – thereby protecting the country's broader interests. But in 2000, House Republican leaders, eager to maintain their slim majority in the face of potential Democratic inroads in the upcoming elections, embraced the bill. Speaker of the House Dennis Hastert (R-Ill.) promised Rogan that he would bring the resolution to a vote on the House floor. He personally placed the measure on House legislative calendar. The House International Relations Committee subsequently approved it by a large margin.

As Rogan, Hastert, and other House members pushed the genocide resolution forward, they gave little thought to the consequences their symbolic gesture would have on broader U.S. interests. The result was escalating tensions with Turkey, a major American ally that among other things let U.S. and British fighter planes use Incirlik Air Base to patrol the skies over northern Iraq. Turkey's president expressed "grave reservations" about the resolution, repeating his country's long-standing insistence that there had been no genocide.[25] Suddenly U.S. defense companies faced the possibility that they might lose sales to Turkey, and the Pentagon the possibility that it would lose the right to fly out of Incirlik. After a barrage of phone calls from Bill Clinton, other administration officials, and senior military officers warning that the resolution would significantly harm U.S. foreign policy, Hastert agreed to put off a vote on Rogan's bill.[26]

25 Quoted in Mufson, "Local Politics Is Global."

26 Juliet Eilperin and Steven Mufson, "Hastert Withdraws 'Genocide' Resolution, Ties with Turkey Cited," *Washington Post*, October 20, 2000; and Mufson, "Local Politics Is Global."

The dispute over the Armenian genocide resolution shows that interest group activity does not always lead to interest group success. Whether interest groups succeed or not depends on the same mix of internal and external factors that determine their ability to influence domestic policy: How many members do they represent? How politically skilled are their leaders? Do they have deep financial pockets? Who, if anyone, opposes them? The genocide resolution ultimately faltered because it antagonized other important domestic interests. U.S. firms were unwilling to lose sales, and the Pentagon was unwilling to risk its basing rights.

The dispute over the Armenian genocide resolution also shows, however, that narrow interests can harm broader U.S. foreign policy interests even when they fail to obtain their objectives because they can greatly strain diplomatic relations and frustrate U.S. policy goals. Ankara responded to the genocide resolution by relaxing its efforts to isolate Iraq and sending an ambassador back to Baghdad for the first time in a decade.[27] This helped to further erode a foreign policy objective that has widespread support in the United States: maintaining the international effort to isolate Saddam Hussein.

September 11

The rise of apathetic internationalism rested on the public's belief that what happened outside America's borders mattered little for their lives. September 11 punctured that illusion and ended America's decade-long "holiday from history."[28] Foreign policy suddenly became a top priority with the public and the news media. Not surprisingly, many interest groups found themselves pushed toward the sidelines, and the pendulum of power swung sharply back toward the White House.

The impact of September 11 on American public opinion was dramatic. Shortly after the attacks, Gallup found that two out of every three Americans named terrorism, national security, or war as the most important problem facing the United States. Foreign policy had reached this level of political salience only twice since the advent of scientific polling – during the early stages of both the Korean and Vietnam wars.[29] Equally important, Americans did not react to the attacks by seeking to withdraw from the world, as figure 1 shows. Quite the opposite. In November 2001, 81 percent of those polled agreed that it would be "best for the future of the country if we take an active

27 Molly Moore, "Turkey Moves to Reestablish Ties with Iraq," *Washington Post*, October 14, 2000.

28 Charles Krauthammer, "The Hundred Days," *Time*, December 31, 2001, p. 156.

29 The Gallup Organization, "Terrorism Reaches Status of Korean and Vietnam Wars as Most Important Problem," November 19, 2001.

part in world affairs." This marked the highest percentage favoring active engagement in the more than half century that the questions had been asked. Nor was the public's reaction particularly unilateralist or militaristic. Nearly 3 in 4 said "it would be better if more countries would join with" the U.S. military operations in Afghanistan. And 86 percent favored – 57 percent strongly – "building goodwill toward the US by providing food and medical assistance to people in poor countries."[30]

September 11 also dramatically altered the stories the news media covered. In the weeks before September 11, the fate of Chandra Levy, a missing intern who had had an affair with a member of Congress, dominated the news. Beginning September 11, terrorism displaced the Levy story – and most everything else – from the news. Virtually every news bureau beefed up its staff, and all the major ones sent reporters and camera crews to the Middle East. Academics, retired generals, and foreign intellectuals took to the nation's airwaves and newspapers to analyze the roots of Islam extremism, the history of Afghanistan, and the politics of Pakistan. This saturation coverage paid off. The cable news channels CNN, Fox News, and MSNBC all saw their audiences at least triple. In the first three months after the attacks, the audience for ABC's main evening newscast jumped 15 percent; CBS's 9 percent; and NBC's 6 percent.[31]

The dramatic change in public attitudes profoundly changed the politics of U.S. foreign policy. On numerous issues, powerful interest groups suddenly found themselves swept aside. The coalition of conservative groups that for several years had frustrated a plan to pay much of the outstanding U.S. dues to the United Nations saw Congress suddenly appropriate the money. Human rights groups and democracy activists watched the Bush Administration do two things that would have been unthinkable only a month earlier – lift the sanctions that the United States had imposed on Pakistan after General Musharraf seized power in 1999 and begin to side rhetorically with Russia in its brutal fight in Chechnya. With the public now watching, politicians who wanted to resist interest group pressure understood that they had the freedom to do so. Those who preferred to protect the status quo backed off. They understood that they risked being seen as courting special interests at the expense of the national interest.

The main beneficiary of the dramatic change in the politics of U.S. foreign policy was the White House, not Congress. The reason was simple. The public was not split on what the government should do – as was the case, for example, in the latter half of the Vietnam era – but remarkably unified.

---

30 Program on International Policy Attitudes, "Americans on the War on Terrorism: A Study of US Public Attitudes," November 6, 2001. Available online at http://www.pipa.org/OnlineReports/Terrorism/WarOnTerr.html .

31 Mark Jurkowitz, "Networks May Be Losing the News War," *Boston Globe*, December 10, 2001.

George W. Bush's public approval ratings soared to 90 percent – a figure seen only once before, and even then only fleetingly, when his father successfully waged the Gulf War.

With the public firmly behind the president, members of Congress who might have preferred to be elsewhere on policy grounds quickly decided they had to be there as well. Three days after the attack, a near unanimous Congress gave the president a blank check retaliate against the terrorists, authorizing him "to use all necessary and appropriate force against those nations, organizations, or persons he determines planned, authorized, committed, or aided the terrorist attacks that occurred on September 11, 2001, or harbored such organizations or persons." Congress surrendered on other issues as well. Before September 11, Senate Democrats hoped to reprise the Star Wars debate of the 1980s – which had been politically profitable for them – by making the Bush Administration's plans for missile defense the centerpiece of debate. Following the attacks, they dropped their effort to cut missile defense spending and limit missile defense tests. President Bush's December 2001 announcement that he was withdrawing the United States from the 1972 Anti-Ballistic Missile (ABM) Treaty caused barely a ripple on Capitol Hill.

As the ABM Treaty withdrawal attested, President Bush made the most of his newfound power during the fall of 2001. But in taking these and other decisions he was carrying out his agenda, not the public's. While the public knew it wanted to win the war on terrorism, it had few well-formed opinions on how to achieve that end. Indeed, the results of the multitude of polls taken in the weeks following September 11 could be read to support a broad array of different strategies for dealing with terrorism, ranging from those that emphasized military force to those that gave long-term economic and political aid an equal priority. What mattered in political terms was that the public was willing to support President Bush in whatever he did, as long as his strategy appeared to be working, or at least not clearly failing.

Conclusion

The 1990s saw the rise of apathetic internationalism among the American public. Events overseas remained *objectively* important but their *political* importance faded. The shifting of the public's attention to domestic issues transformed the incentives facing the news media, interest groups, and most important, politicians. The temptation to ignore foreign policy and cater to groups with narrow but intense preferences became strong, both on Capitol Hill and in the White House. What resulted was a foreign policy more fractious, inconsistent, and shortsighted than it had been in the past.

September 11 shattered America's apathetic internationalism. Foreign policy again became a priority for the American public, and the politics of

U.S. foreign policy reflected it. Most of the domestic political obstacles that had hobbled foreign policy making during the 1990s were swept away. Gone was the talk of the president as a Gulliver tied down by Lilliputians. Back was talk about the second coming of the imperial presidency.

The open question is how long the new, White House dominated politics of U.S. foreign policy will last. In all likelihood, it will prove fleeting in its extreme form, regardless of whether the war on terrorism goes poorly or well. If more attacks occur – especially if it appears the Administration missed the chance to stop them – or if the war on terrorism begins to go badly – say, because an effort to overthrow Saddam Hussein goes awry – public confidence in the president's leadership will decrease even as its fears about events overseas increase. Conversely, if no further attacks occur, the political relevance of September 11 will slowly fade. Indeed, in January 2002 the share of the American public identifying terrorism as the country's most important problem dropped to 35 percent.[32] As the public's concern about terrorism subsides, the Administration's critics will see fewer costs in criticizing the White House. This is especially true for foreign policy issues not immediately connected to terrorism. Indeed, when President Bush was riding high in the polls during the fall of 2001, he managed to win House approval of a bill granting him trade promotion (formerly fast-track) authority by a single vote, and even then only after applying heavy political pressure on wavering members.

This is not to say, however, that foreign policy making will soon revert back to its pre-September 11 form. It will not, at least not any time soon. While President Bush will almost inevitably confront greater political opposition at home as the attacks recede in time, September 11 gave a lasting boost to his influence in foreign policy. Fighting terrorism will likely be the focal point of American foreign policy for years to come, and potential congressional opponents will operate with the residual fear that, if not done exactly right, their criticisms could be portrayed as unpatriotic. In a country newly sensitized to the importance of patriotism, that is an advantage the White House will put to use.

32 Frank Newport, "Terrorism Fades as Nation's Most Important Problem," Gallup Organization, January 14, 2002.

Gebhard Schweigler

Domestic Sources of US Foreign Policy[1]

American foreign policy at any time can only be understood with reference to its domestic sources. These, in turn, reflect not only current concerns and interests, but also long-standing traditions of foreign policy behavior and orientations. Such traditions by no means determine policy choices. But they structure the debate, both in the public realm as well as in the decision-making bodies, and thus influence policy outcomes. They tend to make some policies more likely than others. Therefore, a proper understanding of foreign policy traditions helps to reduce always-present uncertainties about where the United States might be heading.

The first president, George Washington, set the first important traditions. With the French revolution in full swing and all of Europe in political upheaval, Washington saw himself faced with the issue whether to side with France, whose just decapitated king after all had concluded an alliance with the United States that had helped the struggling new nation to defeat Great Britain and gain independence, or to align itself with its mother country with which it still shared so many ties and values. The conflict over America's foreign policy orientation led to sharply escalating domestic turmoil, fed by the main protagonists and stirred up further by the French envoy to the United States. The leader of the British faction was Alexander Hamilton, Secretary of Treasury, who wanted the United States to pursue a foreign policy of conservative realism, guided by narrowly defined political and commercial interests. He was opposed by Thomas Jefferson, leader of the French faction and Secretary of State, who in the spirit of his Declaration of Independence insisted that the United States honor its alliance commitments (even though concluded with the *ancien regime*) and support the lofty goals of the French revolution. The President, faced with conflicting advice and rapidly proliferating domestic passions, eventually decided that the best thing

1 This article reflects the personal opinion of its author. It does not represent the opinions of the National War College, the Department of the Army, the Department of Defense, or the United States government.

to do would be to stay out of the European conflicts altogether and to pursue a policy of neutrality.

Washington's neutrality policy founded one of the seemingly most enduring traditions of American foreign policy: to avoid entangling alliances (as Jefferson so felicitously put it when he became President four years later and happily endorsed a policy that kept the United States from having to support Napoleon's imperialistic goals). Not until NATO would the United States enter again into formal alliance obligations. And to this day, America's alliance partners wonder whether the United States' presumably natural or at least deeply ingrained tradition of isolationism might, before too long, reassert itself once again, either in the guise of an outright withdrawal from world affairs or in the – more likely – form of heavy-handed unilateralism.

A less well noticed, but similarly important and controversial tradition set by the first President has to do with the interplay of domestic factions and international factors. His policy of neutrality, after all, was determined as much by a desire to avoid domestic unrest as by calculations of foreign policy interests. This pattern would hold true, or was violated only with serious domestic repercussions. On the one hand, the United States did get involved, politically and even militarily, in areas of the world from which it would not admit immigrants: Until well into the 20th century, there were few Americans of Latin American or Asian origin who could foment domestic turmoil in cases where the U.S. did intervene in Latin America or Asia. On the other hand, when the United States entered the two world wars of the 20th century, it found it necessary to suppress the large German community during the First World War and to (thoroughly illegally) imprison the small Japanese community in isolated camps during the Second World War. In acknowledging its shameful guilt many years later and by offering surviving Japanese-American victims of incarceration a token sum of restitution, the United States rediscovered the importance of this tradition. There is much speculation, now that massive waves of Latin American and Asian immigrants have so radically changed the demographic make-up of American society (as revealed in the stunningly surprising results of Census 2000), that a more diverse America might pursue a different foreign policy – one less focused on Europe and directed more towards the South and the Pacific. The long tradition of caution, if not indeed outright neutrality, in international conflicts that might incite domestic turmoil suggests that such speculation might well be premature, perhaps even wrong. Internal diversity is as much a prescription for caution as for coercive intervention.

Precisely in order to avoid the corrosive problems of domestic factions, the framers of the Constitution had designed a political system that would negate the need for, or the pernicious effects of, political parties. Or so they thought. Political reality caught up with them even while they were running the country they had founded. In the process they established yet another important tradition: Despite their best intentions, politics does not stop at the water's edge. Or, as a later adage would have it: All politics is local. Foreign policy is subject to the interplay of domestic forces, much to the dislike of Presidents (who, with flimsy evidence, continue to argue that the Constitution grants the executive branch a dominant role in foreign policy) and even more to the consternation of foreign leaders who have to deal with the United States (and who do not understand how a superpower can tolerate such a presumably outdated system of government).

The elections of 1800 were a harbinger of party politics to come. The presidential contest pitted the incumbent President, crusty realist John Adams standing for the rights and "energy" of the federal government against the firebrand idealist Thomas Jefferson who believed "that government governs best that governs least." In a development considerably more dramatic and entertaining than the elections 200 years later, Jefferson eventually prevailed in the House of Representatives, but only after his arch-rival Hamilton had thrown his support to Jefferson against the challenge of Aaron Burr (who, as Jefferson's candidate for Vice President, had emerged as contender for the presidency due to a quirk of the Constitution's election provisions that was quickly remedied). Adams left Washington in a huff as Jefferson was inaugurated; the two, old friends from revolutionary times and diplomatic service in Europe, would stay out of touch with each other until shortly before they both died on July 4, 1826. Hamilton and Burr, who had their political base in New York, engaged in deadly enmity that resulted in Hamilton being killed by Burr in a duel. So much for a political system without partisanship.

Jefferson's two terms as President were not marked by many successful foreign policy undertakings. Due to a stroke of luck (Napoleon lost Haiti to rebelling slaves and he needed cash for his war efforts) Jefferson was able to purchase the Louisiana Territory west from the Mississippi to the Rocky Mountains. But America's policy of neutrality in the European wars led to increasing conflicts with both France and Great Britain. Jefferson sought to solve these conflicts (mostly involving American shipping interests) by imposing an embargo on all shipping to and from the warring parties. He thus established another tradition: to use sanctions as a coercive instrument in order to avoid having to go to war. Such efforts failed then as much as they have failed since. Great Britain did not give in, while at home the commercial interests in the New England states, much hurt by the embargo, came close to seceding from the United States. Eventually, the embargo was lifted. But now it was the "War Hawks" in the West, where Great Britain allegedly stirred up trouble by instigating Indian raids against white settlements, who clamored for teaching the Brits a lesson. When war came in 1812 during the presidency of James Madison, it was the Americans who learned a lesson, especially after British troops had burned down the few public buildings just erected in Washington City. It was the last time the United States suffered the indignity of a foreign invasion. Ever since, the United States has, at times almost pathologically so, insisted on the primacy of "homeland defense."

Taking care of America first in general is an uncontroversial proposition. It has, and does, become a matter of controversy, however, where and when demands for American intervention elsewhere are rejected in the name of an "American first" realism as too idealistic and therefore not in America's interest. A classic case of such a clash of interests occurred in 1821, just after James Monroe had become President (and John Quincy Adams, the son of President Adams, his Secretary of State). Greece was engaged in a struggle to throw off the yoke of the Ottoman Empire. There was a great deal of agitation (primarily on college campuses) for the United States to come to the help of the Greek freedom fighters. Secretary Adams felt it necessary to counter such agitation. He used the occasion of a July 4 (1821) oration to remind his audience that: "Wherever the standard of freedom and independence has been or shall be unfurled, there will her [the United States'] heart, her benedictions, and her prayers be. But she goes not abroad in search of monsters to destroy."[2]

The domestic struggle between realists and idealists over the pursuit of foreign policy goals is as old as the American Republic itself. But John Quincy Adams's historic soundbite – "goes not abroad in search of monsters to destroy" – reflects another long-standing tradition of American foreign policy. For in fact, the American public is never more ready to approve of international interventions than when there are identifiable monsters to be destroyed. As a corollary to this rule, foreign policy elites like to – indeed, feel compelled to – justify interventions in terms of "monsters to destroy," from the Kaiser to Hitler, Stalin, Saddam Hussein, Slobodan Milosevic and Osama bin Laden. The very personal demonization of opponents is a reliable tradition of American foreign policy.

John Quincy Adams, the real author of the Monroe Doctrine (1823) that sought to keep European monsters out of the Western Hemisphere (but allow the United States a relatively free hand there), ran for President in 1824. His opponent was General Andrew Jackson, the hero of the battle of New Orleans (1814), where his troops defeated advancing British forces after a peace treaty had already been signed (news of which, however, had not yet reached the United States). Once again, the outcome of the election was thrown in doubt by a result that saw Jackson leading in the public vote, but not gaining enough support in the Electoral College to claim victory. Eventually, Adams was elected by a majority in the House of Representatives that he was able to gain by offering one of the other contenders the position of Secretary of State in exchange for his support. Jackson cried foul and swore revenge. Which he

2 Quoted according to Walter LaFeber, *The American Age. United States Foreign Policy at Home and Abroad since 1750* (New York: W.W. Norton, 1989), p. 80. LaFeber's book offers an excellent introduction to the history of domestic-foreign interrelationships.

got four years later, when he and his forces of Western populist democracy took over the presidency and ushered in a new era in American politics.

Jackson, an ardent Indian fighter, was a militant expansionist, focusing less on foreign policy issues and more on getting rid of native Americans who stood in the way of expansion. His policy of "Indian removal," an early form of ethnic cleansing, constitutes another shameful episode in American history. To speak of a "Jacksonian tradition" in American foreign policy is therefore not entirely correct.[3] Yet in a larger sense there is just such a tradition, which might also be called the "hillbilly tradition" in American politics. (Its essence is captured in a famous country-and-western song: "Oh Lord, it's hard to be humble when you're perfect in every way.") At its heart is the populist notion that the people are always right and that the American people are the best. From this sense of righteousness follows a foreign policy tradition that encourages the United States to get what it wants, if the U.S. can claim a right to it (Indian lands, a Panamanian isthmus, a colony in the Philippines), or is right in doing it (fighting the Kaiser, Hitler, Stalin, Saddam, Osama bin Laden). In pursuit of such goals, traditional niceties of diplomacy or the finer arts of *Realpolitik* need not be applied. Instead, apply full force in order to maximize the chances of success (and minimize the risks of loss of lives on your own side).[4] Once the goal has been accomplished, get out, if necessary leaving the dirty clean-up job to others. It is readily apparent that this Jacksonian tradition is alive and well in the United States today, as evidenced in the ongoing debates over the use of massive force (Weinberger and Powell Doctrine, as applied in the Gulf War or in the air wars against Serbia over Kosovo and Afghanistan against Taliban and al-Quaeda) and the requirements to minimize one's own losses at all costs (including those imposed on the opponent).

The American public as a whole does not live comfortably with all aspects of the Jacksonian tradition. It does, after all, clash with some self-perceptions that see the United States as morally superior to other countries.

---

3 See Walter Russell Mead, "The Jacksonian Tradition," in: *The National Interest*, 58, Winter 1999/2000, pp. 5-30 (also accessible at: http://www.nationalinterest.org/issues/58/Mead.html). Mead's article brilliantly captures this important element in the interplay of domestic and international forces.

4 "For the first Jacksonian rule of war is that wars must be fought with all available force. The use of limited force is deeply repugnant. Jacksonians see war as a switch that is either 'on' or 'off'. They do not like the idea of violence on a dimmer switch. Either the stakes are important enough to fight for – in which case you should fight with everything you have – or they are not, in which case you should mind your own business and stay home. To engage in a limited war is one of the costliest political decisions an American president can make – neither Truman nor Johnson survived it." (Mead, "Jacksonian Tradition")
"The second key concept in Jacksonian thought about war is that the strategic and tactical objective of American forces is to impose our will on the enemy with as few American casualties as possible." (Mead, "Jacksonian Tradition")

How can that be true when the United States blatantly engages in aggressive warfare, as President James K. Polk did in 1846, when he sent American forces to occupy Mexico in order to force that unfortunate neighbor to give up New Mexico and California to the United States (which itself was in pursuit of a "manifest destiny" seeking to establish the United States from "sea to shining sea")?

Polk succeeded in almost doubling the size of the United States, yet there are no monuments in monument-rich Washington to celebrate that achievement. He is the best forgotten president – conveniently forgotten because to remember him would force a confrontation with unpleasant truths.[5] Theodore Roosevelt is not quite that forgotten. But he is better known for his exploits as a "rough rider" – leading the charge up San Juan Hill in Cuba – than for the fact that he, as Assistant Secretary of the Navy, almost single-handedly got America into the Spanish-American War in the first place (1898). The United States emerged from that war not only as a great power, but also as a greater power, having acquired a number of territories (including Hawaii and Puerto Rico) in the process. Roosevelt, riding the fame of his "rough rider" exploits, eventually became President and went on to win the first Nobel Peace Prize for an American when he mediated between Japan and Russia after their war of 1904. The term "rough rider," however, remains an appropriate description of a foreign policy approach based on the Jacksonian tradition.

The Jacksonian tradition is an amalgamation of different values and orientations that is unique to the United States. That uniqueness derives in the second instance from immigration patterns (Mead attributes the origins of this tradition to largely Scottish immigrants who settled in the Appalachian mountains), but in the first instance from immigration itself. As a country of immigrants, the United States, unlike most other countries around the world, cannot define itself in terms of ethnic origins. Its national identity must therefore be based on other characteristics. Despite many problems of consistency and credibility, these identifying characteristics are the values on which the United States was founded and which it continues to protect and project.

5 Domestic support for the war against Mexico was overwhelming, but not total. Abraham Lincoln, a young Congressman from Illinois, spoke out against it. Henry David Thoreau tried to encourage his fellow-Americans to practice "civil disobedience" (such as refusing to pay taxes) against it. And John Quincy Adams, the only president ever to be elected to the House of Representatives after his presidency, railed against it. When the House of Representatives voted to award parade swords to the winning generals, Adams got so upset that he suffered a stroke on the floor of the House and lapsed into a coma from which he did not recover. That Adams would die in protest over an award of parade swords to generals who had gone "in search of monsters to destroy" (the monster being General Santa Anna, the Mexican dictator, who had refused to accede to American demands) is one of the enduring ironies of American politics.

Among these values are individualism – the firm belief in individual rights (especially vis-à-vis the state) and the basic equality of individuals within society – and democracy in a multi-layered political system. In combination, such values amount to a belief in American exceptionalism: the conviction that America is, or should be, Number One in the world.

In terms of these underlying values, public opinion has always influenced the conduct of foreign policy. So has published opinion, as the press played a decisive role in formulating public opinion and helping to set the national agenda, from Thomas Paine's pamphlets during the struggle for independence to Harriet Beecher Stowe's *Uncle Tom's Cabin* (that set the stage for the Civil War), from the "Yellow Press" (that pushed the United States to intervene in Cuba against the fading Spanish empire) to CNN, whose pictures of human suffering would not let the United States stay out of Somalia or Bosnia. The "CNN-factor" may be new in terms of the medium, but it is not all new in terms of the media's and the public's mutually reinforcing role in U.S. foreign policy. Yet it is also evident that the precise nature of that influence cannot accurately be predicted at any point in time, or for any concrete case. For the underlying values are split in such a way that concrete policy recommendations may often be completely contradictory, just as the emergence of specific value coalitions can often be surprising.

In regard to specific orientations towards the outside world (but often reflecting deeply held personal and political convictions), Americans are split between realism and idealism. Realism (whose classic proponents range from John Quincy Adams to Henry Kissinger) argues for the hard-nosed pursuit of strictly defined national interests along the lines of traditional European *Realpolitik*, without regard for any kinds of passion or "sentimentality" (Kissinger's preferred term). Idealism pleads for the primacy of values over interests, for the reality of passions, for the dreams of a better world. Realists are basically pessimistic, idealists optimistic. Not least for that reason, but also because their country is, after all, founded on ideals, idealism has always enjoyed hearty support among Americans.

In regard to specific orientations toward their own country, Americans are split between those who claim that America should come first – that strictly American interests should predominate – and those who believe that America should be Number One in the world – that it should set an example, and serve as a role model, for a different kind of behavior, for a better kind of political system, in short, for a more perfect world. "America First" proponents claim the singularity of American interests. "America Number One" adherents believe in the exceptional qualities of their country Both are American nationalists; but the nature of their nationalism differs in significant ways.

The interplay of international orientations and nationalist values yields (at least) four distinct types of foreign policy approaches. These are (in the Weberian sense) ideal-types; in reality, they may be less than clear-cut and the boundary lines among them can be quite fuzzy. Still, these four types more often than not conform to actual policy positions (taken, for instance, by candidates for public office and their voters).[6] The first typical foreign policy approach is best described as "Fortress America." It results from the interplay of realism and "America First." Its essence was captured – and represented – perfectly by Pat Buchanan when, in the course of his unsuccessful run for the presidency as the candidate of the Reform Party in 2000, he suggested it was time for the United States to pull its troops out of Kosovo in order to station them at the border to Mexico. "Fortress America" advocates are classical isolationists, who do not want the United States exposed to the evils of the world (which might infect it with such alien ideas as socialism) and who see no role for the United States to fight the evils of the world.

By contrast, the second typical foreign policy approach could be termed "Battleship America" (or, in more modern terms, "Carrier Battle Group America"). This policy preference results from the interplay of realism and the "America Number One" nationalism. As such, it comes closest to the Jacksonian tradition. Its advocates much prefer unilateral American action, swift and decisive where necessary, but without any constraints of sentimentality or, for that matter, of international law. America must do what is right (for it), and it must do it right. It should not be tied down by other considerations, or propelled into action by outside obligations. Such appeals to righteous unilateralism can find deep resonance in the American body politic.

The third ideal-type of U.S. foreign policy might be called (with apologies to President Lyndon Johnson, who did not mean it that way) "Great Society." It results from the combination of idealism and "America First" nationalism. Unlike conservative isolationists, its advocates insist that the United States live up to its own ideals first before it gets involved in outside activities. "Great Society" adherents want to see significant domestic change, and they do not want to have it impeded by costly foreign policies. Typical for this position were Martin Luther King and his followers in the civil rights movement, who opposed the War in Vietnam for precisely those reasons, long before such opposition had become politically correct. A more recent variant of this approach is (re)presented by Ralph Nader, presidential candidate of the Green Party in 2000, who ran on a platform of resistance to allegedly anonymous global forces (such as the WTO) and of support for the perfection of American society and politics along environmental and classical populist lines.

---

6 For a more extensive exploration of these public opinion characteristics see Gebhard Schweigler, "'America First'? Die öffentliche Meinung und die amerikanische Aussenpolitik," in Matthias Demibinski, Peter Rudolf, Jürgen Wilzewski (eds.), *Amerikanische Weltpolitik nach dem Ost-West-Konflikt* (Baden-Baden: Nomos, 1994), pp. 23-67.

For want of a better term, the fourth ideal-type could be termed "Global Society." It combines idealism with "America Number One" nationalism. Its proponents embrace the argument that it is not only in the United States' very own interest, but also an American duty to help remake the world in America's image. Not only would that result in a better, more prosperous and more peaceful world (not least because democracies do not fight each other and market economies help each other), but it would also reaffirm America's exceptional position as a role model for the rest of the world. Not surprisingly, "Global Society" adherents believe in the magic powers of globalization in general, and the Internet in particular. They also point to the United States' obligations in helping to alleviate problems of a global nature (such as the spread of AIDS or the increase of emissions resulting in global warming).

As the election results of 2000 have shown, it is quite evident that there is relatively little support among the American public for "America First" approaches. Neither Pat Buchanan nor Ralph Nader were able to garner even minimalist support for their positions and their parties. Thus there is no indication that the United States, under pressure of public opinion, could backslide into any kind of isolationist foreign policies. On the other hand, the extremely close election between Al Gore (who won the popular vote) and George W. Bush (who won the bare majority of the Electoral College with some friendly help from conservative judges on the Supreme Court) indicates how deeply split Americans are along a number of dimensions – including that of foreign policy approaches. Both candidates and their parties firmly fell into the category of "America Number One," but their realist and idealist impulses and inclinations differentiated them.

By and large, the majority of American public opinion supports "Global Society" goals, even though most Americans – and their policy-makers – show little understanding of the facts or of each other's opinions.[7] But, along the lines of the Jacksonian tradition, they are susceptible to unilateralist appeals. President George W. Bush, as he amply demonstrated after the events of September 11, 2001, has shown a certain willingness to go it alone, and to ride rough. It is likely that the American public will give him considerable leeway – at least for a while, and up to a point. Should the new President stray too far, however, or not be successful with his "Battleship America"

---

7 See, for instance, "Americans on Foreign Aid and World Hunger. A Study of U.S. Public Attitudes,"
February 2, 2001; "Americans on the Global Warming Treaty" (Principal Investigator: Steven Kull). November 27, 2000; "American on Globalization: A Study of US Public Attitudes," March 28, 2000. Reports by the Program on International Policy Attitudes (PIPA), University of Maryland, College Park, MD, accessible at: http://www.pipa.org/index.html. PIPA also conducted a fascinating survey of public attitudes and their (very false) perception by policy-makers: Steven Kull and I. M. Destler, *Misreading the Public: The Myth of a New Isolationism* (Washington: Brookings Institution, 1999).

approaches, public opinion quite possibly will rein him in. The idealist impulse as much as the realities of globalization will impose that constraint upon him.

When the United States declared their independence from Great Britain in 1776, they appealed to a "decent respect for the opinion of mankind" in justifying their action. Ever since, a decent respect for public opinion in general has characterized the American political process. Despite all the vagaries of that process, and the seeming fickleness of public opinion, the United States and the rest of the world has been well served by that reliance.

Part II
U.S. Leadership and the Reform of Western Security Institutions

Peter W. Rodman

"U.S. Leadership and the Reform of Western Security Institutions: NATO Enlargement and ESDP"

Introduction

The November 2000 elections in the United States have produced a divided national government, which will be a source of many problems. Nevertheless I thought I would try to begin on a more reassuring note – stressing the degree of bipartisan consensus that I am convinced exists on American international engagement, and particularly on the U.S. commitment to Europe. Both the Clinton Administration and the Republican Congress have expressed themselves on the issues before us, on a number of occasions, in a bipartisan and (I would say) constructive manner. This is no guarantee of a bipartisan and constructive future, but it is the logical starting point of any discussion of the new domestic context in the United States.

Not only is the United States not isolationist in this post-Cold War period; not even the much-maligned Republican Congress can fairly be called that. Don't be misled by some of the exuberant rhetoric of our domestic debate, particularly in a campaign year. Clinton's is not the first administration to throw the label "isolationist" around rather freely while struggling with those who disagree with some of his policies. The Congress has demonstrated by its support for NATO enlargement, for a strong global U.S. military posture, and for free trade (NAFTA, WTO, MFN for China, etc.) that it is internationalist on the most important strategic issues.

In fact, what we have had in the recent period between the Clinton Administration and the Republican Congress is not a clash between internationalism and isolationism, but between a more Wilsonian philosophy of internationalism and a more strategic-minded internationalism. The name of Woodrow Wilson has long been associated with an idealistic faith in multilateral institutions, in disarmament, and in humanitarian engagement, as opposed to what are disparaged as raw calculations of power, strategy, and national interest. Thus the Clinton Administration's great initial faith in the United Nations (in what Madeleine Albright called a U.S. policy of "assertive multilateralism")[1], and in

1 Amb. Madeleine Albright, Statement before the U.S. House of Representatives, Committee on Foreign Affairs, Subcommittee on International Security, International Organization, and Human Rights, Washington, June 24, 1993.

international law, multilateral arms control, and humanitarian military interventions from Haiti and Somalia to Bosnia and Kosovo. (Forty percent of all the UN Security Council resolutions since 1945 have occurred in the Clinton Administration.) The President was reported to dismiss the more classical geopolitical considerations as "Old Think."[2]

The Republican answer to this is to reassert a strategic view and a principle of national interest. This includes a more classical appreciation of the role of power in the world, and therefore less faith in multilateral institutions or international law to deter aggression and assure security, especially in a world in which the likes of Iraq, Iran, and North Korea still pose challenges. Export promotion and the ozone layer have not yet completely replaced the traditional security agenda. The principle of national interest may mean less of our idealistic exuberance, but also a bit less self-righteousness about America's ability to improve the rest of the world.

The Republican instinct is also to reserve U.S. combat troops for missions of strategic importance to the international order – preserving the balance of power in vital regions such as Europe, Asia, and the Gulf, and preferring that the international community find other cooperative ways to deal with the rash of humanitarian crises that have plagued the past decade. When these arise, the United States should be willing to help, but should prefer that other capable and like-minded nations take the lead to organize an international response. East Timor, in that sense, is a model. In fact, there is growing bipartisan support for this approach. [3] The fear is that the United States will only exhaust itself if its troops are the first ones called upon to deal with every international crisis, including those of more humanitarian than strategic importance.

Republicans in Congress have, to be sure, resisted important international agreements such as the Kyoto Protocol, the Comprehensive Test Ban Treaty, the anti-personnel land mines convention, and the International Criminal Court. There is not sufficient space here to explore all these controversies. I would simply note that the Clinton Administration itself rejected the latter two documents, and that on all four of them the Republican opposition featured many who would generally be deemed moderates and who had serious substantive objections on national-security grounds. There may be a serious divergence of perspective developing across the Atlantic – witness the abortive recent meeting at The Hague on the Kyoto Protocol – but it cannot be explained simply in terms of partisan politics in the United States.

---

2 Jim Hoagland, "Russia Into the Vacuum," *Washington Post*, November 21, 1997, p. A27.

3 See, e.g., the report of the bipartisan U.S. Commission on National Security/21st Century, *Seeking a National Strategy: A Concert for Preserving Security and Promoting Freedom* (Washington, DC: April 15, 2000), pp. 6, 13, at www.nssg.gov.

Congressional Republicans have also, as noted, been strong supporters of free trade. Protectionism is much stronger a force in the Democratic Party. The issue of using free trade agreements to try to impose standards of environmental protection and labor rights is not yet resolved. The November elections, however, showed that Pat Buchanan, Ross Perot, and possibly Ralph Nader have been marginalized.

Republicans were divided over the Balkan crises. But when Sen. Robert Dole was Senate Majority Leader, he urged a *more* assertive policy in Bosnia than either Europeans or the Clinton Administration wanted (lifting the arms embargo and arming the Bosnians); it was hardly a case of Republican isolationism. In the end, the Congress expressed its disagreements but did not thwart President Clinton's Bosnia policy.[4] The same was true in the case of other Clinton interventions – a more honorable course, I would say, than that of past Democratic Congresses that worked ferociously to undermine Republican Presidents' policies in Indochina and Central America by all means available. The more recent debate over reducing U.S. troops in Bosnia, originating in some statements by Gov. George W. Bush, is really more of an issue of timing. Americans share European hopes that European forces can take on a greater role in peacekeeping in such cases. But all agree that any further transfer of responsibility ought to be a matter of consultation and agreement.

The NATO enlargement debate in America in 1997-98 is more instructive. NATO enlargement was an idea, in fact, that originated among Congressional Republicans in 1994-95 (again, hardly an isolationist impulse) and soon gained bipartisan support. But the arguments made for the first wave of NATO enlargement during our great national debate of 1997-98 show an interesting philosophical difference between the two parties. The Clinton Administration emphasized Wilsonian themes – how NATO enlargement was good for democracy and ethnic harmony, and even good for Russia. As President Clinton listed the arguments in a 1997 speech, NATO enlargement was necessary:

- to help address local conflicts that "threaten the common peace of all" (like Bosnia),
- to help "secure the historic gains of democracy" in Central and Eastern Europe,
- to "encourage prospective members to resolve their differences peacefully," and
- to help (along with Partnership for Peace and special arrangements with Russia and Ukraine) to "erase the artificial line in Europe that Stalin

4 Dov S. Zakheim, *Congress and National Security in the Post-Cold War Era* (Washington, DC: The Nixon Center, October 1998), Chapter II.

drew, and bring Europe together in security, not keep it apart in instability."[5]

The Republicans did not disagree with these goals, but in the U.S. Senate's resolution that accompanied its advice and consent to ratification of NATO enlargement, they insisted on strengthening the *strategic* rationale for the enterprise. That resolution declares bluntly that "NATO is first and foremost a military alliance," and the first mission listed for NATO is to prevent "the re-emergence of a hegemonic power confronting Europe."[6] Whether the reasons are more strategic-minded or more Wilsonian, nevertheless, the bottom line is that the United States intends to remain a power in Europe, and that this is a bipartisan commitment.

The particular issues at hand are the European Security and Defense Policy (ESDP) and the question of further NATO enlargement. Let me deal with these in turn.

European Security and Defense Policy

On ESDP, too, I would stress that what concerns have been expressed in the United States have been bipartisan. I see three kinds of problems – a rhetorical problem, an institutional problem, and a capabilities problem. I list these in ascending order of difficulty, though I think they are soluble.

By *the rhetorical problem*, I mean the temptation in Europe to use the United States as a foil as the European Union (EU) strives to construct its new institutions. As the EU struggles, especially, with the frustrating contradictions of trying to broaden its membership and deepen its central institutions at the same time, there is a temptation in some quarters in Europe to stress the need for Europe to be a "counterweight" to the United States, to be more of an equal to the United States, or to be more independent of the United States. The positive motivations for European integration are, of course, obvious and they predominate. But the temptation clearly exists in some quarters in Europe to build Europe on a platform of differentiation from the United States.

It was always inevitable that if Europe did more to strengthen itself, it would do so for its own reasons, not just to "share America's burdens." This is perfectly natural. If carried beyond a certain point, however, using the United States as a foil can be corrosive to Alliance relations and contrary to

5 President Bill Clinton, remarks at the United States Military Academy commencement, May 31, 1997.

6 Protocols to the North Atlantic Treaty of 1949 on the Accession of Poland, Hungary, and the Czech Republic, Resolution of Ratification, May 4, 1998, *Congressional Record*, pp. S4217-4220, especially Section 3.

Europe's own long-term interest. One danger, of course, is that it could trigger a corresponding irresponsibility on the American side of the Atlantic. There *are* isolationists in America, who, if they heard that Europeans no longer valued the Alliance, would be quite pleased to reciprocate the sentiment. Scholars at the libertarian CATO Institute in Washington, for example, have long been arguing that, with the end of the Soviet threat, there is no region of the world whose peace and security cannot already be handled adequately by the regional countries or by a natural regional balance of power. So we can come home.[7] The U.S. Congress, too, for all its current commitment to Europe, might give way to other impulses if it thought that Europeans themselves were eager to dispense with what they saw as American imposition.

It is not hard to find examples of what I mean, and they are not all in French. The French do, indeed, state the issue most acutely. When Foreign Minister Hubert Védrine complained famously about the American *"hyperpuissance"* (hyper power), the interesting part of his remarks was not the word *"hyperpuissance"* (I accept his contention that it is not really an invidious usage), but the statements which accompanied it, to the effect that America is too powerful, with hegemonic tendencies, and that the EU must labor mightily to be a "counterweight" in order to restore a much-needed "multipolarity" to the international system. To a conference of French ambassadors in August 1997, Mr. Védrine declared:

> Today there is one sole great power – the United States of America.... When I speak of its power, I state a fact...without acrimony. A fact is a fact....But this power carries in itself, to the extent that there is no counterweight, especially today, a unilateralist temptation...and the risk of hegemony.[8]

France's policy, he went on to say, was:

> to contribute...to the emergence of several poles in the world capable of being a factor of equilibrium....Europe is [such] an actor, a means of influence absolutely necessary for such a multipolar world to come about.[9]

In an interview with *Liberation* two years ago, Mr. Védrine complained again that "a major factor in the world today" was "the overriding predominance of the United States in all areas and the current lack of any counterweight." Again, Europe had to be that counterweight:

> We have to have nerves of steel. We have to persevere. We have to methodically broaden the basis for agreement between Europeans. We have to coordinate with

7 E.g., Ted Galen Carpenter, *The Case for U.S. Strategic Independence*, Foreign Policy Briefing No. 16 (Washington, DC: CATO Institute, Jan. 16, 1992).

8 Minister of Foreign Affairs Hubert Védrine, remarks to a conference of French ambassadors, Paris, August 28, 1997.

9 Ibid.

> the United States all along the line on a basis agreed by all European states, combining a friendly approach with the need to be respected, and defending organized multilateralism and the requirements of the Security Council under all circumstances. Finally, we have to plan politically, institutionally, and mentally for the time when Europe has the courage to go further.[10]

There are other such statements. The Economic and Monetary Union (EMU), of course, was meant to enable Europe to be a stronger competitor and to be more equal to the United States. German Chancellor Helmut Kohl argued in 1996:

> [W]e all need Europe to be competitive in the global market. Only together are we able to assert ourselves against the trade blocs of the Far East and North America, and with the Mercosur pact that Latin America will join as well.[11]

Dutch Prime Minister Wim Kok spoke of EMU as "forming the foundation for Europe's increased power in the world."[12] Former German Chancellor Helmut Schmidt welcomed EMU as something that would "change the whole world situation so that the United States can no longer call all the shots."[13]

As for the EU's Common Foreign and Security Policy (CFSP, forerunner to ESDP), Wim Kok in 1998 made it explicit that it was meant to provide a "counterweight to the United States."[14] After the Kosovo war of 1999, even though it was seen as a success, the reaction was not that it vindicated the Atlantic Alliance but that it was all the more reason to spur the building of Europe's independent institutions in the security field. After the Bremen ministerial meeting of the Western European Union (WEU) in May 1999, for example, an official German account of the discussion reported:

> Foreign Minister Joschka Fischer and Defense Minister Rudolf Scharping urge a rapid buildup of common EU forces to master crises and conflicts in Europe even without participation of the United States. The Kosovo conflict expresses how urgent and indispensable this buildup will be for the future of Europe, declared Fischer.[15]

---

10 Jacques Amalric and Pierre Haski, "Védrine: 'The Era of Symbolism is Over,'" *Liberation*, November 24, 1998, pp. 8-9, in FBIS-WEU-98-328, 24 November 1198.

11 Helmut Kohl, address at Catholic University, Louvain, Belgium, February 2, 1996, excerpted in *Internationale Politik*, August 1996, p. 82.

12 Wim Kok, "Euro Is Crowning Glory of Long Process," lecture at the University of Leiden, March 9, 1998, excerpted in *Handelsblad* (Rotterdam), March 9, 1998, in FBIS-WEU-98-070, 11 March 1998.

13 Schmidt quoted in Lawrence F. Kaplan and Joshua Muravchik, "Family Feud: Western Europe Tells the East: Keep Quiet," *Wall Street Journal Europe*, April 3, 2000.

14 Wim Kok quoted in *Der Standard* (Vienna), October 27, 1998, p.2.

15 Foreign Minister Joschka Fischer and Defense Minister Rudolf Scharping at the WEU ministerial in Bremen, May 10, 1999, quoted in *Bundespresseamt Bulletin*, May 11, 1999.

Kosovo seemed only to demonstrate again to many Europeans how painful it is to be so dependent on the United States. A German Green Party document hailed the ESDP as the beginning of Europe's "emancipation" from the United States:

> Especially in the context of the war in Kosovo, many voices have called for the emancipation of the European states from the USA, and the development of an independent European security policy.[16]

The rhetoric surrounding the Nice EU summit suggests that Europeans are divided on how far to push this. The French stress ESDP's "independence"; the British and others stress complementarity. If the anti-American reflex can be kept under some restraint, the rhetorical problem can be contained. Both sides of the Atlantic can then go about the serious business of ensuring that ESDP is built in the most constructive fashion.

This brings us to *the institutional problem*. The institutional problem is how to define the relationship between the new European defense organization and NATO. Up to now we have had one defense organization in the West; now we are about to have two. Given the decision that Europe has made, the issue today is not whether this comes about, but how. It is important that these institutions be complementary and not competitive. And especially at the formative stage of a new institution, it is important to get the theology right. If this makes me a Cartesian, so be it. Reassurances that "it will all work out in practice," while admirable for their pragmatic spirit, will not help us if, years from now, discrepancies that now seem minor turn out to become bigger divergences.

These concerns have been bipartisan in America as well. You are all familiar with the "three D's" enunciated by Secretary of State Albright – her cautions against duplication, decoupling, and discrimination.[17] Republicans in Congress have expressed the same concern, and, again, with bipartisan support.

A year ago, both houses of Congress passed, by overwhelming majorities, non-binding resolutions on the Atlantic Alliance and the European defense identity. The House of Representatives passed a resolution on November 2, 1999, by 278 to 133, stating that "the Alliance should welcome efforts by members of the European Union (EU) to strengthen their military capabilities and enhance their role within the Alliance through the European Security and Defense Identity (ESDI)." It went on to say that "it is essential that security arrangements elaborated under the EU's Common Foreign and Security Policy (CFSP) complement, rather than duplicate NATO efforts and in-

---

16 Heinrich Böll Foundation, "A New Foreign and Security Policy for Europe?" conference brochure, 1-2 December 1999, Berlin.

17 Secretary of State Madeleine Albright, statement to the North Atlantic Council, Brussels, December 8, 1998.

stitutions, and be linked to, rather than decoupled from NATO structures, and provide for full and active involvement of all European Allies rather than discriminating against European Allies that are not members of the EU."[18]

A similar resolution passed the Senate, by unanimous consent, on November 8, 1999. It stressed that "NATO should remain the primary institution through which European and North American allies address security issues of transatlantic concern." It "acknowledge[d] the resolve of the European Union to have the capacity for autonomous action so that it can take decisions and approve military action where the Alliance as a whole is not engaged," and also called upon NATO and the EU to "promulgate... principles that will strengthen the transatlantic partnership, reinforce unity within NATO, and harmonize their roles in transatlantic affairs." The Senate resolution, too, counseled against discrimination, decoupling, and "unnecessary duplication." It also recommended that NATO have a kind of right of first refusal, suggesting that "on matters of trans-Atlantic concern, the European Union should make clear that it would undertake an autonomous mission through the European Security and Defense Identity only after the North Atlantic Treaty Organization had declined to undertake that mission".[19] It is noteworthy that the sponsors of this Senate resolution included a remarkable bipartisan mix: Senators William Roth, Richard Lugar, Joseph Biden, Jon Kyl, Chuck Hagel, Gordon Smith, Joseph Lieberman, and Jesse Helms.

The institutional problem, at this writing, is the subject matter of negotiations between the EU and NATO. In the French EU Presidency, these negotiations seem to have been contentious. But this problem, too, is soluble, and I expect any U.S. administration would seek to solve it.

A proper solution will require three elements. One is some acknowledgment that the Alliance has a strong claim on being the principal forum for European-American deliberation in a serious crisis, and not limited to Article 5 cases. It may not be the formal "right of first refusal" that the U.S. Senate asked for, but the EU's favored phraseology – "where NATO as a whole is not engaged" – leans somewhat in that direction, with due regard to the EU's sensitivities about not being subordinate to NATO. However, some further clarity on this would be a good idea.

Second is procedural cooperation and transparency. If regular procedures can be developed that ensure transparency of deliberations, liaison at many levels, dual-hatting of key officials, and collaboration on a routine basis, problems will be minimized in practice. The involvement of the Deputy SACEUR is one pivotal element.

---

18 House Resolution 59, 106th Congress, 1st Session, passed November 2, 1999, paragraphs 7, 9.

19 Senate Resolution 208, 106th Congress, 1st Session, passed by unanimous consent November 8, 1999, Section 1 (a), (1), (4), (5) and (b) (1).

Third is avoiding duplication. The U.S. position has retreated from the original "no duplication" to the more elastic "no unnecessary duplication." But Washington has become more vocal lately, in advance of the Nice summit, about what it sees as creation of a duplicative EU military planning staff: "What we don't want to see is a separate planning bureaucracy established that is independent and separate from that of NATO itself," U.S. Secretary of Defense William Cohen said at an October meeting of defense ministers in Birmingham.[20] U.S. Ambassador to NATO Alexander Vershbow echoed this sentiment in a speech in Belgium soon after.[21] More bluntly, in Brussels in December 2000, Secretary Cohen warned that "NATO could become a relic of the past" if NATO and the EU turned into competing organizations attempting "uncoordinated, inefficient, and ad hoc responses" with scarce defense resources.[22] A formal, just published Defense Department strategy document attempted to put it positively:

> NATO and the EU must work cooperatively to develop (and avoid unnecessary and costly duplication of) the military assets and capabilities required by both organizations. This cooperation should extend to the creation of a common, coherent, and collaborative defense planning review process, a complex area where NATO has proven tools and is willing and able to assist the EU in meeting its Headline Goal.[23]

The significance of these expressions is that the Pentagon, SACEUR, and other elements of the U.S. governmental establishment clearly remain concerned about the practical complications of this enterprise, and these views will continue to have bureaucratic weight in any new U.S. administration.

The U.S. Senate and House resolutions both placed considerable emphasis on *the capabilities problem*. The House resolution stated, for example: "[T]he key to a vibrant and more influential ESDI is the improvement of European military capabilities that will strengthen the Alliance."[24] Congress's "burden sharing" complaints are familiar, and perhaps annoying to Europe. But in this context, they reflect a positive sentiment: The United States is

---

20 Secretary of Defense Willam S. Cohen, DoD news briefing, Birmingham, UK, October 10, 2000. See also the quotes from SACEUR Gen. Joseph Ralston in Michael R. Gordon, "Europe Acts to Build Own Military Force," *New York Times*, November 21, 2000, p. A8.

21 Amb. Alexander Vershbow, address to the Centre d`Etudes Europeene, Waterloo, Belgium, October 19, 2000.

22 Secretary of Defense William S. Cohen, press conference at NATO Headquarters, Brussels, December 5, 2000 (DoD News Briefing); Douglas Hamilton and Charles Aldinger, "EU Force Could Spell NATO's End, Cohen Says," *Washington Post*, December 6, 2000, p. A28.

23 U.S. Department of Defense, *Strengthening Transatlantic Security: A U.S. Strategy for the 21st Century* (Washington, DC: Department of Defense, December 2000), p. 21.

24 House Resolution 59, Section 8. See similar language in Senate Resolution 208, Section 1 (b) (2).

saying emphatically that it *does not want* a Europe that is weak; it does not want a Europe that is divided; and it does not want a Europe that is incapable of acting autonomously and effectively in the military field. In other words, it will support the new EU defense entity provided that the relationship with NATO is clarified and that real military effectiveness is achieved. As Secretary of State Albright and Foreign Secretary Robin Cook have put it: "Dangers to NATO and the transatlantic link are far more likely to come from European weakness than European strength."[25] The worst of all worlds would be a new institution that complicates NATO's cohesion but without providing new capabilities.

To sum up, and to try to predict the American view in the coming period:

- We *want* our European allies to be capable of acting autonomously and effectively in the military sphere. And we will encourage – even badger – the Europeans to build the real capabilities to do it.
- We respect our European allies' decision to do this through the EU rather than NATO. But we will continue, I hope politely, to work with the EU to minimize the disruption to NATO. The expressions of U.S. concern in my view have had a beneficial effect. It cannot be in the interest of the United States to undercut, by its silence, all those in Europe who value the Atlantic Alliance and share the same concerns.

NATO Enlargement

Further NATO enlargement also remains a bipartisan goal. The Republican and Democratic Party platforms endorsed it, as did both candidates during the 2000 campaign. Governor George W. Bush reaffirmed the commitment in a statement issued on November 1, which declared, inter alia:

> [T]he enlargement of NATO to include other nations with democratic values, pluralist political systems and free market economies must surely continue. Neither geographic nor historical circumstances should dictate the future of a Europe whole and free. Governor Bush will lead our European Allies to advance the process of NATO enlargement at the next Alliance Summit in 2002. Russia must never be given a veto over NATO enlargement.[26]

You are familiar with the options being discussed among advocates in the Washington policy community: a "big bang" bringing several new members in at once; a more incremental approach in the next round; a more passive

25 Secretary of State Madeleine Albright and Foreign Secretary Robin Cook, "Euro force will beef up NATO," *The Observer*, November 26, 2000.

26 "Governor Bush's Policy on NATO and NATO Enlargement," statement issued at Austin, Texas, November 1, 2000.

approach waiting for the EU to go first; and so on. I will not go into these options in detail, but I will venture a few observations about the likely American debate.

First, the political support that exists in the United States for a new round of NATO enlargement clearly includes the Baltic states. The Molotov-Ribbentrop pact is not regarded as binding on U.S. policy. The argument will also be made that a reappearance of Russian pressures on Baltic independence would pose a strategic problem for all of northern Europe, which NATO needs to address by one means or another. An option that did not include at least one of the Baltic states would probably be criticized by advocates as a cop-out. (I say "at least one of the Baltic states" because of the idea championed by Zbigniew Brzezinski that admitting Lithuania in an early round would serve to break the taboo against Baltic membership.)[27]

Second, the U.S. Senate will nevertheless approach a new round of NATO enlargement with deliberation. There were Republican Senators the last time around (John Warner, Kay Bailey Hutchison, and others) who expressed reservations even though it passed by an overwhelming margin (80-19). Senate Democrats, if they are in opposition to a Republican President, may be less stalwart on the question this time than they were when following the leadership of a Democratic President. This Senatorial caution may apply to an incremental option as much as to a "big bang" option. Thus it is to be hoped that the new administration will engage the Senate at an early stage of its own internal policy formulation, to maximize the likelihood that whatever option is put forward has broad support. (The House of Representatives also needs to be engaged. Last time, it was an important source of political support for NATO enlargement.)

Third, the substantive arguments brought to bear against NATO enlargement will be mostly familiar from last time. Many liberals will respond to the negative view of George Kennan, concerned about Russian reactions and disparaging as anachronistic the expansion of military commitments in the post-Cold War era. Some on the Right will ask about the military feasibility of forward defense in the Baltic region. Others, who focus on the emerging challenge of China, will share the liberals' concerns about the accumulation of quarrels with Russia (BMD, proliferation, the Balkans, and Caspian pipelines, in addition to NATO enlargement). There will be a lively debate on these questions.

Fourth, the evolution of an allied consensus will have an impact on the U.S. domestic debate. Therefore, consultation within the Alliance should proceed simultaneously with consultation with the U.S. Senate. The United States

27 Cf. *U.S. Policy toward Northeastern Europe*, Report of an Independent Task Force Sponsored by the Council on Foreign Relations (Zbigniew Brzezinski, chairman; F. Stephen Larrabee, project director), (New York: Council on Foreign Relations, 1999), p. 43.

should not be as peremptory in its approach to the allies on this question as it was last time.

In sum, I would say that another round of NATO enlargement has significant political impetus in the United States. The leadership of both parties has committed itself, and the Senate has set a precedent of sorts by its overwhelming vote last time. But the real debate has not yet begun. The experts will again be split. And there are a number of new political variables, including what degree of comity our evenly-divided Congress is able to achieve, and how far the Democratic Party drifts to the Left if it is in opposition.

There may be another new factor in the debate, however – namely, what perception U.S. Senators will have of the ESDP enterprise we have been discussing. The effect of this is unpredictable. If the perception arises that the EU is being built on the basis of opposition to the United States, some in the United States will be more disillusioned with the whole U.S.-European relationship, and more skeptical about NATO. Others, in contrast, especially on the conservative side, may intensify their advocacy of NATO enlargement as a kind of counterstrategy.

There were disturbing reports last winter and spring that France, and to some degree Germany, were putting pressure on Poland to be a "good European" (i.e., less close to the United States) if it wished to be admitted to the European Union. President Chirac (and reportedly also Foreign Minister Fischer) were said to have criticized Polish Foreign Minister Bronislaw Geremek for expressing concerns about ESDP. Czech and Hungarian officials have allegedly been subjected to similar pressures. These reports inevitably made their way back to Washington.[28]

If this sort of thing persists, NATO enlargement may become more compelling for some Americans as a way for the United States to consolidate its position in Europe in response. An environment of competition between Europe and the United States is not the healthiest context for common consideration of a major step such as further NATO enlargement, but it may happen. In the first-round debate in America on NATO enlargement, attitudes toward Russia were the pivotal issue; next time, perceptions of the EU might have equal weight.

So, our discussion comes full circle, and we are back to the core question: how healthy is the transatlantic partnership? It is one thing to acknowledge that Europeans are more likely to put effort into defense if they are asked to do so for the sake of European unity, rather than for Atlantic partnership. That is an argument for the EU project. It may sadden Americans, but it is probably true. Both sides of the Atlantic need, nevertheless, to see it as a priority to preserve the European-American partnership in the security field. The alliance of the Atlantic democracies is one of the successes of

---

28 Kaplan and Muravchik, *loc. cit.*

Western history, and the end of the Cold War has not terminated its value, strategic or moral. Maintaining the balance of power in Europe still requires an American contribution. Today's is a turbulent world of emerging new powers, proliferation of weapons of mass destruction and ballistic missiles, ethnic violence, a volatile global economy, and a host of new geopolitical and other challenges. In this environment, as before, Europeans' and Americans' first recourse should be each other. With respect to most of those major challenges, whether on the continent of Europe or elsewhere, our interests are fundamentally parallel; there is also no doubt that the effectiveness of our respective policies would be multiplied many times over if we worked together. I believe that is the preference of most Americans. I hope it remains true in Europe as well.

Charles A. Kupchan

Recasting the Atlantic Bargain

America's relationship with Europe has been the anchor of U.S. foreign policy for much of the past century. The Atlantic link promises to be equally important to America during this century, but the U.S-European relationship is headed into a new and more difficult era. The United States and the European Union must map out complementary strategies for ensuring the integrity and vitality of their relationship.

We are at a fluid moment in history, one in which the outlines of a new geopolitical landscape have yet to emerge. Such fluidity provides America and its partners an enormous opportunity to shape that new landscape. But at the same time, it denies us a readily available set of guiding assumptions upon which to base U.S. foreign policy. The enhanced threat of terrorism adds to the complexity of formulating a coherent and comprehensive strategy. Accordingly, this paper begins with a set of guiding assumptions in thinking about the future of U.S.-European relations. It then turns to an examination of specific areas of American policy.

Guiding Assumptions

The emerging Atlantic relationship will be quite different than over the past fifty years because of two fundamental changes in the geopolitical landscape. The first fundamental change is the rise of a stronger and more self-confident Europe. The European Union is reaching a new stage in its evolution that will lead to increased political cohesion, more autonomy, and a desire for greater influence in the international arena. This assessment is based on the following observations.

- The EU has completed the creation of a single market and a single currency. The euro declined over 20 percent after its introduction, largely due to the booming U.S. economy and the outflow of European capital to the United States. The euro is now likely to strengthen as a result of the U.S. slowdown, gradually evolving into one of the world's major reserve currencies. The EU is also expected to enjoy stronger economic growth than the United States in the near term. The entry of new members will ensure that the collective GDP of the EU soon surpasses that of the United States.

- The EU is continuing to pursue internal reforms that will provide for more efficient and collective decision-making and prepare the way for enlargement. The Nice Summit fell short of expectations on this front. However, the EU is expanding the use of qualified majority voting, strengthening the power of the EU parliament, and taking steps to reinforce the identity of Brussels as its collective capital. A debate is also underway on the drafting of an EU constitution. The approach of enlargement promises to give urgency to institutional reform.
- The EU has embarked on a serious effort to forge a common security policy and acquire the military forces needed to back it up. Javier Solana is the first High Representative for Foreign and Security Policy, and the EU is in the midst of building a rapid reaction force of some 60,000 troops. The EU has also been flexing its diplomatic muscle by offering to increasing its engagement on the Korean peninsula, taking the lead during the crisis in Macedonia, and enhancing its role in the Middle East. It is also working hard to strengthen its ties to Russia.
- Great Britain, after decades of keeping its distance from Europe, is gradually becoming one of the EU's leading members. Prime Minister Tony Blair was a key player behind the new initiative on the defense front. He intends to guide Britain into the euro zone with the strong mandate he received in the election of June 2001. The EU will be immeasurably strengthened by enhanced British participation.
- The EU enjoys enormous allure among Europe's new democracies. All the countries of Central Europe are preparing for membership, providing the EU a great deal of influence throughout the region. The EU promises to do for Europe's east what it succeeded in doing for its west – locking in democracy, prosperity, and peace.
- European politicians are beginning to use arguments about Europe's place in the world to legitimate the project of European integration. For the past fifty years, the need to escape Europe's bloody past was the main justification for integration. This argument now carries little weight among younger Europeans, who have no past from which they seek to escape. The new legitimating task for the EU is focused on the future and projecting Europe's voice on the world stage. As Tony Blair has stated, "Europe's citizens need Europe to be strong and united. They need it to be a power in the world. Whatever its origin, Europe today is no longer just about peace. It is about projecting collective power."[1]

---

1 Speech to the Polish Stock Exchange, October 6, 2000, available at <http://www.number-10.gov.uk/news.asp?NewsId=1341&SectionId=32>.

In light of the maturation of the EU, the United States has in Europe a stronger and more capable partner. At the same time, as Europe seeks a new station and a voice commensurate with that new station, the potential for rivalry with the United States also increases. Both sides will need to work to ensure that partnership prevails over rivalry.

The second fundamental change in the geopolitical landscape is the emergence of a new and more selective brand of internationalism in the United States. U.S. internationalism has reached a high-water mark and will be on a downward trajectory in the years ahead. Since the Cold War's end, the United States has been the chief guardian and peacemaker in virtually every quarter of the globe – a level of engagement that is likely to prove unsustainable over the long term. From this perspective, the activist and wide-ranging foreign policies of the 1990s are more likely to be an aberration, a legacy of the Cold War, rather than a good predictor of the future. This evaluation is based on the following considerations.

- The United States today faces the threat of terrorism, but it is not confronted by a major external adversary – a peer challenger. This strategic environment, as it cycles through domestic politics, is likely to induce the country to seek to lighten the burden of global engagement.
- The war against terrorism and the priority assigned to homeland defense will come at the expense of America's focus on more traditional missions – in particular, at the expense of America's strategic role in Europe. The more time U.S. troops spend defending the homeland the less time they will spend abroad.
- George W. Bush has pledged to pursue a more selective foreign policy than his predecessors. He began by reducing America's role in mediating conflicts on the Korean peninsula, and in the Balkans, Middle East, and Northern Ireland. He has also pledged to reorient U.S. foreign policy toward America's own hemisphere.
- The U.S. economy has begun to slow after successive years of unprecedented growth. The accompanying constraints on resources and political will promise to contribute to the emergence of a less ambitious brand of internationalism.
- American foreign policy is also becoming increasingly unilateralist in tone and substance. The Bush administration withdrew from the Kyoto Protocol and the ABM Treaty, and has made clear its opposition to the International Criminal Court and other multilateral institutions. This impulse has deep roots in America's individualistic political culture – and should not be seen as a passing phenomenon. Ideological, regional, and sectional divides are reemerging as powerful domestic forces shaping foreign policy.
- President Bush was elected by states in the south and west that have historically been less enthusiastic about liberal internationalism than states

in the northeast and on the west coast. These states are also some of the fastest growing in the country in demographic terms. The political preferences of these regions partly explain the unilateralist and neo-isolationist tones of President Bush's foreign policy.

- Americans who came of age after the Cold War are now entering the work force and rising to positions of prominence. They will not bring to the table the historical experiences of World War II, the rebuilding the Europe, and the fall of the Berlin Wall that had provided a ready foundation for U.S. internationalism over the past decades. Younger Americans, raised in a globalized world, are unlikely to be isolationist, but they may well support a more discriminating brand of international engagement than their elders.
- The threat of terrorism has to some extent countered the emerging unilateralist and neo-isolationist tone to U.S. policy. But terrorism will not serve as a solid foundation for robust internationalism in the same way that the Cold War did. Terror represents an elusive enemy; victory will be hard to measure. And the struggle against terrorism does not evoke the same sense of unity and sacrifice as America's confrontation with the Soviet Union.

The forging of a new and more selective brand of internationalism, if handled correctly, need not lead to a dangerous isolationism. Rather, it may represent a necessary search for a new level of international engagement that befits a new strategic environment and that is politically sustainable over the long term. Indeed, deliberately crafting a new internationalism is the best way to avoid the isolationism that could potentially result from an America that overextends itself.

Europe, precisely because of the success of the European Union in bringing prosperity and peace to the continent, is the part of the world that will feel the strongest effects of this new brand of U.S. internationalism. Europe is today no less important to the United States than during the previous half century, but it remains hard to make the case that the United States should remain Europe's primary guardian when the EU's collective wealth is surpassing that of America and when the United States faces far more pressing threats in the Middle East and East Asia. America's reluctant participation in the war over Kosovo and its continuing ambivalence toward the peacekeeping mission in the Balkans are clear signs that America is in the midst of altering its strategic priorities and reconsidering its dominant strategic role in Europe.

The rise of a stronger Europe and the evolution of a more prickly and selective brand of U.S. internationalism promise to have a profound effect on the Atlantic link. Indeed, the traditional Atlantic bargain – America keeps the peace while the EU focuses on economic and political integration – is rapidly coming undone. If the Atlantic link is to remain strong, a new and more balanced bargain is urgently needed, one that will require hard work by both sides.

Europe will have to redouble its efforts to forge a common position on foreign and defense policy. It will also have to devote sufficient political and economic resources to ensure that it builds its rapid reaction force in a timely and effective manner. The United States will have to make room for a stronger EU and accord it more influence in step with increases in Europe's collective political will and military capabilities. The United States will also need to resist unilateralism if it is to build a more balanced and cooperative relationship with Europe. If the Atlantic link is to remain strong in this new century, it must evolve into a more mature partnership. The next few years represent a critical window of opportunity for both Europe and the United States to get right this important transition.

Completing the European Project

During the current period of transition in the Atlantic relationship, the United States and Europe should together address the three remaining tasks needed to complete the European project: managing the emergence of ESDP, finishing the stabilization of Southeastern Europe, and enlarging Europe eastward.

ESDP. As indicated above, a robust European defense force capable of operating independently of U.S. forces is not just tolerable from an American perspective, but essential to maintaining the vitality of the Atlantic link. Far from undermining NATO, ESDP is critical to bringing about the more equal sharing of burdens that will keep America in Europe, give the alliance more capability to combat terrorism and other threats to collective interests, and make NATO relevant to meeting new challenges. Some American analysts argue that ESDP will mean the end of the alliance. They contend that the United States will see an autonomous European defense force as finally providing an opportunity for U.S. forces to withdraw from the continent. This analysis assumes just the opposite. Five years hence, Americans and their elected representatives are far more likely to support the Atlantic link if Europe carries its fair share of the burden than if Europe continues its excessive strategic dependence upon the United States.

Accordingly, the United States should give Europe an unequivocal green light on ESDP and outline a new Atlantic bargain that consists of the United States granting Europe more influence in return for Europe's acquisition of military capability. Washington is right in insisting on close and transparent defense links between the United States and the EU. Washington is also justified in arguing that NATO should have the right of first refusal and that the EU may act independently only when the United States chooses not to engage. After all, consultation before action is what a mature and balanced partnership is all about.

Most U.S. reservations about European defense are simply misplaced. American officials have told Europeans not to duplicate existing assets, but they must do so if they are to develop the capability to operate without U.S. forces. American officials have told the EU not to caucus and form a collective position, but Europe must do so if it is to act with a single, coherent voice. American officials express concern that Europe will go off on its own when it has the ability to act autonomously. But it is Europe, not the United States, that should be the worried suitor. Europe is building what will still be a small military force, and will want U.S. participation in virtually every conceivable operation. The main threat to the Atlantic link stems from too little Europe, not too much. The United States should welcome, indeed it should insist upon, a robust and effective European defense force.

In return, Europe has the right to expect that its views and interests will be carefully considered as the United States develops its policies. The development of a missile defense system is a case in point. If well handled, missile defense has the potential to strengthen the Atlantic link. If mishandled, it has the potential to strain the relationship and polarize the debate over ESDP. The United States should observe three guidelines as it seeks to manage the ongoing debate over missile defense.

- Consult early and often. Just as the United States expects and deserves to be fully consulted as ESDP moves forward, the EU expects and deserves to be consulted as America's missile defense program develops. The EU has recently changed its position; rather than opposing deployment, it is now prepared to engage the United States in substantive dialogue. The United States should take advantage of this opportunity to work toward a common position.
- Proceed slowly and deliberately. The Europeans were justifiably concerned by the extent to which the pressures of an election year led to a rushed and incomplete U.S. debate on missile defense. Especially because tests are still proceeding and missile defense technology is still in a developmental stage, the U.S. should take a paced and measured approach to a decision about both the timing and nature of deployment.
- Develop boost-phase technology and focus on multilateral deployment. A boost-phase system, by intercepting missiles soon after launch rather than as they approach a target state, protects all potential target states, not just the one deploying the system. In this sense, its benefits are shared by all and its deployment therefore is more likely to win widespread approval. Boost-phase intercept is also far more difficult to circumvent than intercept later in flight. Deployment of joint, multilateral systems will ease fears that the United States is seeking to protect only itself or gain unilateral strategic advantage, thereby substantially decreasing the likelihood that deployment will trigger a new arms race.

The United States should explore with the EU and with Russia proposals for sharing of early warning systems and intercept technology.

*Southeastern Europe***.** Europe's southeastern flank remains its most troubled region. The sources of instability run deep; the history of the area has left behind complicated and volatile relationships among national identity, religion, and ethnicity. The new regime in Serbia and the uneasy peace that now holds throughout the former Yugoslavia provide a window of opportunity for the region finally to leave behind its troubled past. The United States and Europe need to stay the course to ensure this is the case. Otherwise, Europe will continue to be plagued by instability and violence in the region, distracting the EU from other important tasks. To ensure that the Balkans have finally experienced their last war, the United States should be guided by three principles:

- Prepare for a long stay. Integration into Europe's mainstream offers the best hope for a lasting peace in the Balkans. Although the EU is already playing a leading role in peacekeeping and reconstruction, it will take a long time – perhaps generations – before integration works its pacifying effects. In the meantime, the United States should be prepared to stay the course and keep at least a small contingent of troops in the region. American participation is important to the credibility of and momentum behind the mission. Even after the bloodshed has receded into the past, neither the United States nor Europe can afford to let the region fall off the political radar screen.
- Keep an open mind on the question of redrawing borders. The United States and its partners in the Balkans have understandably been reluctant to broach the subject of redrawing borders; doing so has the potential to provoke a new round of instability and bloodshed. At the same time, the issue will not go away and addressing it sooner rather than later would facilitate efforts to attain a self-sustaining regional order. Kosovo has already achieved de facto independence from Serbia. It is very likely to end up either as an autonomous republic in a very loose Yugoslav federation or as an independent state. Montenegro may ultimately move toward independence as well. In Bosnia, the Dayton process and years of political pressure and economic assistance from the international community simply have not produced the multiethnic integration necessary to establish a self-sustaining, unitary state. If the political stalemate in Bosnia continues, it will at some point make sense for the international community to consider other options, including the redrawing of boundaries.
- Place more emphasis on rapprochement between Greece and Turkey. Greek-Turkish rapprochement, which gained steam after the devastating 1999 earthquake in Turkey, has lost some of its momentum. The United States and the EU should urgently press both parties to resume the process of reconciliation. Rapprochement between Ankara and Athens would backstop the improving chances for resolution of a divided Cyprus,

would facilitate peace efforts in the Balkans, and would repair an age-old political cleavage that continues to plague Southeastern Europe.

NATO and NATO Enlargement. Since the end of the Cold War, NATO has gradually changed its core mission and character. Although it still provides for collective defense as an insurance policy, NATO on a day-to-day basis is now fulfilling two other critical functions – carrying out peace enforcement and peacekeeping in the Balkans, and serving as the primary vehicle for integrating Europe's new democracies into the Atlantic security order. This adaptation has been key in keeping NATO relevant to a rapidly changing strategic landscape.

Whether to continue NATO enlargement and which countries to include in a second wave of expansion are becoming pressing issues on the NATO agenda. Prior to the first wave, the case for enlargement was not a compelling one. The prospective gains to security achieved by enlarging the alliance simply did not outweigh the potential risks. Enlargement threatened to jeopardize a top priority for U.S. policy, the integration of Russia into a new Atlantic security order. The end of the Cold War affords a historic opportunity to democratize and pacify Russia, goals that are central to building a stable and peaceful Europe.

Now that the first round of enlargement has been completed, it is important that the process move forward. NATO has established itself as the main vehicle for establishing a new Atlantic security order, and expectations of entry have been raised throughout Central and Eastern Europe. The prospect of membership also provides NATO a great deal of leverage in these regions; countries hopeful of joining are settling border disputes, proceeding with democratization, protecting their minority populations, and undertaking other welcome preparatory steps.

The continuation of NATO enlargement must be predicated, however, on the following important shift in policy. NATO enlargement must become a vehicle for Russia's integration into Europe, not a cause of its alienation and exclusion. Current NATO policy maintains that the alliance is open to all European countries that qualify. The time has come to take this statement seriously and to begin laying the groundwork for Russia's eventual inclusion in the alliance.

Russia remains far from meeting the criteria for membership; indeed, anti-democratic forces have strengthened under President Putin. At the same time, in the countries of Central Europe, including the Baltic states, the desire for NATO membership runs strong and has proven to be a powerful incentive in promoting political and military reform. This desire deserves to be fulfilled. However, the prospect of a continuing process of NATO enlargement that succeeds only in alienating Russia from the West and redividing Europe is a troubling one. To be sure, NATO is a defensive alliance and has no intention of doing harm to Russia, but international politics is very much about perceptions. Russia is justified in feeling uncomfortable with the expansion of NATO toward its borders, just as the United States would be if a third party formed a military alliance with Canada and Mexico.

Starting to work sincerely on Russia's inclusion in NATO is the best way to square America's commitment to the continuing enlargement of the Atlantic Alliance with Russia's legitimate security concerns. Doing so would elevate to a top priority Russia's attachment to Europe – the ultimate prize of the end of the Cold War. It would also make it far easier to integrate the Baltics and others in future waves of enlargement; they will be joining with rather than against a Russia that has come to see NATO not as a threat but as a key to its own security. And Russia made clear during the war against the Taliban and Al-Qaeda that it can contribute substantially to common Western interests.

These suppositions lead to the following approach to NATO's continuing enlargement. NATO should proceed with a second wave of enlargement in 2002. But Russia should be included in the list of prospective members. Other aspirants should gradually begin preparations for accession, buying time for Russian reform to proceed. Even though Russian membership may be years off, the beginning of the second round should coincide with a serious dialogue with Russia about its eventual membership. A detailed work plan should be drafted. A timetable should be drafted, with perhaps 2010 as an initial target date for Russia's accession.

It is entirely plausible that Russian reform will fail, foreclosing the option of joining NATO and entering Europe. But at least the West will have made a sincere effort to bring Russia in and expose it to the pacifying effects of military and political integration. There are few risks with Russia having a say in NATO only as its reforms substantially advance. But the payoffs of success would be huge with Russia's democratization, pacification, and integration into Europe.

At this point in time, the idea of Russia joining NATO has as little support in the Duma as it does in the U.S. Congress. However, many Russians strongly believe that this need not be the case and that beginning a serious dialogue with Moscow about eventual NATO membership may ultimately provide an answer to the strategic dilemmas posed by the continuation of NATO enlargement. President Putin, after all, has made clear his western orientation and his desire to make Russia part of Europe. Just as the prospect of joining NATO has helped induce reform and discipline in Central Europe, it could also help keep reform in Russia on track and counter the return of anti-democratic forces.

Should Russia ultimately join NATO, the alliance would function quite differently than it does today. It would by then have a host of new members from Central and Eastern Europe. Rather than being focused on the territorial defense of members, it would serve as a more informal and flexible vehicle for coordinating military activities and preserving peace across Europe. This looser and broader NATO would be in keeping with a Europe that is no longer so dependent upon the United States to ensure its security and a strategic setting in which terrorism poses a more serious threat to European security than traditional national rivalries.

The Atlantic link is in the midst of transformation. There is cause for optimism that the integrity of the Atlantic bond can be preserved. However, achieving this important objective requires both Americans and Europeans to recognize the profound changes that are taking place, to get ahead of the curve, and to work together to build a free and united Europe.

Peter Rudolf

U.S. Leadership and the Reform of Western Security Institutions: NATO Enlargement and ESDP

At the end of the Clinton presidency, NATO's dual transformation from a collective defense organization with uncertain prospects to the core of an enlarged security community and an instrument of conflict and crisis management was well advanced.[1] For the Clinton Administration, NATO served as the central vehicle for continuing the traditional American role as Europe's "benign hegemon." The Administration remained wedded to the old rationale of American foreign policy according to which the United States was needed as Europe's "pacifier," to use Josef Joffe's words, in order to forestall the reemergence of the security dilemma within Europe and the return to the old rivalries – a development which, in this view, would entail grave consequences for American security and economic interests.[2] Thus, the emergence of a "European Security and Defense Policy" (ESDP) was primarily seen as threat to the institutional primacy of NATO and the traditional American leadership role.

Since September 11, 2001, NATO seems to have lost the former salience for American security policy. Neither strong U.S. leadership for a further transformation of NATO, nor strong opposition to the Europeanization of European security can be expected. With strategic perspectives diverging on both sides of the Atlantic, transatlantic security relations will drift towards a de-facto division of labor.

---

1 Joseph Lepgold, "NATO's Post-Cold War Collective Action Problem," *International Security*, vol. 23, no. 1, Summer 1998, 78-106; in addition, see David S. Yost, "The New NATO and Collective Security," *Survival*, vol. 40, no. 2, Summer 1998, 135-160.

2 For a critical analysis, see Benjamin C. Schwarz, "'Cold War' Continuities: US Economic and Security Strategy Towards Europe," in Ted Galen Carpenter, ed., *The Future of NATO. The Journal of Strategic Studies* (Special Issue), vol. 17, no. 4, December 1994, 82-104.

NATO Enlargement and American Leadership

On the American side, there were a variety of motives for opening NATO to new members.[3] Liberal ambitions – the creation of a democratic security community – mixed with realist concerns about a power vacuum in East Central Europe; domestic political imperatives, namely neutralizing a politically useful, potentially highly controversial issue, coincided with the strategic interest to preserve the American leadership role at a time when the Bosnian conflict had raised serious doubt about NATO's role in dealing with this kind of new conflicts.

NATO enlargement was a bipartisan project pushed forward by the Republican leadership in Congress and by a Democratic administration that carefully managed the issue and, in this case, was astonishingly apt at creating and broadening public support. But the first round of NATO enlargement was supported by a very heterogeneous domestic coalition which could be maintained because some hard and potentially very controversial issue were "finessed:"[4] foremost the costs of enlargement and the future role of NATO.

The Bush Administration is continuing NATO's "open door" policy for all of "Europe's new democracies, from the Baltic to the Black Sea and all that lie between."[5] Yet the ingredients for a strong American leadership role in the new round of enlargement are missing.[6] Domestic incentives are little; pressure within NATO even less. A convincing strategic rationale for making a decision about the nine aspirants is hard to find. There is no "obvious" candidate as Poland was in the first round in terms of domestic and alliance interests. But from the start of the new administration, it was hardly conceivable that George W. Bush would spend his political capital to persuade the U.S. Senate just to support the accession of Slovenia or the Slovak Republic

3 See James M. Goldgeier, *Not Whether But When: The U.S. Decision to Enlarge NATO* (Washington: Brookings Institution Press, 1999).

4 Goldgeier, *Not Whether, But When*, 172

5 As President George W. Bush stated in his speech at Warsaw University on June 15, 2001: "All of Europe's new democracies, from the Baltic to the Black Sea and all that lie between, should have the same chance for security and freedom – and the same chance to join the institutions of Europe – as Europe's old democracies have. I believe in NATO membership for all of Europe's democracies that seek it and are ready to share the responsibility that NATO brings. " (U.S. Department of States, International Information Programs, Washington File, 15 June 2001; available at http://usinfo. state.gov).

6 See Robert E. Hunter, "NATO Enlargement: Decisions for the New President, " in Frank Carlucci, Robert Hunter, and Zalmay Khalilzad, eds., *Taking Charge: A Bipartisan Report to the President Elect on Foreign Policy and National Security – Discussion Papers* (Santa Monica: RAND 2000), 28-37; Jeffrey Simon, *The Next Round of NATO Enlargement* (Washington: Institute for National Strategic Studies, National Defense University, Strategic Forum No. 176, October 2000).

to NATO, while not at least having a "Baltic dimension."[7] In the domestic debate in the United States, this would have been portrayed as the recognition of a Russian sphere of interest. This certainly holds true for those who see NATO enlargement as proactive containment of Russia.[8] This even holds true for some who foremost conceive NATO enlargement in terms of promoting stability and democracy.[9] But for others, extending NATO's security commitment to the Baltic states held the prospect of undermining NATO as a collective defense system, since the Baltic states could not be credibly defended and could not contribute anything meaningful to collective defense.[10]

At least before September 11, it seemed likely that the new round of NATO enlargement would most likely lead to controversial debates in the United States. But in its wake, the political context of the debate has changed. The aftermath of September 11 has, as Francois Heisbourg rightly pointed out, demonstrated the "death" of the "old" NATO. Article V was invoked, but neither side of the Atlantic interpreted this as an obligation to military assistance. NATO "is no longer a defense organization, but a security and defense-services institution." This development has made NATO enlargement easier, since an enlarged NATO, which in fact is no longer a collective defense organization, will be seen as less of a threat by Moscow.[11] Further enlargement in turn will strengthen NATO's development away from an alliance towards a "security organization." As Anthony Foster and William Wallace noted: "Having led the push for NATO enlargement, American policy-makers must accept that this will create a more diffuse organization, less militarily capable as a collective entity and mainly focused on the security of its own region."[12]

---

7 For this argument, see Frederick Kempe, "Like It Or Not, NATO's Expansion Debate Is Back," *Wall Street Journal Europe*, February 21, 2001.

8 See, Jesse Helms, "Towards a Compassionate Conservative Foreign Policy," Speech delivered to the American Enterprise Institute, January 11, 2001 (available at http://usinfo.state.gov).

9 Ronald D. Asmus, "The State of the North Atlantic Alliance," Statement before the Subcommittee on European Affairs, Senate Foreign Relations Committee, February 27, 2001 (htttp://www.senate.gov/~foreign/testimony/wt_asmus_010228.txt).

10 For this line of argument, see Kent R. Meyer, "US Support for Baltic Membership in NATO: What Ends, What Risks," in *Parameters*, vol. 30, no. 4, Winter 2000-01, 67-82.

11 Francois Heisbourg, "Europe and the Transformation of the World Order," in *Survival*, vol. 43, no. 4, Winter 2001-02, 143-148, quotes on pp. 144-145.

12 Anthony Forster and William Wallace, "What is NATO For?," *Survival*, vol. 43, no. 4, Winter 2001-02, 107-122, quote on p. 117.

The Europeanization of European Security

NATO is the only multilateral institution of importance still appreciated by conservative Republicans in Congress – not because they like the "new" NATO intervening in regional conflicts, but, as the NATO enlargement debate made clear, because they value NATO as the vehicle for American leadership in European security affairs and as a collective defense organization, still needed in case a new hegemonic power (most would think of Russia) were to threaten European stability.[13] As the Kosovo intervention has shown, NATO is – despite the necessity of finding common ground – an organization with a dominating American influence.[14] Had NATO in the end not been so lucky in the Kosovo case – winning the war before the decision about sending in combat troops on the ground had to be taken – the alliance could have easily become a target of unilateralists in Congress. The extension of NATO's tasks – originally seen by many as a way of keeping the organization alive ("out of area or out of business") – might undermine rather than buttress support for it in Congress. But how long will this support last in the face of Europe's strife towards greater weight and autonomy in security affairs?

In Europe, one major lesson has been drawn from the political and military weakness the Kosovo crisis made plain: the European Union must increase its capability to act autonomously in the process of preventing and managing crises in Europe so that Europe gains "real equity" ("*wirkliche Gleichberechtigung*") with the United States.[15] In the aftermath of the Kosovo war and fed by the general perception that U.S. foreign policy has been drifting towards unilateralism, it has almost become a dogma that only a stronger Europe will get a hearing in Washington.

---

13 As the Senate made clear in its resolution ratifying the accession protocols: "NATO enhances the security of the United States by embedding European states in a process of cooperative security planning, by preventing the destabilizing renationalization of European military policies, and by ensuring an ongoing and direct leadership role for the United States in European security affairs." And: "It is the sense of the Senate that (i) the central purpose of NATO is to provide for the collective defense of its members." The text of the ratification resolution can be found in *United States Policy Information and Texts*, May 7, 1998, 2-6 (quotes on pp. 2 and 3).

14 See Ivo H. Daalder and Michael E. O'Hanlon, *Winning Ugly: NATO's War to Save Kosovo* (Washington: Brookings Institution Press, 2000).

15 Rudolf Scharping, "Europäische Sicherheitspolitik und die Nordatlantische Allianz," Speech on July 5, 1999 in Berlin; in addition, see the speech by Joschka Fischer, May 10, 1999 in Presse- und Informationsamt der Bundesregierung, *Bulletin*, May 26, 1999, 335.

Thus the Kosovo war gave new impetus to the old vision of a common European security policy; it acted as a "catalyst"[16] for the development of a "European Security and Defense Policy" (ESDP), which, for many supporters, lies in the political logic of the European unification process. In the German view, ESDP is seen as the basis for a new atlanticism, for a real partnership based upon greater European strength.[17] Skeptics still have good reason to doubt whether Europe will get its act together. The final outcome of this secular process of Europeanization is open and success is by far not certain.[18] But the momentum is great. As some have pointed out, this time Europe cannot afford failure since so much political capital has been invested into this project and Europe's credibility is at stake.[19]

In effect, the development of ESDP has eroded the "basic bargain" struck by the Clinton Administration and the EU in the mid-nineties, guided by the idea of "separable but not separate" forces and translated into the concept of Combined Joined Task Forces, thereby securing the institutional primacy of NATO.[20] ESDP reactivated those irritations and concerns about the security dimension of the European integration project and its potential effects upon NATO that the first Bush Administration had unmistakably expressed in the early 90s when it was confronted with European attempts to upgrade the WEU. The Clinton Administration articulated those concerns in the now famous three D`s: "no decoupling, no duplication, no discrimination."[21]

Although senior members of the incoming Bush administration shared those concerns in substance,[22] they struck a more conciliatory tone, thus

16 Rudolf Scharping, "Die Kosovo-Krise wirkt wie ein Katalysator," *Frankfurter Allgemeine Zeitung*, March 24, 2000, 12

17 See Karsten D. Voigt, Coordinator for German-American Cooperation, Foreign Ministry, "The Discussion of a European Security and Defence Policy: Labor Pains of a New Atlanticism," Speech on 8 March 2000 in Washington, D.C. (http://www.auswaertiges-amt.de/6_archiv/2/r/r000308a.htm).

18 Werner Link, "Europäische Sicherheitspolitik. Der Ausgang Europas aus seiner selbstverschuldeten Unmündigkeit," in *Europa oder Amerika? Zur Zukunft des Westens*, Sonderheft Merkur, vol. 54, no. 9/10, September/October 2000), 916-928.

19 See Christoph Bertram, "Partnerschaft und Divergenz. Die amerikanische Außenpolitik und die Zukunft der transatlantischen Beziehungen," in Peter Rudolf and Jürgen Wilzewski, eds., *Weltmacht ohne Gegner: Amerikanische Außenpolitik zu Beginn des 21. Jahrhunderts* (Baden-Baden: Nomos, 2000), 395-400.

20 See Michael Brenner, *Terms of Engagement. The United States and the European Security Identity* (Westport, CT: Praeger 1998), 32-34.

21 See, Deputy Secretary of State Strobe Talbott, "The State of the Alliance: An American Perspective," Brussels, December 15, 1999 (http://www.state.gov/www/policy_remarks/19997991215_talbott_nac.html).

22 For a broad collection of foreign policy pronouncements, including about NATO, by Secretary of State Colin Powell, Secretary of Defense Donald Rumsfeld, and National Security Advisor Condoleezza Rice, see "U.S. National Security: The Bush Team," in *U.S. Foreign Policy Agenda. An Electronic Journal of the U.S. Department of State*, volume 6, no. 1, March 2001.

avoiding transatlantic frictions over the issue. Confident about America's power resources, little interested in getting involved in those missions of crisis management and peacekeeping that ESDP is foremost about and lacking the ambition to transform NATO into a globally acting alliance, the Bush Administration could be more relaxed about European security policy.[23]

Nevertheless, for those conservatives in the American foreign policy elite who predominantly perceive the world (even the Western world) through the "realist" lens and who fill the upper ranks of the second Bush Administration, ESDP is seen as part of a long-term process of building the EU into a "counterweight to United States."[24] But given the high degree of economic interdependence and the broad realm of common strategic interests the result will hardly be a form of antagonist balancing, but rather a form of cooperative balancing.[25] Whatever the substantive effects of Europe acting as counterweight will be, one effect is likely: Some sort of the highly feared "European Caucus"[26] in NATO will change the structure of transatlantic interaction – from hegemonic leadership relying upon the traditional "multiple bilateralism"[27] to a new form of cooperation based upon greater equity. This will lead to a "redistribution of power in the alliance."[28]

But balancing is not the only motive for this process of Europeanization. It also stems from a sober realization that for domestic reasons American leadership in European security affairs can no longer be taken for granted. And here we face the transatlantic dilemma. On the one hand, Europe has to prepare for contingencies where the United States might opt to stand aside or

---

23 Kori Schake, *Constructive Duplication: Reducing EU reliance on US Military Assets* (London: Centre for European Reform, Working Paper, January 2002), 6-7.

24 Peter W. Rodman, *Drifting Apart? Trends in U.S.-European Relations* (Washington: The Nixon Center, June 1999), 4. On the perception of ESDP, see U.S. Congress, House, Committee on International Relations, *European Common Foreign, Security and Defense Policies: Implications for the United States and the Atlantic Alliance*, 106th Congress, 1st Session, November 10, 1999 (Washington: Government Printing Office, 2000).

25 See Link, "Europäische Sicherheitspolitik."

26 "[T]here can be no question of an "EU Caucus" inside NATO: NATO decisions must continue to be reached in real collective discussion, so that NATO will remain, in fact as well in rhetoric, the principal forum for security consultation." Testimony of Franklin D. Kramer, Assistant Secretary of Defense for International Security Affairs to the Senate Foreign Relations Committee, Subcommittee on European Affairs, March 9, 2000 (mimeo), 10. In addition, see William S. Cohen, "Preserving History`s Greatest Alliance," *The Washington Post*, January 8, 2001, A19.

27 Michael Brenner and Phil Williams, *Europa und die Vereinigten Staaten. Amerikanische Sicherheitspolitik in den neunziger Jahren* (Sankt Augustin: Forschungsinstitut der Konrad-Adenauer-Stiftung, Mai 1992), 13.

28 Ernst-Otto Czempiel, "Nicht von gleich zu gleich? Die USA und die Europäische Union," in *Europa oder Amerika?*, 901-915, quote on p. 910.

where the "new American way of war"[29] – basically strategic coercion by airpower – is ill suited to the conflict and "boots on the ground" are needed. On the other hand, the process of Europeanization might erode domestic support in the United States for the continuation of the role as Europe's pacifier.[30]

Shifting Strategic Priorities and its Consequences: A Global Division of Labor?

For strategic reasons, doubts about a consistent American role in European security were appropriate even before September 11 and the resulting focus on the war against terrorism. Of course, for a long time, the United States has been a European and an Asian power, but given the lack of threats to vital interests in Europe, and the likelihood that China will emerge as a serious regional competitor within the next 15 years or so, American strategic priorities will more and more shift to Asia. Current policy towards China is already a mixture of "engage and hedge," a combination of economic integration and military containment.[31] Under the Bush Administration, the second strand will become more accentuated, since from the perspective of those realists who occupy the upper echelons of the administration it remains all too doubtful whether economic engagement will in the end really bring about a democratic, more cooperative and non-threatening China as the Clinton Administration seemed to hope.

Although there is still some talk about a global U.S.-European partnership as the foundation of a new transatlantic bargain, political and strategic realities on both sides of the Atlantic make this sort of bargain even less likely than in the mid-to late-nineties when it seemed to gain some attraction in the Clinton Administration.[32] A new transatlantic bargain will have to accept two political facts. On the one hand, Europe will be preoccupied by European conflicts and reluctant to assume new military commitments out-

---

29 Michael Ignatieff, "The New American Way of War," *The New York Review of Books*, July 20, 2000, 42, 43, 45, 46.

30 As John R. Bolton, now serving in the Bush administration, put it some time ago: "If the E.U. were really capable of a united security policy, which is doubtful both politically and militarilly, it would undermine the sole remaining argument for an American military presence in Europe, which is that the Europeans cannot handle these critical questions themselves." "The Next President and NATO," *The Washington Times*, July 21, 1999 (available at http://www.aei.org/ra/rajbr27.htm).

31 See Zalmay Khalilzad, et al., *The United States and a Rising China: Strategic and Military Implications* (Santa Monica: RAND, 1999).

32 Ronald D. Asmus, Robert D. Blackwill, and F. Stephen Larrabee, "Can NATO Survive?," in *The Washington Quarterly*, vol. 19, no. 2, Spring 1996, 79-101.

side Europe, although September 11 was, as an American observer put it, a "tragic reminder" that in an dangerous world, the capability to wage distant military operations might also be necessary for Europe.[33] On the other hand, the United States, facing more urgent security challenges to vital interests in East Asia and the Persian Gulf region, and fighting terrorism and what George W. Bush called "terror states," will be drifting towards minimal engagement in Europe.

Thus, a global division of labor[34] is the only realistic alternative option in the longer term although the Bush Administration quickly dropped its election campaign slogan of a "new division of labor" in order to appease allied anger about being left alone in the Balkans. With the focus on the Greater Middle East and the fight against terrorism, there is additional impetus for disengagement from the Balkans. The number of American soldiers on the ground in Bosnia and Kosovo had even been reduced before September 11, 2001.[35]

The debate about a new transatlantic bargain will continue since the "new division of labor" idea reflects a widespread concern among conservatives that the "new NATO" engaged in crisis management and peace-keeping foremost serves European, but not American interests, and that these undertakings are detrimental to otherwise more needed American military capabilities.[36] Assuming progress on ESDP, Europe will probably be more willing to accept the logical implications of its own vision of a greater role in European security affairs: the development of autonomous military capabilities. With U.S. strategic priorities shifting towards the Middle East, Asia, and the fight against terrorism, a decreasing importance of NATO in U.S. global strategy and a more unilateral American approach to security, assured access to NATO military "assets," which are mainly expensive and scarce American assets such as strategic intelligence collection, communications equipment, and airlift capabilities, cannot be taken for granted for European forces acting in a crisis in which the United States does not want to get involved. Thus, a certain duplication of military assets, especially for logistics and intelligence, and an independent planning capacity will be necessary if Europe wants to act independently of the United States. As Kori Schake noted: "Without

---

33 Philip H. Gordon, "NATO After 11 September," in *Survival*, vol. 43, no. 4, Winter 2001-02, 89-106 (98ff.).

34 On these options, see David C. Gompert, "U.S. Alliance Relations in the Global Era," in Carlucci et al., *Taking Charge*, 39-48.

35 Marta Dassù and Nicholas Whyte, "America's Balkan Disengagement?," in *Survival*, vol. 43, no. 4, Winter 2001-2002, 123-136.

36 See, John C. Hulsman, *A Grand Bargain With Europe: Preserving NATO for the 21st Century* (Washington: The Heritage Foundation Backgrounder, No. 1360, April 17, 2000); Kim R. Holmes, *The United States and Europe in the 21st Century: Partners or Competitors?* (Washington: The Heritage Foundation, March 20, 2000, Heritage Lectures, No. 657).

having genuinely autonomous military forces, Europe's needs are subordinate to US priorities. The EU is left hostage to the concerns and potential veto of the US and Turkey, both of which may well evaluate their interests as opposed to an EU operation. More generally, the lack of an EU military capability forces Europe into continuing dependence on the US, which is politically unhealthy in states as powerful and independent-minded as those of the EU."[37]

Under a global division of labor NATO, would remain an "insurance policy" just in case American involvement would again become necessary. But basically NATO would become a "mechanism to manage a division of labor between the EU and the United States"[38] and would coordinate policies on a more balanced and equal basis. This strategic vision poses a clear challenge to the form of hegemonic leadership the United States is used to.

37 Schake, *Constructive Duplication*, 28.
38 Gompert, "U.S. Alliance Relations," 42.

Part III
U.S. Leadership in Crisis: The Balkans, Russia and China

David Ryan

'With One Hand Tied Behind Our Back': Collective Memory, The Media And US Intervention From The Gulf War To Afghanistan

At the end of the Vietnam War the proverbial Cold War consensus on US foreign policy was shattered. The United States emerged from the conflict into an uncertain world. Over 58,000 Americans had been killed, their names inscribed on Maya Lin's black granite memorial on the Mall in Washington, D.C., and up to four million Indochinese were killed during the successive Vietnamese wars. Washington was severely damaged: the outcome was a humiliating defeat which discredited its reputation; allies in Europe and Asia were alienated; the financial costs were tremendous as was the opportunity cost of the 'Great Society' programme; and widespread division further undermined US society. Since that period there has been a constant search to reconstruct consensus.[1] US 'world leadership' was being challenged, though its need to assert power and intervene abroad had not diminished. The broader moral and fundamental lessons that could have been addressed were ignored so as not to upset the direction of US policy and its leadership of the 'western' world. Instead, tactical and instrumental lessons have dominated policy makers' considerations. These popular lessons suggested that next time, better instruments would be used, and different tactics would be followed. Next time the media would not be allowed such a free hand. The war would not be lost on the 'home front'.[2] The battle for the 'hearts and minds' of the American people became crucial to subsequent intervention. Where possible the use of US troops was avoided and any images of casualties were controlled. Eventually during the 1990s airpower became the preferred in-

1 Richard Melanson, *Reconstructing Consensus: American Foreign Policy since the Vietnam War*, (New York: St. Martin's Press, 1991). Despite the unending debate on Vietnam there have been persistent attempts to reshape the narratives of the war. See for instance: David W. Levy, *The Debate Over Vietnam*, (Baltimore: Johns Hopkins University Press, 1995). Academic debate aside, presidential rhetoric has been profoundly influential in reshaping the American consciousness of the effects of Vietnam on contemporary crises. The post-Vietnam presidents have tried to reshape the past and to forward certain limited lessons on the war. See Trevor McCrisken, *American Exceptionalism and the Legacy of Vietnam: US Foreign Policy Since 1974* (London: Palgrave, 2002, forthcoming).

2 See for instance, Earl C. Ravenal, *Never Again: Learning from America's Foreign Policy Failures*, (Philadelphia: Temple University Press, 1980), pp. v, 55-74.

strument of direct intervention. It not only provided television images that made the war appear precise, but it also limited US casualties and dealt with the enemy from a safe altitude. Conventional warfare made little sense under such circumstances and by 2001 horrific acts of terrorism, a crime against humanity, were perpetrated in New York and Washington. There are multiple causes, but 11 September 2001 was, according to Halliday, 'the most spectacular case ever of the policy espoused by anarchists from the 1880s onwards of "propaganda of the deed", an iconic destruction against the clear blue sky.'[3] The magnitude and horror of the event helped undermine but not eliminate the 'Vietnam Syndrome' that had been so pervasive hitherto.

After Vietnam, if the executive branch tried to limit the lessons and become more sophisticated and pro-active in shaping public opinion through the media, US collective memories also exercised a considerable constraint on executive options to intervene abroad. Most famously the War Powers Act was passed in 1973 limiting the duration that US troops could remain involved in a conflict without congressional approval. But also the resurfacing and reconsideration of Vietnam throughout the 1980s during Reagan's intervention in Nicaragua and El Salvador, the hasty retreat of US Marines from Lebanon after 1983 and throughout the 1990s, the Vietnam syndrome exercised an impact on the US decisions to intervene.[4]

After the Cold War, Washington did not significantly alter its foreign polices, especially on US intervention in regional conflicts. Obviously one of the restraining factors, the Soviet Union, had collapsed, but Washington continued to insist that its 'leadership' was vital. That remained clear from the Gulf in 1991 to Afghanistan in 2001, though exceptions were found in the early part of the Bosnian crisis and in Rwanda. Otherwise, in many conflicts Washington downplayed the importance of a diplomatic solution in preference for a military response and by the 1990s the Bush and then Clinton administrations could rely, imperfectly, on US technology to overcome or limit the effects of the Vietnam syndrome.

When US national interests can be clearly identified and plausibly presented to the public, Washington asserted its leadership and took charge of the response. Alternatives such as UN led or EU initiatives were sidelined because they stressed the importance of diplomacy or economic sanctions. By and large Washington has come to expect to lead and to expect that US personnel will be in command. Thus, despite the constraints imposed through the Vietnam syndrome, Washington eschewed the isolationist option for one

3 Fred Halliday, *Two Hours That Shook the World: September 11, 2001: Causes and Consequences* (London: Saqi Books, 2002), p. 32.

4 David Ryan, 'Asserting US Power' in Philip John Davies (ed.), *An American Quarter Century: US Politics from Vietnam to Clinton* (Manchester: Manchester University Press, 1995), 103-126.

of continued 'independent internationalism'[5] and, when the effective outcomes were likely to be met, through multilateral operations. But costs casualties and US interests determined above all the extent of US involvement and leadership.

This article will examine the impact of the Vietnam syndrome on the decisions to intervene throughout the 1990s and in Afghanistan in 2001. The conflicts are considered chronologically, first examining the Gulf War of 1991, then the tentative responses in Somalia, Rwanda and Bosnia from 1992 to 1995. Kosovo will illustrate a return to more decisive intervention. The US intervention in Afghanistan after September 11 will further illustrate the partial perseverance of the Vietnam syndrome. Presidential rhetoric and the media were essential in shaping public opinion and creating a consensus on intervention. One of the basic and misused lessons from the Vietnam War was that the media was in part responsible for the US defeat. Thus, prior to US intervention in the Gulf conflict, President George Bush indicated 'we don't need another Vietnam. ... No hands are going to be tied behind backs ... It will not be a long, drawn-out mess.'[6] Instead the media would be controlled through a pool system so that domestic constraints would essentially be limited through the types of images they would see or the type or reporting to which they would be exposed.

Even though US intervention occurred after a failure in US policy in Iraq, Bosnia and Kosovo, there generally was a strong tendency to support the president in a time of crisis. Especially if US interests could be directly linked to and convincingly presented to a wary public, a patriotic response usually resulted in the initial stages of the crisis even if the effects of the Vietnam syndrome played a greater role if the crisis was protracted.[7] Moreover, the US media shared US ideologies and acted through, what Michael Hunt describes as,'integrated and coherent systems of symbols, values, and beliefs' arising from 'socially established structures of meaning'[8] which tended to mean that they also responded within a nationalistic framework, largely supporting US intervention.

Thus public opinion overall did not set the agenda or directly influence the construction of policy, though it did exercise considerable restraint on the

---

5 For a survey of this option used throughout the twentieth century see Joan Hoff, 'The American Century: From Sarajevo to Sarajevo' *Diplomatic History* 23, no. 2 (Spring 1999), pp. 285-319.

6 Quoted in Bob Woodward, *The Commanders* (New York: Simon and Schuster, 1991), p. 339.

7 Richard A. Brody, 'Crisis, War, and Public Opinion: The Media and Public Support for the President,' in W. Lance Bennett and David L. Paletz (eds.), *Taken by Storm: The Media, Public Opinion, and U.S. Foreign Policy in the Gulf War* (Chicago: University of Chicago Press, 1994), pp. 212-214.

8 Michael H. Hunt, *Ideology and US Foreign Policy,* (New Haven: Yale University Press, 1987), p. 12.

executive. All of the decisions to intervene during the 1990s, from the Gulf War, through Somalia, Rwanda, Bosnia on to Kosovo and Afghanistan in 2001, were influenced by the Vietnam Syndrome, the restraints imposed from 'lessons' learned, and from reactions to opinion polls. After the collapse of the Soviet Union, it was no longer 'anti-Communism', but humanitarian issues, US credibility and interrests which propelled intervention, this propulsion needs to be set against the influence of the Vietnam Syndrome and the liklihood of US casualties.[9]

The Gulf War 1990-1991

The Vietnam syndrome exercised considerable influence throughout the 1980s and the 1990s. As George Bush was inaugurated on 20 January 1989 he indicated that 'The war cleaves us still ... But friends, that was begun in earnest a quarter century ago. Surely the statue of limitations has been reached. ... The final lesson of Vietnam is that no great nation can long afford to be sundered by a memory.'[10] In other words if the United States continued to aspire to the status of a superpower, it had to over come the syndrome which limited its ability to use the full range of its military capability. Moreover, there was a certain tension in the vast amounts spent on the US defence budgets during the 1980s and the continued reservations on its use.

Though Iraq and Saddam Hussein had facilitated US interests and policies of containing Iran during the 1980s, Iraq's invasion of Kuwait on 2 August 1990 changed the regional balance of power almost instantaneously. Saddam Hussein made the grave miscalculation that the United States would not respond in a similar manner that it adopted in Panama 1989. When Saddam Hussein met with the US Ambassador April Glaspie on 25 July 1990, days before the invasion, he inferred that the United States would not go to war over the disputed territory. Perhaps with Vietnam in mind, Hussein told Glaspie, 'yours is a society which cannot accept 10, 000 dead in one battle.' He was obviously aware that Iraq could not defeat the US, but he also clearly indicated that should conflict arise, 'we too can harm you' and that 'we cannot come all the way to you in the United States but individual Arabs may reach you.' The account of the meeting released by Iraq was characterised by the State Department as 'essentially accurate' though it contained omissions. In the document Glaspie makes clear that the United States was concerned about the Iraqi troops gathering in the south, she congratulated Hussein on

9 Richard Sobel, *The Impact of Public Opinion on US Foreign Policy Since Vietnam: Constraining the Colossus*, (New York: Oxford University Press, 2001), p. 234.

10 Jonathan Mirsky, 'Reconsidering Vietnam,' *New York Review of Books* XXXVIII, no. 15 (10 October 1991): p. 44.

the advances in the diplomatic track and indicated that she had a 'direct instruction from the President to seek better relations with Iraq.' Hussein probably read Glaspie's message as a green light to take action after she indicated 'we have no opinion on the Arab-Arab conflicts, like your border disagreement with Kuwait.' And further that Secretary of State 'James Baker has directed our official spokesman to emphasize this instruction.' Though after the war, in March 1991 Glaspie insisted that her message made clear that any solution should not involve aggression.[11]

Despite the failure in US policy because it neither deterred nor satisfied Hussein[12] public opinion rallied around Bush in the weeks after the Iraqi invasion. Presidential approval ratings moved upward and after the initial deployment of troops to Saudi Arabia and the imposition of the naval blockade support for US policy shot up to 80%.[13] Such responses were normal as long as the situation was presented in terms of US national interests. Moreover, the media concentrated on the issues of troop deployment, coalition building, UN resolutions and international co-operation. Elite establishment criticism of US policy and any media coverage of it were extremely limited during August 1990.[14]

By October elite criticism increased, some protest in US cities against involvement also took place. As criticism increased, media coverage followed suit and President Bush's approval ratings dropped. Most Americans (69%) felt that UN imposed sanctions should be given a longer time to work and further diplomacy should be pursued. The opposition to a military solution remained stable to early November, but Bush clearly indicated that he did not think there was sufficient time to pursue a diplomatic route or wait to see if sanctions were enough to remove Iraq from Kuwait.[15] By 8 November a second contingent of US troops were deployed which moved the forces far beyond the numbers necessary to defend Saudi Arabia. At this point Congressional members became increasingly wary of Bush's intentions. They asserted their constitutional right to declare war, criticised the lack of clarity in administration policy, and suggested that the additional deployment of 200 000 troops undermined the other options. Vietnam became an increasing reference point among congressional members and the media. Bush and congressional Republicans suggested that the open debate on whether the US should go to war might actually undermine the cohesion of US opinion and

---

11 Meeting between President Saddam Hussein and the American Ambassador to Baghdad, 25 July 1990, document 01482, fiche 223, *Iraqgate: Saddam Hussein, US Policy and the Prelude to the Persian Gulf War, 1980-1994,* National Security Archive, Washington, D.C., 1995; Thomas L. Friedman, 'Envoy to Iraq, Faulted in Crisis, Says She Warned Hussein Sternly,' *The New York Times*, 21 March 1991.

12 Brody, in *Taken by Storm*, p. 214.

13 Sobel, *Public Opinion*, p. 144.

14 Brody, in *Taken by Storm*, p. 215.

15 Sobel, *Public Opinion*, pp. 145-6.

play into Hussein's hands. Still, congress needed to be appeased. And to that end James Baker was sent to meet with Iraqi officials before 15 January. Senator William Cohen, was adamant that the US divisions should not be ignored, 'we should not try in any way to gloss over those doubts or divisions. ... Simply passing resolutions which profess to claim that there is unity, when in fact there is not, I do not think serves us well.'[16] Opinion polls indicated that people thought diplomacy and sanctions should be given more time and effort. The congressional, public and media criticism had some effect. After the second troop deployment Bush's approval ratings on the Gulf dropped to 54%.[17] It appeared as if he was approaching the war option with undue haste.

Public opinion and some congressional opposition did influence policy; at least in terms of policy presentation. Here the media played a crucial role. From August to January Iraq indicated several times that it was willing to talk, though their proposals were summarily dismissed. The French put forward prominent initiatives supported in the UN Security Council by Belgium, Germany, Spain, Italy, Algeria, Morocco, and Tunisia though rejected by the US, UK and USSR. The Baker-Aziz meeting in Geneva produced absolutely no compromise as Baker indicated they would not negotiate backwards from the UN Security Council Resolutions demanding complete withdrawal to the August 1990 border. Even UN Secretary General Javier Perez de Cuellar's meeting with Hussein in which compromise positions were offered produced no change. The US media failed to analyse the diplomatic tracks in sufficient depth. Thus when the Bush administration argued that diplomacy had been tried and had failed they could do so with some credibility, though the public remained sceptical,[18] even though some diplomatic options were considered viable in the State Department.

The worries of another Vietnam continued throughout the period prior to the war. Bush invested considerable effort to dispel the notion of another Vietnam, arguing that the conflict was expected to last a matter of days rather than months and that US casualties were expected to be relatively low. Bush assured the country that 'this will not be another Vietnam. This will no be a protracted, drawn out war.' Still, 62% polled thought that the situation would be somewhat like Vietnam.[19]

---

16 Carroll J. Doherty, 'Uncertain Congress Confronts President's Gulf Strategy,' *Congressional Quarterly* 48, no. 46 (17 November 1990), pp. 3879-3882; Carroll J. Doherty, 'Public Debate on Persian Gulf Poses Challenge for Members,' and Pamela Fessler, 'Bush Quites His Critics on Hill By Sendinfg Baker to Iraq,' *Congressional Quarterly* vol. 48, no. 48 (1 December 1990), pp. 4004-4008.

17 Sobel, *Public Opinion*, p. 146.

18 Douglas Kellner, *The Persian Gulf TV War* (Boulder: Westview Press, 1992), pp. 30-37.

19 Sobel, *Public Opinion*, pp. 147-8.

Ultimately, until days before the war the nation remained divided. On 12 January Congress provided the authorisation to use force by 250 to 183 in the House and 52 to 47 in the Senate. Within days as the war began and the very selective television coverage provided pictures of the 'smart' weapons, Bush's ratings shot up once more into the low 80s, an increase of around 20 points within a matter of days. Sobel points out that the terminology used was important. While the bombing campaign in Vietnam had been called 'Rolling Thunder', the operations in Desert Storm were referred to as 'Instant Thunder', again allaying the fears of a protracted conflict.[20]

During the 1980s US Secretary of Defense Caspar Weinberger developed a set of criteria that had to be met before the United States committed troops abroad. Generally, vital US interests had to be at stake, political will and the strength of force had to be sufficient, objectives had to be clearly identified, congressional and public support had to be assured and ultimately that force was used as a last resort.[21] Later the so-called Powell Doctrine largely emerged from these constraints and the lessons of Vietnam. Washington employed overwhelming power and a new military strategy of inside-out warfare in which the regime is paralysed and its communications systems destroyed from the outset.[22] The war from the air ensured that US casualties were kept to a minimum, and as the initial days passed without significant coalition or US losses, US public opinion began to shed their fears of another Vietnam. Wider problems remain relatively unconsidered in the US. One of the logical assumptions of the use of overwhelming power is that the enemy forces will be relatively weak. What this does to the UN Charter, which requires a proportionate response, has not been officially addressed.

The media in the field were pooled; their output was scrutinised and was approved before release. Generally, the media was very supportive of the US led war. Their coverage was extremely selective. Viewers in the west were left with the impression that the war was a 'painless Nintendo exercise' as Edward Said suggested[23] whereas the death toll ranges to estimates of up to 200 000. The smart weapons impressed the US viewers and dispelled the Vietnam syndrome for a time, but according to the US Air Force some 93.6% of bombs dropped were unguided and of the 7000 tons of guided bombs, a substantial proportion missed their targets.[24] Washington was able to control

---

20 Sobel, *Public Opinion*, p. 152.

21 McCrisken, *American Exceptionalism,* Palgrave, 2002, forthcoming; Caspar Weinberger, *Fighting for Peace: Seven Critical Years at the Pentagon* (London: Michael Joseph, 1990).

22 John Andreas Olson, 'Operation Desert Storm: An Examination of the Strategic Air Campaign,' Ph.D. dissertation, Department of historical and International Studies, De Montfort University, Leicester, UK, 2000.

23 Edward Said, *Culture and Imperialism* (London: Chatto and Windus, 1993), p. 365.

24 Paul Walker, 'The Myth of Surgical Bombing in the Gulf War,' in Ramsey Clark et. al., *War Crimes* (Washington, D.C.: Maisonneuve Press, 1992), p. 87.

the images and the output because as Philip Taylor argues most of the media were 'essentially dependent' on the coalition military forces for their information. Even when the media was not subjected to the pool system they were 'supportive, largely uncritical and generally reflected the official line.' Viewers were not initially permitted to see the pictures of the carnage at the receiving end of the bombing. Though the war was popularly remembered as CNN's war, Taylor concludes that the 'conflict belonged to the coalition's armed forces, and to the victors went the spoils of the information war.'[25] As a study from the Center on the Press, Politics and Public Policy argues, 'in the Gulf, live television pictures did not dictate policy or force changes. They distorted public impressions and confirmed the war strategy being carried out... However in Somalia and Bosnia gruesome images did – on occasions – weaken the political consensus for military involvement.'[26]

Still, because of the attendant fears lingering from Vietnam, once the stated objectives had been met the war was terminated. The option to go on to Baghdad to get Saddam Hussein was rejected, especially after the protracted hunt for Manuel Noriega just over a year earlier. Similarly, at the time of writing the hunt for Osama Bin Laden is proving problematic.

Somalia, Rwanda and Bosnia

Questions of intervention and the ghosts of Vietnam plagued the first Clinton administration. Throughout the campaign of 1992 Bill Clinton criticised President Bush on his lack of effective action in the continuing Balkan crises. For his part Clinton saw the US role as preventing 'mass violence against civilian populations.' This humanitarian theme continued into his inaugural period when he declared that 'when our vital interests are challenged, or the will and conscience of the international community is defied, we will act – with peaceful diplomacy whenever possible, with force when necessary.'[27] Of course rhetoric is always more ambitious than confronting the reality of intervention and the commitment of US troops.

Not only was Bosnia becoming increasingly problematic with the widespread human rights abuse and 'ethnic cleansing', but days before relinquishing the presidency Bush intervened in Somalia to provide famine relief.

25 Philip M. Taylor, *War and the Media: Propaganda and Persuasion in the Gulf War* (Manchester: Manchester University Press, 1998), pp. 268, 287.

26 Nik Gowing, 'Real-Time Television Coverage of Armed Conflicts and Diplomatic Crises: Does it Pressure or Distort Foreign Policy Decisions,' The Joan Shorenstein Barone Center on the Press, Politics and Public Policy, John F. Kennedy School of Government, Harvard University, Working Paper 94-1 (June 1994), p. 13.

27 President Bill Clinton, Inaugural Address, 21 January 1993; Martin Walker, 'Withdrawal Symptoms,' *The Guardian* (London), 7 May 1994.

Other strategic interests were also pertinent. Some 30 000 US troops ensured the distribution of supplies and pushed various military factions aside to facilitate the process.

In Somalia Bush introduced the US troops, but in Bosnia Clinton had to make the fateful decisions. While on the one hand he was determined, at least rhetorically, to prevent ethnic cleansing, he felt constrained by the State Department, Defense Department and the National Security Council not to introduce US troops. Despite US Ambassador to the UN, Madeline Albright's frequent references to an 'assertive multilateralism' in US policy, the European allies opposed Clinton's suggestion of the 'lift and strike' policy: lifting the arms embargo of the Bosnians and striking Serb positions. Even though 61% of Americans favoured striking Serbs they insisted that the action should be part of a multilateral effort. However, the Europeans were particularly concerned not to militarise the situation further and endanger their troops that were on the ground. Apart from these early suggestions Clinton's latitude was comparatively limited because of the European dominance. But Clinton also ignored Bosnia, preferring to deal with the domestic agenda and the media largely ignored the situation unless explicit military action was taken or there was news of further ethnic cleansing.[28]

As the problems on intervention continued the Clinton administration worked on the Presidential Review Directive 13 (PRD-13). From April 1993 as horrific scenes were filling the airwaves from Srebrenica, criteria emerged that would condition any US intervention. Four essential criteria had to be met: there had to be a clear military mission, a strong likelihood of success, domestic support and a clear exit formula. Such criteria precluded the introduction of US troops into the Balkans, and the Europeans had effectively vetoed the option of air strikes at this stage.[29] Ground forces were an unpopular option. As Secretary of State, Warren Christopher points out 'Memories of Vietnam caused many, especially those in the military, to resist a commitment to a dangerous and uncertain mission in a confusing and complicated conflict.'[30]

In Somalia the exit strategy and the objectives became more problematic. The US mission shifted from the distribution of medical and food supplies to a more militaristic approach and the obsessive hunt for Mohammed Farrah Aideed. Aideed was accused of murdering twenty-four Pakistani soldier of the UNOSOM peacekeeping force. The intensive hunts for Aideed lead to further militarisation of US tactics and cast the US presence in the country in

---

28 Nicholas Guyatt, *Another American Century? The United States and the World After 2000* (Sydney: Pluto, 2000), p. 75; Sobel, *Public Opinion*, p. 186; David Halberstam, *War in a Time of Peace: Bush, Clinton and the Generals* (New York: Scribner, 2001), pp. 163, 196.

29 Ryan, 'Asserting US Power,' p. 120.

30 Warren Christopher, *In the Stream of History: Shaping Foreign Policy for a New* Era (Stanford; Stanford University Press, 1998), p. 347.

a more combative and imperial guise. The former US ambassador to Somalia, Frank Crigler, testified to congress in July 1993 that the change in tactics would be disastrous for the United States. The humanitarian response and diplomacy had given way to a military action that antagonised the Somali people. By October 1993 after constant raids on Aideed's supporters in Mogadishu, US forces confronted widespread resistance from Somali soldiers, women and children. After the exchanges of 3 October, US indiscriminate shooting killed more than 1000 Somalis and eighteen US Rangers died in Mogadishu.[31] One US Ranger was dragged through the streets, relayed on television, producing widespread US reaction. Again the fears of 'mission creep' were discussed as was the new 'Somalia Syndrome' or 'Vietmalia'.

By the spring of 1994 as the Clinton administration withdrew US troops from Somalia and the Bosnian nightmare continued Washington concluded its study PRD-13 and crafted PDD-25 (Presidential Decision Directive). If the four criteria of PRD-13 were not enough, after Somalia a fifth was added in early 1994. In the final version in the document on US intervention it became clear that the United States would not get involved unless there was an explicit threat to the international community. If the interests were marginal to the US the response too would be marginal. If the violence in Bosnia could be contained there was little to fear from the conflict. Former US Secretary of State, James Baker, however, argued that European stability was a vital US interests and that should the conflict spread to say Macedonia, 'if we do get a wider Balkan war, we'll be back.'[32]

Thus far the Bosnian crisis had not threatened the stability in Europe, though US credibility and leadership was under increasing scrutiny. As media attention increased after the mortar shell exploded in the market in Sarajevo in February 1994, a majority of Americans favoured the use of US troops in peacekeeping activities and by May 1994 US aircraft in NATO undertook its first offensive action, downing four Bosnian-Serb planes.[33]

Simultaneously the Clinton Administration remained aloof from the horrific genocide that began in Rwanda in April 1994 after President Juvénal Habyarimana's plane was shot down. As the majority Hutus murdered the Tutsis at an unprecedented rate in modern history, killing over half a million people in 100 days and over a million by the time the killing stopped. But after PPD-25 US real interests and the stability of the world community were not at stake, furthermore there was insufficient domestic interest in the humanitarian crisis and genocide to propel US policy towards intervention. By

---

31 Guyatt, *Another American Century?* pp. 78-9.

32 Martin Walker, 'Generals Get New Mission Statement,' *Guardian Weekly* (London), 17 April 1994; Patrick Cockburn, 'Air strikes Point to New US Strategy to Save Troops,' *Independent* (London), 14 July 1993; Martin Walker interview with James Baker, 'Mad as Hell over what they've done to America,' *The Guardian* (London) 25 June 1994.

33 Sobel, *Public Opinion*, pp. 188-189.

May Albright told the House of Representatives that they would not go along with a UN mission that was not in the US interests.[34]

After Somalia, Clinton was not willing to risk further US casualties. And within days of the disaster at Mogadishu, Washington tried to inject US troops into Haiti in part of an operation to restore Jean-Bertrand Aristide. As the USS *Harlan* tried to dock Haitians jeered the US troops, some shouting, 'Somalia'. The ship retreated amidst negative media coverage describing the impotence of US tactics. By mid-October the media covered the story along side Senatorial calls to withdraw from Somalia. In the words of Halberstam, 'rarely had the United States looked so impotent, its mighty military driven away from a banana republic by a pip-squeak dictator and a hired mob.'[35]

In 1994 Clinton was careful to avoid the term 'genocide' to describe the killing in Rwanda because that would have mandated a response under international law. But by 1998 on his tour through Africa, at his stop in Kigali he explained:

The international community, together with nations in Africa, must bear its share of responsibility for this tragedy, as well. We did not act quickly enough after the killing began. We should not have allowed the refugee camps to become safe havens for the killers. We did not immediately call these crimes by their rightful name: genocide. We cannot change the past, but we can and must do everything in our power to help you build a future without fear and full of hope.[36]

Though little was done in Rwanda, by the summer of 1995 US public opinion and congressional support had grown for a much tougher approach in Bosnia. US support for strikes against Serb targets grew to 71% in the summer of 1995 and NATO threatened disproportionate strikes if the Serbs threatened Gorazde. When the Serbs continued to shell Sarajevo, NATO forces initiated heavy bombing of Serb positions in August 1995. The cease-fire in October and negotiations in Deyton, Ohio finally produced agreement through US mediation.[37]

---

34 Guyatt, *Another American Century?* pp. 80-86; see also Philip Gourevitch, *We Wish to Inform You that Tomorrow We Will Be Killed With Our Families* (London: Picador, 1999).

35 Halberstam, *War in a Time of Peace*, pp. 272-273.

36 President Bill Clinton, Remarks to Genocide Survivors in Kigali, Rwanda 25 March 1998, Public Papers of the President, William J. Clinton, 1998, vol. 1, pp. 431-434.

37 Sobel, *Public Opinion*, pp. 190-191; Michael Ignatieff, 'The Missed Chance in Bosnia,' *The New York Review of Books* 43, no. 4 (29 February 1996), p. 8.

Kosovo

Even though the Dayton process rehabilitated Miloševíc, by 1998 he had turned his attention once again to Kosovo, largely to shore up his domestic position through the abuse of nationalist sentiments. Further ethnic cleansing was carried out against the dominant Albanian population, whose autonomy had been rescinded. The Bosnian conflict had been contained within its borders, but the conflict in Kosovo threatened to affect Macedonia and therefore possibly Greek or even EU stability. Such a prospect would require an immediate US response. As early as 1992 the Bush administration sent a 'warning' to Miloševíc, 'in the event of conflict in Kosovo caused by Serbian action, the United States will be prepared to employ military force against the Serbs in Kosovo and in Serbia proper.' As James Baker had warned in the mid-1990s if the war spread the United States would be back. As far as Washington was concerned Bosnia and Croatia could burn out, but Kosovo reached the geo-political limit in Europe, the 'red line' that could not be crossed according to the Clinton administration.[38]

Miloševíc refused to accept the western conditions in the Rambouillet document, which included the rights of NATO personnel 'unrestricted passage and unimpeded access throughout the FRY' (Federal Republic of Yugoslavia). Though on 23 March 1999 the Serbian National Assembly did call for negotiations 'towards the reaching of a political agreement on a wide-ranging autonomy for Kosovo…' and indicated a 'willing to review [the] size and character of international presence.'[39] After the failed exercise in coercive diplomacy, force was considered necessary to bring Miloševíc back to the negotiating table.

The bombing campaign was expected to last a matter of days. Secretary of State Albright made it clear on the McNeil-Lehrer hour, 'I don't see this as a long-term operation' and Lieutenant General Mike Short, directing the bombing programme, was told 'you're only going to be allowed to bomb two, maybe three nights.' No contingency plans had been made. And the option of ground troops was out of the question. Without counter-force ground operations, Serb ethnic cleansing accelerated, as did the flood of refugees. On 27 March 1999, US NATO commanding officer, General Wesley Clark, indicated that it was 'entirely predictable' that violence would intensify after the bombing and that 'the military authorities fully anticipated the vicious

---

38 Mark Danner, 'Endgame in Kosovo,' *The New York Review of Books* (6 May 1999), p. 10.

39 Michael Albert, 'The "Diplomatic Scene" in Brief, as of May 8' www.zmag.org/dipscene.htm, 10 May 1999.

approach that Milosevic would adopt, as well as the terrible efficiency with which he would carry it out.'[40]

Again the Vietnam syndrome operated extensive influence. The option of ground troops was ruled out in Washington. The Clinton administration was divided on the issue, but they saw no support for ground troops in congress, the media or from public opinion. Clark disagreed with the air strategy. But explicitly and publicly limiting the strategy to airpower was essential to its success. The Clinton administration generated support by ruling out ground troops, whereas Clark thought it was imperative to leave Miloševíc under the impression that the full force of the US military might be used. Only such a threat might induce compromise. Clark's request for Apache helicopters was hotly disputed. If one were downed, would that not require a rescue mission and possibly the introduction of further support? The Pentagon resisted Clark suspecting the request was the thin edge of the wedge that would ultimately lead to the necessity of ground troops. It was only after the mid-phase of the war had been reached that Clinton changed his mind. By this time the bombing alone was coming under some media criticism, the refugee exodus turned to crisis, more and more targets were being missed, most devastating the bomb that hit a refugee column, and the politically damaging bombing of the Chinese Embassy. Once President Clinton and British Prime Minister Tony Blair had made up their mind to see the project through, Clark was given permission to draw up plans to introduce troops. And after 7 May NATO started bombing targets in Belgrade, which ultimately induced capitulation.[41]

The option of using overwhelming power as in the Gulf conflict or aerial bombardment from virtually safe altitudes as in Kosovo, 'makes it easier to be more frivolous in the use of extremely powerful weapons' according to Eric Hobsbawm. The technology developed by the United States provides the executive with the only viable anti-dote to the Vietnam syndrome, in the absence or the reluctance to pursue negotiations and sanctions to their logical conclusion. The technology of the precision weapons allows the executive to overcome the democratic constraint on going to war. As Ignatieff argues,

If violence ceases to be fully real to the citizens in whose name it is exercised will they continue to restrain the executive resort to precision lethality? This becomes an urgent issue in the context of overwhelming American military superiority. If one side of a future conflict is shielded from the reality of war and its consequences, why should it continue to be guided by restraint?[42]

---

40 Halberstam, *War in a Time of Peace*, p. 425; Noam Chomsky, *The New Military Humanism: Lessons from Kosovo* (London: Pluto Press, 1999), pp. 20-21.

41 Halberstam, *War in a Time of Peace*, pp. 424, 463-471.

42 Eric Hobsbawm in Roundtable: The Global Order in the 21st Century, *Prospect* (August/September 1999), p. 50; Michael Ignatieff, *Virtual War: Kosovo and Beyond* (New York: Picador, 2000), p. 163.

Of course after Somalia this was the particular attraction of using this kind of force. It was a remarkable precedent in the history of war that the NATO forces did not suffer one casualty during the conflict. In such circumstances and the inability of the Serbs to properly engage NATO forces the battle moved to the media, as it did in the Gulf conflict. Miloševíc as did Hussein used the western media in an attempt to undermine western morale by taking them to the bombed out sites of television stations, refugee columns and so forth. Near the conclusion of the Kosovo bombing, less than 50% of the US public supported the campaign and it was estimated that it could not be sustained much longer.[43] On the other hand NATO had to concentrate on providing a seemingly credible explanation for the so-called 'collateral damage' to try to maintain morale and support for the tactic of war with impunity.

In the post-Vietnam era, and especially the post-Somalia period perhaps the only way to obtain acquiescence for intervention has been to convince congress that, in line with the sentiment of the War Powers Act, the intervention will be short and decisive and that ground troops will not be required in direct warfare. But such tactics assume the use of disproportionate power and often lead to disproportionate casualties.

The Independent Commission on Kosovo considered that the NATO campaign was neither a success nor a failure. The Serbs were forced to withdraw and accept an agreement close to the original proposed, and the Kosovar oppression was eventually halted. But the tactics accelerated the ethnic cleansing and the refugee crisis resulting in thousands of deaths.[44]

Afghanistan 2001

The Vietnam syndrome continued to exert its influence after the horrific events of 11 September in New York and Washington. Despite the huge and instant public response to George Bush's approval rating and the huge support for military action, the US response fitted within the patterns that had been established during the 1990s. President Bush's approval ratings jumped from 51% in early September to a high of 90%, and began to drop slightly before the aerial bombing of Afghanistan began on 7 October. Similarly, the country was squarely behind (82-88%) taking direct military action in Afghanistan throughout late September and into October. Moreover, Americans accepted that the war would be a prolonged affair unlike the short sharp action in Kosovo or the Gulf conflict. The Bush administration enjoys wide-

43 Ignatieff, *Virtual War*, pp. 191-195.

44 Guyatt, *Another American Century?* pp. 148; The Independent International Commission on Kosovo, *The Kosovo Report* (Oxford: Oxford University Press, 2000), p. 5.

spread support for the actions take to date. In comparison, by the early 1970s 61% thought it was a mistake to send US troops to Vietnam, whereas only 6% think it was a mistake to send troops to Afghanistan.[45]

This high level of support remained despite the elusive nature of the 'war on terrorism'. Perhaps the enormity of the events of 11 September has allowed some of the enduring principles of both the Weinberger and Powell Doctrines to lapse. If one considers the guiding principles that found their way into of PDD-25, and the reluctance to commit US troops previously by the incumbent Secretary of State, Colin Powell, we see that only some are fully adhered to. US interests were obviously at stake. Congressional and public support was clearly behind administration actions. Objectives had been defined, but they are too open-ended. But while the military mission has a clear intended outcome, the methods are questionable, the likelihood of success somewhat dubious, and an exit formula somewhat elusive in such an on going, broadly defined 'war on terrorism'. George Bush did spell out his objectives quite clearly, that the leaders of Al Qaeda must be delivered to the US, that every terrorist training camp must be closed in Afghanistan, that every terrorist must be handed over, and that the United States should have full access to the training camps.[46] But few of these can be achieved within the criteria developed during the 1980s and 1990s.

Still, the methods of aerial bombardment, before diplomacy had been exhausted and the use of cluster bombs and 'daisy cutters' moves away from the notion of a discriminate and proportionate response. While the Taliban regime obviously did succumb to the power of the US response, their removal was not part of the original objectives, bringing up fears of 'mission creep' that has undermined previous US interventions. The hesitancy of using ground troops similarly testifies to the continued prevalence of the Vietnam syndrome, now almost institutionalised within the US system. While Fred Halliday is right to argue that the provisions of the Weinberger and the Powell doctrines were 'one of the casualties of 11 September',[47] perhaps a more effective US response would have involved the pursuit of diplomacy, economic engagement and the selective use of ground troops. Retired US Gen-

45 Mark Gillespie, 'Most Americans Still Rallying Behind Bush and War on Terrorism,' Poll Analyses, The Gallup Organization, www.gallup.com, 16 October 2001; Jeffrey M. Jones, 'Americans Showing Patience in War on Terrorism,' Poll Analyses, The Gallup Organization, www.gallup.com/poll/releases/pr011015, 15 October 2001; Frank Newport, 'Terrorism Fades as Nation's Most Important Problem,' Poll analyses, The Gallup Organization, www.gallup.com/poll/releases/pr020114, 14 January 2002. See also Fred Halliday, *Two Hours That Shook the World: September 11, 2001: Causes and Consequences* (London: Saqi Books, 2002), p. 33.

46 President George Bush, Address to a Joint Session of Congress and the American People, www.whitehouse.gov/news/releases/2001/09/20010920, 20 September 2001.

47 Fred Halliday, *Two Hours That Shook the World: September 11, 2001: Causes and Consequences* (London: Saqi Books, 2002), p. 33.

eral Anthony Zinni was quick to point out that 'you can't just go in and devastate a country. A military approach that strikes and leaves will only perpetuate the problem.'[48] But since 1989 and 1991, the use of airpower has become the preferred option.

The collective memories of the Vietnam War had a profound impact on US intervention during the 1990s. In all cases Washington went to great lengths to avoid US casualties, even though this meant inflicting a disproportionate amount of casualties on the various opponents. The media has been tremendously influential for both US strategy and for the strategies of its opponents. In the Gulf conflict, the media was pooled into controllable systems of information output, in Bosnia and Somalia images of the suffering impelled some reaction, and when operations turned to disaster in Mogadishu in October 1993, the media images augmented the reluctance to intervene on the ground in future conflicts.

There are a couple of ironies that follow. Given the inability to inflict significant damage on US forces, both Saddam Hussein and Slobodan Miloševíc used the media to great effect in an attempt to undermine US morale and public support for the bombing campaigns, their targeting policy, mistakes. The preferred US tactic of overwhelming power has also meant that terrorism and asymmetric violence was the chosen response for 11 September. Yet the enormity of the violence of that day has also meant that Washington and Americans more generally have sacrificed some of the lessons learned since Vietnam. If George Bush senior could proclaim, 'by god we've kicked the Vietnam syndrome', George Bush junior faced atrocities that made Americans willing to put aside selected parts of the syndrome.

48 CDI, 'Zinni Urges Economic, Diplomatic Moves,' Center for Defense Information, www.cdi.org/terrorism/zinni-pr, 17 October 2001.

Paul S. Shoup

U.S. Policy Toward The Balkans: The Role Of Domestic Factors And Lessons Learned

I. Introduction

We are all generally familiar with the role played by domestic factors in shaping foreign policy decision making in the United States, ranging from the most general and diffuse (cultural influences, historical perceptions) to the highly specific (the role of special interest groups). On the one hand, cultural and historical factors express themselves in the tension between isolationism and internationalism; on the other, narrowly focused interest groups, with Congressional support, seek to gain economic advantages abroad, and ethnic groups such as the Cuban or Armenian Americans are highly influential in shaping policy vis-à-vis their country of origin. In the case under consideration here – U.S. policy in the Balkans – we are well aware that domestic actors (we include the media in this category) put immense pressure on the Clinton administration to act more decisively in support of the Bosnian government following the outbreak of civil war in the republic in 1992, and then supported U.S. intervention in Kosovo seven years later.

Foreign policy decisions are nevertheless shaped primarily by the actions of foreign, not domestic, actors, and by the nature of the problems being addressed. For our purposes, we can distinguish between two types of policy environments. At one extreme are problems that do not need to be dealt with within a compressed time frame, such as negotiations over the environment or the liberalization of international trade. Such negotiations permit (or should permit) a careful weighing of domestic interests and foreign policy goals, aiming for compromise. Interest groups have a significant role to play in this process, all other things being equal. Such negotiations usually (but not always) elicit a low level of public interest. On the other hand – and this was the case in the Balkans – foreign policy may be made in a pressure-cooker environment, pulled and tugged by events. In the extreme case, as in Bosnia and Kosovo, foreign policy decision-making may take the form of crisis diplomacy, in which a single event (the shelling of Sarajevo, the Racak massacre) demands a quick response. Policies made in this context are highly reactive, leave no time for longer-term strategies to emerge, and are often colored by sensational reports in the press (the "Remember the Maine" syndrome). Public awareness will be high, at least among the articulate public easily mobilized behind humanitarian concerns. Because there is pressure for a quick response, first perceptions of the event, or crisis, are all important (thus the heightened role of the media).

Crisis diplomacy is also characterized by a desire on the part of policy makers to resist being swept away by the emotions of the moment. Thus, typically, policy makers may pay lip service to pressures for intervention in a crisis while in fact acting with caution. In the Bosnian case, Washington reacted with anger to the shelling of Srebrenica in April 1993, yet moved cautiously and did not initiate air strikes against Bosnian Serb forces. On the other hand, policy makers may throw caution to the winds, as happened in response to reports of massacres of thousands of Bosnian Muslim soldiers by Serbian forces in Srebrenica two years later. The strong response, in the latter case, was occasioned not only by domestic pressures, but by the fact that policy makers in Washington perceived the situation as challenging their credibility. At the same time a contradiction existed between the perceived interests of the United States in getting drawn into a conflict in the Balkans (American vital interests clearly were not involved), and the pressure to intervene generated by demands for humanitarian intervention.

How do domestic pressures influence foreign policy under such circumstances? In the case of the former Yugoslavia, crisis diplomacy was accompanied by intense pressures to intervene on the part of humanitarian organizations, the press, and certain ethnic lobbies. The war in Bosnia also gave rise to a rationalization for early involvement as a response to these pressures: the notion of preventive diplomacy. Domestic influences on foreign policy thus took two forms: calls for intervention; and efforts on the part of the policy makers to anticipate these pressures and if possible to prevent a humanitarian crisis from emerging in the first place (preventive diplomacy). We shall examine the problem of how policies were shaped to anticipate crises in Part II of this paper. But first we must examine the situation that prevailed at the outset of the Balkan crisis and how it encouraged domestic forces in the United States to place pressure on Washington to become involved in the Balkan wars.

II. The Role of Domestic Forces in Shaping American Policy in the Balkans

We may begin by noting the absence of any overriding American interest in the Balkans after the collapse of the Soviet Union. During the Cold War,

Yugoslavia had received a great deal of attention from the West. Notwithstanding the authoritarian character of the Tito regime, Western aid flowed to Yugoslavia in order to counterbalance Soviet influence. With the end of the Cold War, Yugoslavia lost her strategic value in American eyes. American diplomats remained favorably inclined toward Yugoslavia, promoting business ventures there and supporting those politicians – especially in the Federal government – who were fighting centrifugal forces within the country. Meanwhile Yugoslavia, and especially Serbia, presented an opportunity to pursue human rights issues at no apparent risk to American global or regional interests, while at the same time satisfying an important domestic constituency. The focus on human rights, evident already in American criticism of the human rights violations of the Milosevic regime in Kosovo in the late 1980s, set the stage for human rights groups to play an important role in the Balkan crises that followed. Think tanks, foundations and human rights groups, reacting to atrocities committed during the conflict, received a sympathetic hearing in Washington. An activist policy toward the crisis was supported by the Helsinki Commission of Congress, which held extensive hearings on all aspects of the war in Bosnia and then in Kosovo, focusing on human rights violations committed by Serb forces in these regions.

This mutually supportive relationship between human rights organizations and the U.S. government became strained in the aftermath of the Kosovo conflict. Human rights organizations criticized the manner in which the United States waged war in Kosovo.[1] There were charges that local elections in Kosovo were undemocratic, followed by criticisms by the OSCE of trials of Serb war criminals in Kosovo in which Albanian judges participated. As we shall see, calls for humanitarian intervention in the recent conflict in Macedonia have been virtually nonexistent. We can anticipate that human rights activists will continue to support efforts at humanitarian intervention in Africa and elsewhere. But in the Balkans, at any rate, enthusiasm for such policies on the part of human rights organizations may be waning, especially following the events of September 11, when the priorities of both the private and public sectors in the West were radically redirected toward the threat of terrorism and events in the Middle East.

Brief mention should also be made of the influence of domestic actors on American policy in Bosnia since the Dayton Peace Accords. As we know, NGOs rushed into Bosnia when the war ended there, and have remained in great numbers, concentrated in Sarajevo. There was indeed a need for non-

---

1 See Human Rights Watch bulletins of May 11, 1999, "NATO's Use of Cluster Munitions in Yugoslavia," and its report "Civilian Deaths in the NATO Air Campaign." Human Rights Watch also criticized the failure of the international community to protect Serbs and other minorities in Kosovo following the establishment of the UN administration. See "Abuses Against Serbs and Roma in the New Kosovo" *Human Rights Watch* (August, 1999).

governmental organizations in Bosnia after the conflict was over. Yet much of the NGO activity in Bosnia was undertaken in haste, and a debate continues over the effectiveness of these organizations. It seems that with certain exceptions[2] American NGOs have not measurably contributed to the long-range goal of creating a civil society in Bosnia, and that the input of this domestic component of American foreign policy, both in Bosnia and Kosovo, has proven something of a disappointment.[3] On the other hand, NGOs and advocacy groups, such as the International Crisis Group (ICG), indirectly influenced American and Western policy in Bosnia by supporting efforts of the Office of the High Representative (OHR), which is designed to strengthen the central government and create a state of all the Bosnian peoples – for example, by supporting the return of refugees to their homes – despite resistance from all three ethnic communities.

There was another, less savory, side to the role of the American private sector in Bosnia: namely, supplying arms to the Bosnian government. The U.S. military, concerned with its own image, has turned over this task to non-governmental operatives acting under American guidance. The most notable of these groups is Military Professional Resources Inc. (MPRI), which stands accused by its critics of encouraging the flow of arms into Bosnia for reasons of self-interest. Efforts to rebuild Bosnia have been marked by the lack of a clear-cut delineation of responsibilities among international organizations, NGOs, and military chains of command. None of these organizations, groups or institutions appears to have built a constituency in the United States that could be mobilized to support, indefinitely, an international presence in Bosnia (or in Kosovo, for that matter). And this in turn has raised the question of whether the Bush administration in Washington, reacting to domestic sensibilities and fears of foreign involvement, will seek to further reduce its commitments in the Balkans.

Meanwhile, no discussion of domestic influences on policy toward the Balkans would be complete without considering the role of the media. For the most part, Western coverage of the war focused on the plight of the Bosnian Muslims. How greatly this influenced policy makers is a subject of considerable debate. Critics of the media accused it of an anti-Serb bias, or at best, of naivety and ignorance, "Like scouts without a compass," in the words of one analysis of the media's role."[4] Yet media attention to the atrocities that took place during the conflict – largely those committed by the Serbs – did not generate any enthusiasm with the American public for U.S. intervention

2 For example, the Central and East European Law Initiative (CEELI), has tried, with some success, to train lawyers and establish an independent judiciary in Bosnia. See *CEELI Update (*Summer 1999), p. 6.

3 See David Chandler, *Bosnia: Faking Democracy After Dayton* (1999).

4 Sylvia Paggoli, "Scouts without a Compass," *Nieman Reports* (Fall, 1993), p. 16.

in the war.[5] One journalist-scholar argued, on the basis of interviews with policy makers in the United States and Britain, that media coverage did not, by itself, substantially alter policies under consideration by decision makers, and that government intelligence sources usually provided policymakers with information in advance of the media.[6] Yet it was the media, above all, which contributed to the atmosphere of crisis with which policy makers had to cope, and it can be suggested that the media's treatment of events – whether selective or impartial – provided the setting within which perceptions of the conflict were shaped.

We may sum up the discussion of domestic influences on American policy in the Balkans as follows: (i) Perceptions of the conflict in the former Yugoslavia were indeed influenced by arguments of the media, human rights groups, and think tanks with ties to the Washington establishment that humanitarian intervention in Bosnia was necessary. The arguments put forward by these actors reinforced the perception that one side was largely to blame (thus simplifying the task of bringing the aggressor in the conflict to heel). (ii) American foreign policy makers, however, were resistant to being dictated to by advocacy groups and only took action in Bosnia when crisis situations arose – such as the massacre in Srebrenica – which challenged the credibility of the United States and the Western alliance. (iii) The violence in Kosovo, which broke out in 1998, was as a consequence viewed in the same somewhat simplified perspective. (iv) Following the occupation of Kosovo by UN forces and reports of Albanian human rights abuses (as well as abuses by the Serbs during the preceding months), domestic pressures on Washington for further intervention decreased, notwithstanding calls of human rights groups for a more active role on the part of the international community in enforcing its mandate in Kosovo. As we shall see, this trend was even more evident in the case of Macedonia

In light of the shortcomings of crisis diplomacy in Bosnia, American policy towards the Balkans underwent a shift of emphasis, from caution to what might be called "preventive activism." U.S. policy makers were more and more determined not to become trapped in situations in which they were at the mercy of events and forced by public pressures into making decisions

5 See Steven L. Burg and Paul S. Shoup, *The War in Bosnia Herzegovina: Ethnic Conflict and International Intervention* (1999), pp. 163-64. For media coverage of the Kosovo crisis, see Steven Livingston, "Media Coverage of the War: An Empirical Assessment," in Albrecht Schnabel and Ramesh Thakur (eds.), *Kosovo and the Challenge of Humanitarian Intervention* (2000), pp. 360-84. For criticisms of the media's role in the Balkan crises, see articles appearing on the web site of FAIR (www.fair.org/international/yugoslavia.html).

6 Nik Gowing, "Real-Time Television Coverage of Armed Conflict and Diplomatic Crises: Does it Pressure or Distort Foreign Policy Decisions," *Working Paper* No. 94-1, the Joan Shorenstein Barone Center on the Press, Politics and Public Policy, Harvard University (June, 1994).

and commitments that they otherwise would have avoided. It was considerations of this nature, re-enforced by the think tanks with ties to American policy makers, that produced the doctrine of preventive diplomacy, or "operational prevention of conflict" in the words of an influential report prepared by the Carnegie Commission on Preventing Deadly Conflict issued in 1997.[7] In brief, in pondering the lessons learned from the Bosnian experience, American diplomats (or at least those activists most influential in the White House at the time) embraced a doctrine that they thought would avoid the shortcomings of crisis diplomacy, while at the same time serving a humanitarian purpose. These "lessons learned" – a product of both perceptions of the policy makers themselves and of domestic advocacy groups – held out hope that the risks of crisis diplomacy in the Balkans (and challenges to the credibility of the United States which followed) could be avoided by early intervention, if necessary by force, to compel a settlement before ethnic cleansing and atrocities against civilians had taken place. Although it was not clearly foreseen at the time, the test of this doctrine was to come in Kosovo in the spring of 1999.

III. Lessons Learned

Rather than reviewing the arguments for preventive diplomacy, which may be found in part in the Carnegie study cited above, as well as in a report issued under the auspices of the U.S. Institute of Peace, *Coercive Prevention: Normative, Political and Policy Dilemmas,*[8] we can pass directly to two questions: first, was the need for early intervention the correct lesson learned from the Bosnian conflict; and second, could this lesson be applied in subsequent crises?

It may be suggested that the arguments for early intervention had serious deficiencies in so far as they attempted to distill the lessons learned in Bosnia into guidelines for dealing with other conflicts in the Balkans. As noted earlier, American intervention in Bosnia was based on the assumption that one party was the aggressor. This assumption was no longer possible following the demise of Milosevic in Serbia.[9] More fundamentally, the fact that the

7 Carnegie Commission on Preventing Deadly Conflict, *Preventing Deadly Conflict: Final Report* (1997).

8 Bruce W. Jentleson, *Coercive Prevention: Normative, Political and Policy Dilemmas,* U.S Institute of Peace, *Peaceworks* No. 35 (October, 2000). See also Alexander George and William E. Simons (eds.), *The Limits of Coercive Diplomacy*, 2nd ed. (1994) and Peter Jakobsen, *Western Use of Coercive Diplomacy After the Cold War (1998).*

9 For the difficulty of engaging in "impartial" interventions, see Richard R. Betts, "The Delusion of Imperial Intervention," *Foreign Affairs*, (November/December, 1994).

Dayton settlement in Bosnia produced a secure peace while the Kosovo solution became mired down in the contradictions of UN resolution 1244 can be related to the fact that in the former instance the exhausted combatants were ready to agree to a compromise settlement in order to end the fighting, while in the case of Kosovo NATO air strikes against Serbia pre-empted negotiations for a permanent settlement agreed to by the parties themselves. Early intervention (or "coercive prevention," in the words of the U.S. Institute for Peace report) did, of course, hold out the promise of preventing bloodshed or even genocide. But it also ran the risk of placing peacekeepers between two warring parties who had agreed to a temporary truce, but not a final settlement. This appeared to be the case in Kosovo, where the presence of UN forces was all that prevented the outbreak of a fresh round of fighting between the Serbs and the Muslims. (Of course, this was still perhaps better than the alternative of a protracted war between Serbia and the KLA, and the present situation is undoubtedly more favorable to Serbia in the long run than if she was still engaged militarily in Kosovo.)

This is not to say that there was *no* case for early intervention. On the contrary, we now see that projecting power in the Balkans did influence the outcome of the conflicts in Bosnia and Kosovo, and further, that the United States was the only member of the NATO alliance that could have organized such an effort. A long drawn-out war between Yugoslavia and the Albanian Liberation Army, with the likelihood of further atrocities on both sides, was avoided. In the last analysis, however, early intervention in Kosovo did not provide a way of escaping the dangers of crisis diplomacy. On the contrary, the decision to intervene in Kosovo was itself an example of crisis diplomacy: a reaction to the Racak massacre, rationalized by the notion--which proved false – that Milosevic would capitulate after several days of air strikes, while little consideration was given to the long term implications of asking the international community to assume responsibility for the administration of the region.

Furthermore, the notion that one could build a stable democracy and a civil society after intervening in a massive fashion in ethnic conflicts now seems less and less convincing, if indeed this argument ever had any validity.[10] In the case of Bosnia this has posed a major dilemma for those in Wash-

---

10 Numerous reports on the situation in Bosnia have appeared since the Dayton peace accords. Note Leo Tindemans et al. *Unfinished Peace: Report of the International Commission on the Balkans (1996);* International Crisis Group, *Is Dayton Failing: Bosnia Four Years After the Peace Agreement* (October 28, 1999); Gordon Bardos, "The Bosnian Cold War Politics, Society and International Engagement After Dayton," *The Harriman Review* (April, 1999); U.S. Institute of Peace Special Report, *Bosnia's Next Five Years: Dayton and Beyond* (November, 2000): and Thomas Cushman (ed.), *Justice and Social Reconstruction in Bosnia Herzegovina in Global Perspective* (1999). Most of these reports accept the premise of the OHR that the Bosnian state must be recreated at the expense of the entities, that is, that the task is

ington who have argued that nation building was the key to creating conditions for the withdrawal of American troops from the region. Nation building was equated, in this view, with re-establishing a strong central government in Bosnia and creating a single army for all of Bosnia Herzegovina. In point of fact, efforts to recentralize the Bosnian government have increased the dependence of the country on foreign forces and transformed the Office of the High Representative into the de facto government of Bosnia.

This is not the occasion to settle the question of what policies might be conducive to the creation of self-sustaining institutions in Bosnia. Rather, the point to be made is that there is no real agreement on the lessons learned – and therefore what policies to follow after intervention takes place – in ethnic conflicts in the Balkans. The deal that ended the fighting in Kosovo was an act of desperation on both sides. NATO faced the prospect of a land war if it was to oust the Serbs from the province. The Milosevic regime, on the other hand, found itself isolated – the Russians had failed to come to its support – and threatened with new air strikes aimed specifically at Belgrade. The outcome was Resolution 1244, which provided for a UN force in Kosovo (the Serbs refused to allow NATO to take on this task), the withdrawal of all Serb forces, and the establishment of a civilian UN administration. In one respect, certainly, justice was served, since the Kosovo Albanians were able to liberate themselves from harsh Serb rule. But in another sense, nothing was resolved, since Resolution 1244, in order to gain Serb consent, acknowledged that the province remained part of a sovereign Yugoslavia. Any permanent settlement of the status of Kosovo was thereby put off to the indefinite future.

The most important conclusion that could be drawn from the preceding analysis is that if a new crisis did erupt in the Balkans, the United States would not necessarily find answers on how to respond by relying on lessons learned from earlier conflicts in the region. The lessons learned from Bosnia and Kosovo were not agreed upon, and in any case did not seem to apply to situations where intervention was not directed against an easily identifiable foe such as Slobodan Milosevic. It was apparent, furthermore, that reliance on air strikes – the only way in which the United States could exercise military power without incurring American casualties – was not likely to prove appropriate in any future humanitarian crisis, once.

Indeed, events in the spring of 2001 bore out these conclusions. Following the overthrow of Milosevic in October 2000, it appeared that the Balkan crisis had finally come to an end. The new democratic government in Yugoslavia, under President Vojislav Kostunica, pledged to cooperate with the UN in Kosovo, although insisting that Kosovo remain part of Yugoslavia.

---

one of "nation building." For the contrary view, that the United States has failed in nation building whenever it has been attempted (including Bosnia), see Gary T. Dempsey, *Fools Errands: America's Recent Encounters with Nation Building (2001)* and David Chandler, *Bosnia: Faking Democracy After Dayton* (1999).

Moreover, the tensions that arose between Montenegro and Yugoslavia, following Montenegrin demands for independence, did not lead to violence. But hopes for continued peace in the Balkans proved premature after fighting broke out in the spring of 2001 between Albanian guerrillas and Serbian police in southern Serbia, and then between Macedonian troops and local Albanians in Macedonia. One might have expected calls for early intervention by NATO to protect Macedonia from the violence, which threatened the stability of the country, yet none was forthcoming.[11] Nor were any steps taken prior to this time to strengthen the Macedonian army against a possible uprising among the Albanians in Macedonia; on the contrary, American policy had favored keeping the Macedonian army small out of an understandable fear that a large military would prove a drain on the Macedonian economy.

Continued fighting in the summer of 2001 threatened the territorial integrity of Macedonia but did not lead to calls for intervention. Instead, the international community pursued a policy that Chancellor Schroeder of Germany called "preventive stabilization." NATO intervention was limited to a symbolic disarming of the Albanian insurgents timed to coincide with the adoption of amendments to the Macedonian constitution aimed at granting the Albanian minority greater rights while depriving the Macedonian people of the symbolic privileges of a "constituent" nationality.[12] This solution was largely the work of a small group of Western diplomats representing the EU, NATO and the OSCE. American input was minimal. Pressure for intervention on the side of the Macedonian government was absent, although calls for greater U.S. participation in the negotiations between the warring parties were common. If anything, the United States projected the image of an indifferent observer. This image was then heightened by the events of September 11 and the American dedication to the war against terrorism that followed.

---

11 Richard Holbrooke, the American ambassador to the United Nations, did call for such a move. But he was no longer speaking for the new Republican administration.

12 These changes were outlined in the Framework Agreement signed by the major political parties of Macedonia under pressure from Western mediators on August 13, 2001. For a description of the agreement and the politics of the Macedonian crisis, see International Crisis Group, "Macedonia's Name: Why the Dispute Matters and How to Resolve It,"(December 10, 2001); and "Macedonia: Filling the Security Vacuum," (September 8, 2001).

IV. Conclusions

The preceding analysis has cast doubt on the validity of certain doctrines that were developed as a way of guiding policy makers through the perils of crisis diplomacy in the Balkans. Indeed, we have suggested that as a consequence of the application of the strategy of early, or coercive, intervention in Kosovo the United States found itself caught in the very dilemmas this doctrine was meant to avoid – hasty decision making without any clear conception of where intervention might lead. Our second argument was that in so far as early intervention did end the fighting and ease the humanitarian crisis – and this was accomplished in Kosovo – the question of the ultimate fate of the region was put on hold. Does this mean that the decision to intervene in Kosovo was a mistake? The answer may only be known if, and when, there is a peaceful resolution of the Kosovo question, although how this is to be accomplished is unclear. The important point for this analysis is that the confusion surrounding policy in the Balkan crisis makes it difficult to agree that the formulas developed within the foreign policy establishment in the United States – including both official Washington, the academic community, and think tanks – have much validity for solving future crises. Those who follow in Washington's footsteps in developing strategy for the Balkans--we are of course thinking of the European Union--must do this without much hope that guidance can be found in the so-called "lessons learned," at least those formulated by the American foreign policy establishment. This appears to be borne out in the case in Macedonia, as we have briefly noted above.

This does not mean that the international community in the Balkans can draw no conclusions from the past ten years of engagement. We can now better predict the conditions under which such crises erupt; we are aware that peaceful solutions require the participation in any settlement of the near neighbors of the country affected; and we see that it is possible to engage in limited coercion by an international force as a prelude to a settlement, *providing* that the basics of a final settlement are already agreed to and that the parties in question do not see any further gains from carrying on the fighting. American support for any settlement is imperative.

On the other hand, the problems that now confront Europe and the United States in the Balkans – whether, for example, to support independence for Kosovo, and what to do if fighting is renewed in Macedonia – arise in an environment radically altered by the events of September 11, the ouster of Milosevic in Serbia, and the determination of NATO not to engage in additional post-conflict nation building in the Balkans. The likelihood that the Bush administration in Washington will seek to further limit the U.S. role in the region following the events of September 11 means that the lessons learned must be distilled and debated in Europe, where, as we have just suggested, the future of the Balkans is likely to be determined.

Will the United States, lacking a firm policy on how to respond to a new Balkan crisis, show a better grasp of conditions in the region? Let us end this discussion on a cautiously optimistic note. Americans have retained a strain of idealism and engagement in the face of crises around the globe, and the Balkans is no exception. We see this idealism and engagement in the work of American NGOs in the Balkans and the participation of American diplomats in the role of mediators acting in the name of the OSCE, or NATO, most recently in Macedonia. In addition, there are a growing number of Americans who have been in Bosnia, and more recently in Kosovo, as election observers, serving in National Guard units, or working for NGOs. They are glad to be home, but their curiosity and sympathy for the Balkan peoples is heartening. The presence of a good number of refugees from Croatia, Bosnia and Kosovo in the United States – hard working people – has contributed to a growing familiarity of the average American with this part of the world. Thus there is some reason to hope that Americans will over the longer term be increasingly receptive to the needs of the peoples of the Balkans, even if, as seems likely, the United States will, in the near future, take a back seat to Europe in the region.

This takes us back to our original subject, the role of domestic forces in shaping American policy in the Balkans. In the last analysis, the interplay between foreign policy and domestic forces in the United States in the case of the Balkans follows a pattern familiar from American involvement elsewhere in the globe: one of hasty and well meaning engagement, followed by withdrawal, but with possible positive aftereffects as the United States develops more concrete links with the peoples of the region in question. If strategic (and abstract) notions of how to respond to crises in the Balkans are replaced with more pragmatic and sober relationships with the countries in question – in cooperation with Europe – we shall all be the winners.

Thomas E. Graham, Jr.

U.S. Leadership and Domestic Factors in Dealing with Russia During the Clinton Administration

Nine years after the breakup of the Soviet Union, Russia has not embodied our worst fears, nor has it fulfilled our greatest expectations. We have not witnessed a return to its totalitarian past, a descent into chaos, or the country's disintegration. Neither have we witnessed steady progress in the building of a democratic society based on a market economy. Russia has not reverted to being a strategic adversary, but neither has it become a strategic partner. Rather, Russia remains suspended somewhere between its Soviet past and an uncertain future, where market democracy and partnership with the West is still a possibility, but hardly the only, nor even the most likely, future.

Such thoughts were cold comfort to the Clinton Administration, which assumed office in 1993 determined, as Deputy Secretary of State Strobe Talbott, the chief architect of the Administration' s Russia policy, was wont to put it, to assist Russia in its transformation into “a normal, modern state - democratic in its governance, abiding by its own constitution and by its own laws, market-oriented and prosperous in its economic development, at peace with itself and with the rest of the world.[1] As late as 1997, the Administration looked upon Russia as one of its success stories. President Yeltsin had been reelected in 1996, burying at last any chance of communist revanchism; the government, headed by the stolid Viktor Chernomyrdin, was dominated by the so-called “young reformers” and the economy was showing the first signs of life after steady decline since the beginning of the reform effort. Russia, Talbott declared in September 1997, was at “the end of the beginning” of its journey toward becoming a normal, modern state. "It may be," he said “on the brink of a breakthrough.”[2] Russia' s financial collapse less than a year later demonstrated that Talbott had been right, but not in the way he had intended.

---

1 Deputy Secretary of State Strobe Talbott, *The End of the Beginning: The Emergence of a New Russia*, Address delivered at Stanford University, Stanford, California, September 19, 1997.

2 Ibid.

Something had obviously gone wrong, although the Administration had steadfastly refused to admit that in public. Part of the reason lies in Russian developments that lay beyond the serious influence of any outside government. But part also lies in the Administration' s policy. A review of the last eight years reveals an Administration that launched a massive effort to help transform Russia, but failed to produce a coherent strategy or build and maintain sufficient domestic support for its policies. It also reveals an Administration turning its back on Russia once its policy had failed, unwilling to rethink it in an effort to retard, if not reverse, a serious deterioration in U.S.-Russian relations.

The Clinton Administration entered office promising change in both the United States' domestic affairs and foreign policy. In foreign policy, the Administration sought to distinguish its approach from that of the Bush Administration, arguing that the end of the Cold War had fundamentally altered the nature of the international system. In dealing with this new system, *Realpolitik* would no longer suffice. A country's external behavior was ultimately an expression of its domestic structure; therefore, the United States needed to have policies that would nudge a country's domestic developments in directions favorable to American interests. President Clinton laid out this perspective in his first major address on foreign affairs as President:

> During the Cold War, our foreign policies largely focused on relations among nations. Our strategies sought a balance of power to keep the peace. Today, our policies must also focus on relations within nations, on a nation's form of governance, on its economic structure, [and] on its ethnic tolerance. These are of concern to us, for they shape how these nations treat their neighbors as well as their own people and whether they are reliable when they give us their word.[3]

Clinton left no doubt that his Administration intended to promote democracy and free markets as fundamental to the advancement of the United States' own long-term interests.

No country was more important for the Administration in this regard than Russia. It saw an historic chance to transform a strategic enemy into a constructive partner working for global peace and prosperity. More mundanely, it sensed an opportunity to improve on the record of its predecessor. During the presidential campaign of 1992, candidate Clinton had sharply attacked the Bush Administration for tardiness in meeting the challenge of Russia's transformation. Clinton's attacks – together with former President Nixon's call for more assistance to Russia – eventually pushed the Bush Administration into cobbling together a $24-million assistance effort. But the effort never got off the ground as the campaign intensified and Bush ultimately lost.

---

3 President Clinton, "A Strategic Alliance With Russian Reform," Address before the American Society of Newspapers Editors, Annapolis, Maryland, April 1, 1993.

The Clinton Administration was determined to act where its predecessor had hesitated. And it did so with a sense of urgency. Shortly before it took office, Yeltsin had replaced his reformist acting Prime Minister, Yegor Gaydar, with Chernomyrdin, then widely seen as a conservative "red director" unsympathetic to genuine reform. Yeltsin and the conservative parliament, the Congress of People's Deputies, were locked in a bitter battle for political supremacy. A popular referendum in Russia on Yeltsin's policies was looming on the horizon. Monthly inflation was running in double digits. As one senior Administration official subsequently argued, when the Administration took office there was a real risk of a Weimar Russia or a return to totalitarianism.[4]

President Clinton devoted his first foreign policy address to Russia, calling for "strategic alliance with Russian reform." The struggle to build a free society in Russia was "one of the great human dramas of our day," he argued. It presented the "greatest security challenge for our generation," and it offered "one of the greatest economic opportunities of our lifetime." Success in Russia would improve our security, create a partner in global problem solving, allow the United States to reduce the pace of defense spending and invest more in its own future, and yield innumerable opportunities for productive trade with and investment in a potentially rich country. To underscore the importance of Russia, Clinton made his first trip abroad – to Vancouver, Canada – to meet with Yeltsin to discuss ways in which the United States, and the West as a whole, could help.[5]

During its first months, the Administration moved quickly to galvanize Western support behind its effort to assist Russia. It took the lead in forging and promoting the so-called "Washington consensus" – a focus on monetary and fiscal measures to achieve macro-economic stabilization – that became the West's guide in pressing economic reform in Russia (and elsewhere around the globe). It put together an assistance package of over $40 billion. As part of this package, it persuaded the G-7 in April 1993 to commit to a $28.4-billion package of multilateral assistance to help Russia restructure key sectors of its economy, divest itself of inefficient state enterprises, finance critical imports, and stabilize the currency. For its own part, the Administration committed nearly $3 billion in bilateral assistance. Finally, the Administration also encouraged the IMF to create a new lending facility with looser conditionality, the Systemic Transformation Facility, to empower it to give credits to Russia before it could qualify for a traditional standby-agreement. The first tranche from this facility – $ 1.5 billion – was disbursed in June 1993.[6]

---

4 Lawrence Summers, Deputy Secretary of Treasury, Foreign Press Center Briefing, July 19, 1993.

5 Clinton, "A Strategic Alliance With Russian Reform."

6 See Strobe Talbott, Ambassador-at-Large and Special Adviser to the Secretary for the New Independent States, "US Must Lead a Strategic Alliance with Post-Soviet Reform." Statement before the Subcommittee on Foreign Operations of the House Appropriations Committee, Washington, DC, April 19, 1993.

The Administration also moved to energize the U.S. Government bureaucracy to support Russia's reform effort. Upon taking office, Clinton appointed his close friend, Strobe Talbott, Ambassador-at-Large and Special Adviser to the Secretary of State for the New Independent States. In this position, Talbott was to oversee all U.S. policy toward Russia, and it was hoped that his close ties to the President would give him the clout to bring recalcitrant bureaucracies into line. To coordinate the massive assistance program – soon over twenty U.S. Government departments and agencies were involved – the office of the coordinator of assistance to the Newly Independent States was created, which reported directly to Talbott.

In addition, the Administration sought to build domestic support for its Russia policy by structuring its assistance programs to the needs of potentially powerful constituencies. So the original assistance package included $700 million in concessional loans for food sales, which would permit a resumption of food exports to Russia and play to the interests of the American agrarian sector. The Administration also proposed a $2 billion Eximbank framework for export credits in the oil and gas industry for the purchase of US equipment and services, a measure intended in part to "support thousands of jobs in US companies that were hit hard by the recent recession [of 1991/92]."[7] Finally, at the Vancouver summit in April 1993, Clinton and Yeltsin agreed to create the "U.S.-Russian Commission on Economic and Technical Cooperation," soon to be known as the Gore-Chernomyrdin Commission after its co-chairmen. The Commission's original mandate focused on space and energy issues, that is, on sectors in which American business had potentially major opportunities in Russia.

While focused on Russia's domestic transformation, the Administration also paid close attention to the traditional security agenda, hoping to produce successes that would help build and maintain support for its broader agenda. There were some important ones. In part because of Administration pressure, for example, Russian troops were withdrawn from Central Europe and the Baltics on schedule in 1994. The Administration played a key role in mediating Russian and Baltic differences, moderating Baltic nationalism, and alleviating Russian concerns about the treatment of ethnic Russians in the Baltics. Likewise, the Administration scored a major success in brokering a deal between Russia and Ukraine leading to the withdrawal of Soviet nuclear weapons from Ukraine to Russia for dismantling. At the same time, the Administration stepped up support for the Nunn-Lugar program, which would help secure and dismantle the Russian nuclear arsenal.

As a result of these efforts, in the first year and a half, the Administration managed to build considerable domestic support for its Russia policy. The Congress gave bipartisan support to the Administration's assistance package. Business looked forward to growing opportunities in Russia. The media was

---

7 *Ibid.*

generally supportive, and the Moscow correspondents of leading American newspapers – *The New York Times*, *The Washington Post*, and *The Wall Street Journal* – sent back reports that reinforced the Administration's view of the state of play in Russia and helped build support for the reformers.

The Administration's success, however, was short-lived. By the summer of 1994, it was already clear that domestic support for its Russia policy was fading away. The reasons lay both in the flaws in Administration policy and policy-making and in developments in Russia.

The ambitious assistance program ran into serious problems almost as soon as it started. The major player was USAID, which had no expertise in Russian matters. Established in 1961, it had worked exclusively on the Third World during the Cold War. Only in the late 1980's did it begin to divert resources and personnel to Central Europe and later, in the 1990's, to the former Soviet Union to meet changing Administration priorities. It was a bad match. First of all, USAID worked on "development", what was occurring in Russia was not development per se, but rather movement away from a misdeveloped Soviet system to, it was hoped, a more Western-styled system. Second, in executing its programs, USAID, like other U.S. aid agencies, relied heavily in the initial years on so-called outside experts with little understanding of Russian conditions; in fact, these were for the most part the same experts USAID had used in the Third World. Third, much of the money in fact never reached Russian entities, as it went into the pockets of expensive Western consultants.[8]

Moreover, the assistance program was never properly coordinated. This was true of the U.S. bilateral effort, in part because USAID remained a world to itself and resisted the efforts of the Special Coordinator at the State Department to exercise effective oversight. But it was especially true of the international effort. Efforts to set up an effective coordinating body ended in failure. Indeed, the Support Implementation Group, set up in 1993 by the G-7 and headed by an American, actually impeded the informal coordination process that had grown up among donors over time, according to the U.S. General Accounting Office. This group was eventually disbanded in 1997.[9]

The problems with coordinating assistance only reflected the deeper problem of coordinating Russia policy in the U.S. Government. The coordination process had worked fairly well as long as Talbott – with his easy access to Clinton – had served as the Special Adviser on Russia policy. But less

---

8 See Peter M. Stavrakis, "Bull in a China Shop: USAID's Post-Soviet Mission." *Demokratizatsiya* 4/2 (Spring 1996); and Janine R. Wedel, *Collision and Collusion: The Strange Case of Western Aid to Eastern Europe 1989-1998* (New York: St. Martin's Press, 1998), pp.15-34.

9 United States General Accounting Office, *Foreign Assistance: International Efforts to Aid Russia's Transition Have Had Mixed Results*, Report to the Chairman and to the Ranking Minority Member, Committee on Banking and Financial Services, House Representatives (Washington, DC: November 2000), pp. 62-63.

than a year into the Administration, Talbott was named Deputy Secretary. With the global responsibilities of that position, he simply did not have the time to pay the close attention to Russia required to coordinate policy effectively. But he refused to delegate that responsibility. Even if he had, it might not have made much difference, for his successor as Special Adviser was a gray career diplomat with little if any clout with other arms of the government.

While the Administration encountered profound coordination problems, developments in Russia itself eroded confidence in Administration policy. Yeltsin's disbanding in October 1993 of the Congress of People's Deputies (whom most American observers saw as a bastion of reactionary, pro-communist opponents of reform) did not lead to the breakthrough on reform that many had hoped for. Zhirinovskiy's ultranationalist Liberal-Democratic Party came in first in the party-list voting for the State Duma, Russia's new parliament, in December 1993. Acrimony between Yeltsin and a democratically elected Duma grew sharper. The economy continued its steep decline. By 1995, Russian GDP was about 65% of the 1991 level. At the same time, there were troubling reports of destabilizing actions by Russian forces in many former Soviet republics, particularly Moldova and Georgia, that raised doubts about Moscow's commitment to their sovereignty and economic development.

Moreover, despite the Administration's urging and assistance, the Russian government did very little to improve the investment climate in Russia. Excessive red tape, pervasive corruption, arbitrary and irrational taxes, poor law enforcement, unreliable courts, and organized crime all dampened any enthusiasm American investors might have had immediately after the breakup of the Soviet Union. Unfortunate stories of American investors being milked by their Russia partners, as well as the murder of one American involved in a dispute with the city of Moscow over control of a luxury hotel in 1995, did nothing to improve the climate.

As was to be expected, the Administration sought to put the best face on developments. While acknowledging the problems, the Administration pointed to what it saw as significant progress on democratic and market reforms. Free and fair elections were becoming an increasingly prominent feature of the landscape. Basic freedoms were guaranteed, and, the Administration pointed out, the press was particularly lively and aggressive in its criticism of the government. On the economic front, the Administration focused on the growing share of private economic activity in GDP and the slow but steady progress in bringing down budget deficits and inflation. Always, the Administration drew a link between this progress and its policies, while suggesting negative developments were the legacy of the Soviet past or reactionary forces inside Russia.

At the same time, two problems emerged in the way the Administration spoke about Russia that were to bedevil it over the following years. First, in its rush to hype the successes of reform, the Administration showed a remarkable lack of curiosity about the reality that lay behind its favorite statistics. It expressed, for example, little concern that declining inflation and budget deficits were in part the consequence of the government's refusal to pay wages and pensions, something that could only erode public support for reform. While praising privatization, it seemed not to notice that the state still owned large blocks of shares in so-called private enterprises and that the vast majority of these enterprises were not being restructured to compete under true market conditions. Rather than growing their enterprises and creating wealth, many owners were shamelessly stripping their assets.

Second, the Administration slowly and perhaps unconsciously substituted the fate of the reformers for the success of reform. Eventually what was important to the Administration was that the reformers with whom it had established close ties remained in power, and it was known from time to time to urge Yeltsin to retain certain key figures in his government when they appeared under threat. This was particularly true of privatization czar Anatoliy Chubays, soon to become a key symbol of the reform effort. The reformers became the guarantee that reforms would continue no matter what the difficulties of the present. In its embrace of the reformers, the Administration was slow to recognize that some of them were growing corrupt and thereby undermining the reform effort as a whole.

In addition, the Administration downplayed growing differences with Russia over its activities in the former Soviet Union, policies in the former Yugoslavia, and arms trade with Iran in a show of support for the reformers (in the Administration's view, these differences arose from the continuing influence of unreconstructed elements in the Russian foreign policy and security elites, to which the reformers had to bend in order to advance political and economic reform).

Despite the Administration's concerted effort to put a positive gloss on Russian developments, Congressional support for the assistance program began to wane in the second half of 1994. In April 1993, the Administration had pledged to provide $1.6 billion in assistance for Russia. That was the high point. Budgets for Russia dropped from $1.0 billion in fiscal year 1994 to $359 million in 1995 to $219 million in 1996. Concerned about the effectiveness of assistance to Russia, Congress started to earmark significant portions of assistance funds for other former Soviet states, notably Ukraine.[10]

Similarly, domestic support for the Administration's Russia policy outside the Congress also began to fade. This was particularly true of the business community, which was supposed to be one of the mainstays for the Administration. Because of the formidable obstacles to doing business in Russia, in mid-1996, only slightly more than 600 American companies had repre-

10 *Ibid.*, pp. 55, 57.

sentative offices in Moscow. Only about one-third of those were engaged in trade and investment, and only half of those had made significant investments.[11] Cumulative U.S. direct investment in Russia in the 1990's amounted to a miserly $2-4 billion. (Few others foreigners were investing either. Cumulative foreign direct investment per capita in Russia is less than one-twentieth the level in Hungary at the end of the 1990's.)

Even big oil soured quickly on Russia. Immediately after the breakup of the Soviet Union, American, along with other Western, firms had rushed into Russia, lured by the sheer sizes of the country's energy resources (Russia accounted for 5% of the world's proven oil reserves and one-third of its proven gas reserves). It was widely believed that Russian firms were inefficient and short of capital and therefore in desperate need of foreign help. However, it turned out that Russia's oil bosses resented foreigners and the government was unwilling or unable to push through production-sharing legislation that would have provided much needed protection for foreign investors. By the mid-1990's, American oil companies had little to show for the hundreds of millions of dollars they had sunk into Russia.[12]

Only for a brief moment in 1996/97 was there considerable investor enthusiasm for Russia. Yeltsin's reelection fueled widespread expectations that Russia was on the verge of a radical breakthrough on reform. Russia emerged as the best performing emerging market, as Western investors poured money in. Mutual funds – such as the Templeton Russia Fund – were set up and began to hype the Russian market. Investment banks and brokerage firms – including Goldman Sachs, Credit Suisse First Boston, Morgan Stanley, Salomon Brothers – stepped up their activities in Russia, buying securities and helping Russian federal and regional government agencies float bond issue. But the enthusiasm evaporated quickly as the global financial crisis spread and deepened in Fall 1997, as it did for other emerging markets.[13] Russia's financial collapse of August 1998 killed any lingering optimism about investing in Russia.

With domestic support for its Russia policy soft, the Administration took a step in 1995 that only created confusion about its goals: NATO enlarge-

---

11 See Deputy Secretary Talbott, "U.S.-Russian Relations: The Next Phase." Remarks to the U.S.-Russian Business Council, Washington, DC, July 11, 1996.

12 On the problems energy firms encountered, see "Russian energy: A dangerous bear-dance, *The Economist* (U.S. edition), August 29, 1998; "Oil firms in Russia optimistic; U.S. companies counting on long-term production." *The Houston Chronicle*, August 29, 1998; John Helmer, "US businesses have a list of concerns for Gore." *Journal of Commerce*, July 23, 1998; Patrick Crow, "Gore becomes pro-oil." *The Oil and Gas Journal*, October 6, 1997.

13 See Edmund L. Andrews, "Capitalism With A Vengeance." *New York Times*, October 5, 1997; David Shirreff, "Dances with bears." *Euromoney*, July 1995.

ment.[14] Almost from the moment it entered office, the Administration was engaged in a furious – and curious – internal debate over this matter, curious because there was no pressure for a debate from any other quarter, including NATO allies, the Congress, or the American public.

As was to be expected, Talbott was initially adamantly opposed to NATO enlargement out of concern that it would only strengthen hard-line elements in the Kremlin and parliament. He managed to head off an early decision in favor of NATO enlargement in Fall 1994 with a forceful memorandum laying out the grave damage such a decision would do to U.S. interests in Russia. As an alternative, he proposed Partnership for Peace, a program intended to promote closer ties between NATO and non-NATO states in Central Europe and the former Soviet Union short of full membership. Talbott won the day, but he and the bureaucracy were slow to flesh out the program in ways that would have made it attractive to Russia.

A year later, however, Talbott reversed himself and came out as an ardent supporter of NATO enlargement. With the decision taken, the Administration moved rapidly to push the process forward. By late 1996, it was conducting substantive negotiations with the NATO allies and Russia on enlargement. These talks culminated in the Founding Act, signed in Paris in May 1997. To placate the Russians, the Act provided for a Permanent Joint Committee, in which Russia and NATO members were to discuss substantive issues of common interests. Nevertheless, as Talbott had argued in 1994, NATO enlargement fueled growing suspicions within the Russian elites of Western intentions vis-à-vis Russia. The view once confined to the communists and Russian chauvinists – that the West was seeking to exploit Russia's weakness for its own strategic advantage – quickly penetrated into reformist circles.

What caused this change of course remains unclear. To be sure, electoral calculations played a role: Americans of central and east European descent numbers some 20 million, and, more important, they were concentrated in fourteen states with a considerable number of electoral votes, including Michigan, Ohio, New Jersey, Illinois, Pennsylvania, and New York. But other factors loomed larger, including concern about stability and the promotion of democracy in Central Europe. The Administration believed that the prospect of admission to NATO would lead central European states to accelerate their internal reforms and improve relations with their neighbors.[15]

---

14 The discussion of NATO draws on Margaret Warner, "NATO Expansion: The Domestic Political Debate." in Kenneth W. Thompson, ed., *NATO Expansion* (Lanham, MD: University Press of America, 1998), pp. 115-135.

15 Deputy Secretary Talbott, "America and Russia in a Changing World." Address at the celebration of the 50th Anniversary of the Harriman Institute at Columbia University, New York City, New York, October 29, 1996.

The Administration was, of course, aware that NATO enlargement would cause strains in relations with Russia, but it had come had come to believe that it could limit the damage to U.S. interests in Russia.[16] Although the Administration never said as much publicly, it thought it could assuage the Russian leadership by trading symbolism for substance. In short, the Administration was prepared to treat Yeltsin as a major world leader and Russia as a great power in exchange for concessions on issues of importance to the United States. Thus: the annual Clinton-Yeltsin summits and the semi-annual Gore-Chernomyrdin Commission meetings, intended to create impressions of an equal U.S.-Russian partnership; U.S. pressure to expand Yeltsin's participation in G-7 summits and eventually turn the seven into an eight; a Russian role in the actual peacekeeping operation in Bosnia, even though the West basically had to pay for that participation; and continued support for Russia's co-chairmanship of the Mid East peace process, even though the United States ran that process with little reference to Russia's interests.[17]

This approach initially produced results in minimizing the Kremlin's objections, for example, to NATO enlargement and to U.S. policy in the former Yugoslavia. But it came at the expense of growing suspicions about American intentions within the broader Russian elites, which saw the Administration's blatant manipulation of a physically and mentally challenged Yeltsin as a sign of disrespect for Russia and its interests. Moreover, this approach was inherently risky, since its success depended on Yeltsin, whose health was increasingly precarious from late 1995 onward. Finally, this approach raised questions about the central thrust of Administration policy: Was it backing lending, particularly IMF credits, to Russia to promote reform or to pay off Yeltsin and the radical reformers for their support of U.S. policies in Europe and elsewhere?

In August 1998, Russia suffered a severe financial meltdown. Despite its intimate ties with leading figures in the Russian government, the Administration had not seen the crisis coming. Indeed, less than a year before the crash, as the first shock waves of the South East Asian financial crisis reached Russia, the Administration was decidedly upbeat about Russia, buoyed by the first upturn in the Russian economy since the Soviet collapse. Even as the pressure on Russian finances mounted in Spring and early Summer 1998, the Administration was convinced that a collapse could be averted. It praised the new government under the untested Sergey Kiriyenko as "the Dream Team-

---

16 *Ibid.*

17 Assuaging Yeltsin's ego was not the only reason for this approach. The Administration was also concerned that Russia, even in its weakened state, could do much mischief in the Balkans, Middle East, CIS, and other places. Giving a Russia a voice on these issues, it was hoped, would reduce the temptation to do mischief and encourage Moscow to play – from the Western standpoint – a responsible role.

II." and it played - at the request of Chubays - a central role in pressuring the IMF to agree to the $22.6 billion package that was intended to tide the Russian Government over for the most difficult period. So confident was the Administration and their Russian allies, that many key officials on both sides were on vacation when the crisis struck in August.[18]

The crisis proved to be a watershed in the Administration's Russia policy and in American attitudes toward Russia. For the Administration, the financial collapse marked the failure of its policy of rapidly transforming Russia into a vibrant democracy and a prosperous market economy along Western lines and with substantial Western assistance. In the immediate aftermath of the collapse, the Administration was at a loss as to what to do. When President Clinton traveled to Moscow for a summit meeting with Yeltsin, which had been scheduled several weeks before the collapse, he could think of nothing better than to urge Russians to stay the course on reform, an exhortation that grossly misread Russia's public mood.[19]

The Administration's apprehension grew exponentially when Yevgeniy Primakov, not Chernomyrdin, replaced Kiriyenko as prime minister. Over the years, the Administration – and particularly Vice President Gore – had grown comfortable with Chernomyrdin. Although not counted among the radical reformers, he was seen as a stabilizing force in favor of moderate reform. Primakov was another matter. Well known in Washington circles from his years as a leading Soviet foreign policy expert, he was seen as anti-American and a throwback to the Gorbachev period. Washington's anxiety only deepened with Primakov's appointment of Yuriy Maslyukov, the last head of Gosplan, as his first deputy prime minister and his nomination of Viktor Gerashchenko, the top Soviet banker once described by a Jeffrey Sachs as "the worst central banker of the century." to head the Central Bank.

Despite this setback, the Administration did not initiate a full-scale review of its Russia policy. That idea was scotched by the State Department, even though it was being urged by several former government officials.[20] Rather a new line was worked out in small meetings of the key policymakers, including Strobe Talbott and Stephen Sestanovich, the State Department's Special Advisor for the New Independent States. That line started from the implicit assumption that the Yeltsin era was over: attention was focused not on Yeltsin, but on Primakov and his government. There was much talk of a "time of troubles" in Russia. Discussions in Russia about printing new money, indexing wages, imposing price and capital controls, and restoring state management of parts of the economy led Secretary of State Al-

---

18 See Chrystia Freeland, *Sale of the Century: The Inside Story of the Second Russian Revolution* (London: Little, Brown and Company, 2000), pp. 291-309.

19 See President Clinton's remarks at the Moscow University of International Affairs, Moscow, Russia, September 1, 1998

20 Jim Hoagland, "Russia: What Went Wrong?" *Washington Post*, November 8, 1998.

bright to wonder "if some members of Primakov's team understand the basic arithmetic of the global economy."[21] Talbott warned that "as Russia asserts its own special needs and distances itself from the West on the economic front, we may be in for heightened tensions over security and diplomatic issues." Despite these forebodings, the Administration stressed its firm intention to remain engaged in Russia in support of reformers and argued that, whatever the short-term problems, reform retained good chances of succeeding over the long run. "Strategic patience" became the Administration's watchword.[22]

Bleaker in its assessments of Russian reform, the Administration began to downgrade Russia among its foreign-policy priorities. Despite repeated Russian objections, the United States took military action against Iraqi leader Saddam Hussein and led the NATO air campaign against Serbia over Kosovo. Significantly, these military campaigns both began on the eve of promised Russian Duma consideration of ratification of the START II Treaty, something for which the Administration had been pressing for several years. Yet when ratification was possible –Primakov had the clout within in the Duma to push the Treaty through – the Administration decided that U.S. interests in Iraq and the former Yugoslavia took precedence over relations with Russia.

To be sure, the Administration eventually helped place Russia at the center of the diplomatic effort to end the Kosovo conflict, but more out of concern for NATO's cohesion than out of a conviction that Moscow had great leverage over Serbian President Milosevic. (Some NATO allies feared that Russia would seek to destabilize the situation in the former Yugoslavia if its interests were not taken into account. Dealing with those fears – by bringing Moscow into the negotiations with Milosevic on NATO's terms – was critical to maintaining sufficient Allied unity to allow the air campaign to continue.) Moreover, whatever good feelings might have resulted from these diplomatic efforts were quickly eroded by Russia's dash to Pristina, the surreptitious occupation of the airport in Pristina to ensure that Russia would play a role in the Kosovo peacekeeping operation.

As the Administration struggled with the implications of Russia's financial collapse, American attitudes toward Russia began to change rapidly. The once prevailing image of Russia as an aspiring democracy gave way to an image of a hapless land mired in deep, pervasive corruption, where organized crime operates unrestrained. That image was reinforced by the eruption in August 1999 of a money-laundering scandal, allegedly involving billions of dollars funneled through the Bank of New York by Russian organized crime

---

21 Secretary of State Madeleine K. Albright, "U.S. Strategy for Responding to Russia's Transformation." Address to the U.S.-Russian Business Council, Chicago, Illinois, October 2, 1998.

22 Strobe Talbott, "Gogol's Troika: The Case for Strategic Patience in a Time of Troubles." Address at Stanford University, Stanford, California, November 6, 1998.

groups. Congress hastily organized a series of hearings on the scandal that only highlighted the pervasiveness of corruption in Russia, including at the highest levels of government. A short time later, Moscow launched a brutal military campaign against Chechnya, which further eroded Russia's standing in American eyes.

Much of the American public and a large part of the political establishment began to suffer from a severe case of Russia fatigue after years of intense focus on the ebb and flow of reform and the constant battles in Russia. In Congress, the "Forget Russia" school gained increasing numbers of adherents. While this school would not gratuitously harm Russia, it was not prepared to spend much time, energy, or money to nurture good relations with Russia because it believed Russia did not matter much in the world any longer. The American business community withdrew from what it saw as an increasingly inhospitable investment climate in Russia. Perhaps the best evidence of this Russia fatigue was the lack of any serious, sustained debate over the Administration's Russia policy or the deteriorating state of U.S.-Russian relations. Even partisan efforts to spark a "Who lost Russia?" debate by and large failed.

Hopes that relations with Russia could be repaired and reform put back on track flared briefly after Putin took over from Yeltsin at the very end of 1999. President Clinton went out of his way to proclaim Putin a man we could do business with. Other senior officials reinforced this view with upbeat assessments of Putin. The great hope was the Putin could be persuaded to cut a grand bargain on the Anti-Ballistic Missile Treaty and START-3 that would allow the Administration to proceed with the deployment of a limited national missile defense system. That deal was to provide the centerpiece of the Clinton-Putin summit scheduled for June 2000.

Several weeks before the meeting, however, it became clear that no deal was in the offing – the Russians remained adamantly opposed to any modification of the ABM Treaty. They saw no reason to compromise with a lame duck Administration, particularly as a major debate was erupting in the United States over national missile defense. More worrying from Washington's standpoint, Russia encouraged – with some success – key NATO allies to voice their own objections more forcefully. Indeed, before and immediately after the summit, Putin traveled to European capitals in an effort to galvanize opposition to U.S. plans.

With no hopes of a deal on national missile defense, U.S.-Russian relations resumed their downward spiral. Washington was disturbed by Putin's efforts to enhance relations with several former Soviet client states, which the United States considered to be "rogues." including Iran, Iraq, Libya, and Cuba. It grew increasingly concerned about Putin's authoritarian tendencies, particularly his attacks on press freedoms, an issue that figured prominently in American press coverage of Russia. An espionage trial of an American citizen, the first in forty years in Russia, was a constant and growing irritation from the Spring and underscored for the American establishment the uncertain prospects for rule of law in Russia. Even Russia's economic upswing – 7% growth in 2000 – did not temper the Administration's increasingly dark view, because it was due in part to high oil prices, which were creating political difficulties for the Administration and Vice President Gore's presidential campaign.

Inevitably, the Administration's Russia policy became entangled in the presidential campaign, which the Republicans were determined to use as a weapon to undermine confidence in Gore's foreign policy skills. In September, a group of Congressional Republicans issued a report blasting the Administration's policy and fingering Gore as the chief culprit. The report charged the Administration with ignoring high-level corruption in Russia and undermining efforts to deal with Russian organized crime, with exacerbating Russia's socio-economic decline, with pursuing policies that encouraged the proliferation of weapons of mass destruction, and with severely damaging U.S.-Russian relations and pushing Russia into a tighter embrace of China.[23] During the presidential debates, Governor Bush, the Republican candidate, charged the Administration with fostering corruption in Russia. Around the same time, official documents were leaked – with clear political intent – that raised questions about the way in which the Administration had dealt with conventional Russian arms sales to Iran. This bitter partisan debate did nothing to improve U.S.-Russian relations.

At the end of the Clinton Administration, the state of Russia and U.S.-Russian relations fell far short of the goals the Administration had set for itself upon entering office. To put it bluntly, the policy had failed on the Administration's own terms. U.S.-Russian relations had sharply deteriorated; while elements of a genuine market economy had been introduced, they had not been consolidated into a functioning system and they had accelerated decline rather than produced growth; and, as the Administration wound down, Putin's actions raised serious doubts about the state of democracy in Russia.

Why did an Administration that initially put so much energy and enthusiasm into helping Russia transform wind up with so little to show for its efforts? Five factors stand out.

First, arrogance, ignorance, and urgency. The Administration entered office convinced it had to act quickly to save Russia's reformers from a burgeoning anti-reform backlash. It put together an assistance program in short order, but without an adequate appreciation of Russian conditions. As Westerners traveled across Russia for the first time in years – during the Soviet pe-

---

23 Speaker's Advisory Group on Russia, *Russia's Road to Corruption: How the Clinton Administration Exported Government Instead of Free Enterprise and Failed the Russian People* (Washington, DC: U.S. House of Representatives, September 2000).

riod as much as three-quarters of Soviet territory was closed to foreigners – it became clear how little the West had really known about Russian realities despite all the scholarly and intelligence work during the Cold War. Moreover, the Administration devised its programs with minimal consultation with the Russian side, and, to make matters worse, many of the Russians it consulted had only a shallow understanding of how their country worked. Arrogance that the West had the solutions combined with ignorance of Russian conditions led to inefficient and often counterproductive policies.

Second, incoherent strategy. The Administration spoke and acted as if democratization, marketization, and integration in the West moved along parallel, reinforcing tracks. Reality, however, demanded trade-offs. The Administration made the trade-offs in practice without ever admitting that it was actually doing just that. As a result, the public presentation of its policy was driven by contradictions, something that cost it public support in the United States. Moreover, this policy sent the wrong signals to the Russians. For example, the Administration's urging Yeltsin to advance reform by using decrees that by-passed the opposition Duma cast doubt upon the United States' commitment to democratic principles. Failure to consult Moscow adequately on matters in the Balkans or the Middle East undermined confidence in the value of "strategic partnership" and integration in the West.

Third, poor policy coordination. With the exception of the first year, Russia policy was never properly coordinated across governmental bureaucracies. As the Office of the Special Adviser to the Secretary of State for the New Independent States was headed by persons with ever less bureaucratic clout, other agencies began to ignore it and pursue their own policies toward Russia. Treasury dominated economic and financial policy toward Russia; Energy usurped the primary role on pipeline issues; and so on. Even within the State Department, policy was not properly coordinated. In the end, there was no unified Russia policy, but a Russian section to policies on other matters, such as NATO expansion, Caspian pipelines, non-proliferation, and the former Yugoslavia.

Fourth, partnership with Russian officials. In short order, a small group of senior Administration officials forged a "partnership" with a similarly small group of senior Russia officials, centered on Yeltsin, aimed at pushing forward an agenda focused primarily on the domestic transformation of Russia. Like all partnerships, this one required constant interaction and a high level of trust to function effectively. The result was that senior Administration officials were tempted to turn first to their Russian partners, rather than to our own internal analysts, for insights as to what was happening in Russia and how to proceed. Moreover, the success of their partners became critical to the success of the enterprise as a whole, and slowly the political survival of someone like privatization czar Chubays became a symbol of the overall success of reform and Administration policy. This approach deprived senior Administration officials of a more complete picture of what was actually happening in Russia and blinded them to the downsides of their policies. This partnership was one of the main reasons why the Administration was caught off guard by the financial collapse in 1998.

Fifth, weak constituencies. Despite much enthusiasm about Russia in the immediate aftermath of the Soviet breakup, the Administration never succeeded in building a strong, broad-based domestic constituency for its Russia policy. The business community soured on Russia fairly early on. Continued socio-economic decline in Russia robbed it of the importance it had once had in elite and public eyes.

But perhaps the central reason for the policy failure lay in the formulation of the task: the domestic transformation of Russia. That goal was set in the belief that a democratic and prosperous Russia would also be a responsible actor abroad and therefore a force for peace and stability and a pillar in America's own prosperity and security. The Administration, however, exaggerated its ability to influence developments inside Russia. As it was to admit as its term drew to a close, America's influence had been marginal at best. Russia was simply too large and too complex and the processes under way there too poorly understood, for it to be otherwise. As a result, the Administration quickly found its policies to be hostage to individuals and events beyond its control; the Administration's success depended on Russians doing the right things. Not surprisingly, Russians were more intent on promoting their own interests than on making the American Administration look good.

Susan L. Shirk

Congressional Politics and U.S. China Policy 1996-2000

The end of the Soviet Union and the disappearance of the Soviet threat fundamentally changed the international strategic context of U.S.- China relations. During the 1970's and 1980's, the two nations reached out to each other after decades of separation to normalize relations and resume cooperation. The ideological divide between them was wide, but they were drawn together by their shared security interest in resisting Soviet power. Their success at achieving cooperation, despite deep conflicts not only of political values, but also of interests over Taiwan, is testimony to the dominance of that security imperative.

Since 1989, however, the original motivation for U.S.-PRC rapprochement has evaporated. Advocates of the relationship on both sides identify new strategic rationales ranging from preservation of the global environment to stabilizing the Korean Peninsula, but none of them provides as strong a strategic attraction as the common threat of the Soviet Union.[1]

As the strategic force drawing them together has weakened, the influence of domestic politics operating on their policies toward one another has grown. A nationalistic public, insecure Communist Party leaders, and an economy dependent on foreign trade and investment have become key factors in Chinese foreign policies toward the United States and other countries. The increasing importance of domestic factors, including Congressional politics, on foreign policy in the United States since the end of the Cold War is a widely observed phenomenon that applies across the board, not just to China policy.

---

1 See Robert S. Ross, *Negotiating Cooperation: The United States and China, 1969-1989* (Stanford: Stanford University Press, 1995), for a study of how the U.S. and China managed to develop and consolidate cooperative relations during the 1970's and 1980's despite significant conflicts of interest over Taiwan.

Distinctive Institutional Patterns

The increased weight of domestic factors in foreign policy-making means that we need to pay attention to the distinctive features of each country's political institutions. My own research agenda is to seek to understand the way China's communist authoritarian institutions, at this stage in their evolution, shape its foreign policies. This chapter attempts to identify some of the significant features of the U.S. Congress that are reflected in recent Congressional actions regarding China. My perspective is that of a political scientist who is not a specialist on American politics, but who as the Deputy Assistant Secretary in the East Asia Bureau of the Department of State, was a participant-observer in the policy process during 1997-2000.

The American Constitution divides foreign policy powers between the President and Congress. This formal structure of divided authority is, as Edward Corwin observed more than fifty years of ago, "an invitation to struggle" for the two branches of government.[2] Scholars of American politics in the 1940's, 1950's, and 1960's, contrasted Congressional influence in domestic policies with Presidential dominance of foreign policies. For example, Aaron Wildavsky noted, "The President's normal problem with domestic policy is to get congressional support for the programs he prefers. In foreign affairs, in contrast, he can almost always get support for policies that he believes will protect the nation – but his problem is to find a viable policy."[3] The President was considered to have an institutional advantage when addressing international issues because of the national security dimension of such issues; only the President, elected by a national constituency, could claim to represent the broad national interests. The President also was perceived to have a much greater ability than individual members of Congress to communicate through mass media and shape public opinion, particularly on foreign policy matters; so much so that Robert Dahl saw the prospect of presidential supremacy producing "a peculiarly American form of modern dictatorship."[4] Although some scholars argue that the executive branch dominance of foreign policy has been exaggerated, it certainly was the case that Congress deferred to the President from the 1940's (World War II) until the late 1960's (Vietnam War) to a greater degree than it does today.[5]

---

2 Edward S. Corwin, *The President: Office and Powers, 1787-1948* (New York: New York University Press, 1948), 208.

3 Aaron B. Wildavsky, "The Two Presidencies," in Aaron B. Wildavsky (ed.), *Perspectives on the Presidency* (Boston: Little, Brown, 1975), ?

4 Robert Dahl, *Congress and Foreign Policy* (New York: Norton, 1950), 116.

5 Randall B. Ripley and James M. Lindsay, "Foreign and Defense Policy in Congress: An Overview and Preview," in Ripley and Lindsay eds., *Congress Resurgent: Foreign and Defense Policy on Capitol Hill* (Ann Arbor: University of Michigan Press, 1993), 4. Some scholars have re-examined earlier history and determined that Congress has been assertive in foreign policy all along or that Congressional assertiveness ebbs and

Although Congress began to assert itself in foreign policy in response to the public backlash against the Vietnam War in the early 1970's,[6] the end of the Cold War has reinforced and sustained the trend. With the Soviet Union gone, the public perceives a reduced external threat to national security and concomitantly a reduced political cost to members of Congress who challenge the President on foreign policy.[7] The foreign policy process is punctuated with fewer crises, when the White House usually takes charge, and characterized by more routine decision-making in which Congress has a major role, just as it does with domestic policy.[8] With security considerations muted, other dimensions of foreign policy, such as human rights, have become more prominent. Human rights concerns are particularly salient for the public and Congress in the case of China, where the Tiananmen crackdown on student demonstrators occurred in a dramatic and well-televised manner in 1989, just as the Cold War ended.

The Tiananmen tragedy shattered the American policy consensus on China and indicated to Americans that the political liberalization that had accompanied the Chinese economic reforms had abruptly ended. The end of the consensus meant that Congress, which had supported Administration initiatives on China during the 1980's, would no longer do so. Since Tiananmen, Congress and the executive branch have clashed repeatedly over China policy. As Kerry Dumbaugh notes, "Both the Bush and Clinton Administrations generally stressed policies of 'engagement' toward China, while their congressional critics have tended to push for a firmer, more sanction-oriented approach."[9]

During the Bush Administration (1988-92), China policy became a highly partisan matter as the Democratic controlled Congress sought to use it to go after the Republican administration.[10] The Bush Administration was

---

flows in a cyclical fashion. See Marie T. Henehan, *Foreign Policy and Congress: An International Relations Perspective* (Ann Arbor: The University of Michigan Press, 2000) 20, 23.

6 Congress repealed the Gulf of Tonkin Resolution in 1971, mandated a pull-out from Vietnam in 1973, and in 1973, overrode President Nixon's veto to pass the War Powers Resolution that requires the President to end any use of U.S. armed forces 60 to 90 days after deployment unless Congress declares war or authorizes the use of the forces.

7 James M. Lindsay, *Congress and the Politics of U.S. Foreign Policy* (Baltimore: Johns Hopkins University Press, 1994), 32.

8 John T. Tierney, "Interest Group Involvement in Congressional Foreign and Defense Policy," in Ripley and Lindsay (eds.), *Congress Resurgent*, 89-111.

9 Kerry Dumbaugh, "Ten Years in U.S.-China Policy: Interest Groups and Their Influence, 1989-2000," Congressional Research Service, RL30768, December 12, 2000, 1.

10 Harry Harding, 'The Sino-American Relationship Today," and Richard C. Bush, "Domestic Political Considerations That Shape U.S. Policy Toward China, Hong Kong, and Taiwan," in David M. Lampton and Alfred D. Wilhelm Jr. (eds.), *United*

strongly criticized for using secret White House diplomacy (i.e. the two Scowcroft missions) to ease relations with China even as he had publicly announced a suspension of all high-level official contacts with it. Congressional opponents depicted the Republican president as more sympathetic to the "butchers of Beijing" than to the young Chinese democracy demonstrators. The annual waiver of provisions under the Jackson-Vanik Amendment of the Trade Act that is required for Chinese goods to receive most-favored-nation tariff treatment by the United States became the focus of Congressional criticism of Beijing and of the White House. In summer 1991, with the Presidential election campaign in sight, House and Senate majorities passed a bill tying MFN renewal to a set of conditions related to human rights, trade and proliferation; the President's veto came close to being over-ridden, and was only saved by a handful of Democratic senators from farm states with important trade interests with China.[11]

Congressional Individualism During The Clinton Administration

During the eight years of the Clinton Administration, Congressional action toward China increasingly became an unstructured free-for-all. Partisan lines became blurred. Each party was internally divided on China issues, and individual members, even junior ones without any foreign affairs committee roles, expressed themselves on China issues through bills, resolutions, hearings, requests for information, and other methods. The annual MFN debate was no longer the focus of the action, which now occurs throughout the year.

Rampant individualism and lack of party discipline have always been more characteristic of legislative behavior in the United States than in parliamentary democracies. The most important thing to remember about the American Congress is that individual members are nominated by local primary elections among voters who are self-declared party members and the members' campaign are self-financed. Members depend on their political party leaders for nothing other than public appearances by these leading politicians in their district during the campaign (and even this favor is sometimes rejected by the candidate as more of a liability than an asset). It follows that when the members come to Washington they behave very independently and Congressional leaders find it difficult to impose party discipline.

States and China Relations at a Crossroads (Lanham, Maryland: University of America Press, 1995).

11 Robert G. Sutter, *U.S. Policy Toward China: An Introduction to the Role of Interest Groups* (Lanham, Maryland: Rowman and Littlefield, p 1998), 42.

This individualism has become increasingly prominent over time as a result of institutional fragmentation in Congress. During the past several decades, institutional reforms, particularly in the House of Representatives, have redistributed power and weakened the committees that used to dominate congressional involvement in foreign affairs. The seniority system has been weakened, the committee structure fragmented, and power has been dispersed to members of the rank and file.[12] Subcommittees have proliferated, and Republicans have established term limits for committee and subcommittee chairs. Power has become so dispersed that "almost everybody is a chairman."[13] Even those who are not chairmen can become foreign policy issue leaders. As Rebecca Hersman notes, "Members of Congress and their staff face few constraints from institutional structures or partisan dictates as they pursue many of their individual foreign policy interests."[14]

Individualism has become more severe in the House of Representatives than in the Senate, which has always had a tradition of individualism. The House, which in the past was characterized by substantial majorities, recently has had very small majorities.[15] As a result, Congressional leaders do not dare discipline members for idiosyncratic behavior because they cannot afford to alienate any member of their party, no matter how junior he or she is; they need each and every vote for key budget bills. The Senate is used to small majorities and has established rules that enable Party leaders to manage them. Senate committee chairs still have authority, and the process in the Senate is less anarchic than in the House.

The House International Relations Committee (HIRC) and the Senate Foreign Relations Committee (SFRC) no longer play the dominant role they once did, having declined in influence relative to the appropriations subcommittees and a whole range of committees (Commerce, Finance, Judiciary, Banking, and Ways and Means) that are playing a greater role. Douglas Bereuter, the chair of the HIRC Subcommittee on Asia, bemoaned the loss of authority over foreign policy from the HIRC and SFRC to the handful of subcommittee chairmen on the appropriating committees. He specifically referred to the ability of human rights advocate Democrat Nancy Pelosi to use her position as ranking minority member of the key appropriations subcom-

---

12 Rebecca K.C. Hersman, *Friends and Foes: How Congress and the President Really Make Foreign Policy* (Washington D.C.: Brookings Institution Press, 2000), 6, 11.

13 Jackie Koszczuk, "A Full Circle," *Players, Politics and Turf of the 105th Congress*, Congressional Quarterly Weekly Report, March 22, 1997, quoted in Jian Yang, *Congress and U.S. China Policy, 1989-99* (Huntington, N.Y.: Nova Science Publishers, 2000), 38.

14 Hersman, 6.

15 104th Congress (1995-97) 230(R)-204(D); 105th (1997-99) 228(R)-206(D); 106th (1999-2001) 222(R)-222(D); 107th(2001-03) 221(R)-211(D).

mittee to block administration Asia initiatives.[16] With the end of the Cold War, foreign policy issues evoke even less citizen interest than previously; seats on the traditional foreign affairs committees are not attractive assignments to most members. The proliferation of committees and subcommittees dealing with foreign affairs provides more points of access for interest groups.

Both the Republican and Democratic Congressional parties contain wide internal ideological cleavages. In the Republican Party there is a massive divide between the economic conservatives, i.e. business-oriented politicians who believe that trade is the best way to promote democratic change in China, and social conservatives, particularly the religious right, who want to punish China for forced abortion and religious persecution. Within the Democratic Party there is a very powerful labor wing (AFL-CIO is the single largest source of campaign funds for Democrats), who opposed the 1990 bill granting China permanent MFN (now called Normal Trade Relations) once China enters the World Trade Organization (WTO), as well as some members who support engagement of China, including bringing China into international institutions like the WTO.[17]

Fractionalization Of The China Policy Debate

Before 1993, differences over China policy were aired largely through the vehicle of the annual debate over China's most-favored-nation status. In 1992 Congress came close to denying renewal of MFN, and in 1993 President Clinton decided to link his decision whether or not to renew China's MFN status to its progress on human rights. Members of Congress realized that although they enjoyed the opportunity to vent their frustrations about China's behavior, the debate might actually result in denying MFN to China, a possibility that would harm American economic interests. Deng Xiaoping gave new impetus to China's market reform drive in 1992; Chinese economic growth accelerated; and American business activity in China picked up. As a result, U.S. companies organized the Business Coalition for U.S.-China Trade to lobby the Executive branch and Congress to retain MFN. Beginning in 1993, Congress became more cautious, and never again came close to voting not to extend MFN. Even after Clinton decided to delink trade and

16 Douglas Bereuter, "Key Issues in Congressional Foreign Policy Making," presentation at the Weatherhead Center for International Affairs, Harvard University, March 1999.

17 Terry L. Deibel (*Clinton and Congress: The Politics of Foreign Policy* (New York: Foreign Policy Association, 2000), 13-22) describes the splits differently: "Idealists" and "Pragmatists" in the Democratic Party, and "Unilateralists" and "Internationalists" in the Republican Party

human rights in 1994, the energy had dissipated from the annual MFN debate.

In recent years, instead of an annual debate, there has been a constant, year-round cacophony of criticisms of China-- and of Executive Branch laxity in pursuing China's bad behavior – involving a great variety of issues, including forced abortion, treatment of dissidents, prison labor, trade in body parts, nuclear and missile proliferation, Tibet, Taiwan, Hong Kong, espionage, religious freedom, and military relations. Members of Congress have a multitude of ways to express their concerns about China. The number of China-related bills is astounding. Many of them are not legislative mandates. Some are "sense of the Congress" resolutions that are largely symbolic expressions of Congressional concerns; and some are House initiatives that members know the Senate will never approve. Once members know that a measure will never become law, it gives them a "free" vote; they can publicly express their values without worrying about any real foreign policy risk to the country.

Beginning in 1997, the religious right and social conservatives in the Republican Party became more actively involved in China policy than in the past. Organizations like the Christian Coalition and the Family Research Council articulated their values by criticizing Chinese religious persecution and forced abortion and the Administration's inadequate policies toward them. For example, Representative Tillie Fowler introduced a bill that would have required the United States to deny visas to any Chinese national or government official who credibly could be determined to have been involved in establishing or enforcing population policies resulting in forced sterilization or forced abortion. Both houses held hearing on the bill and the House passed an amended version, but the Senate never acted. In October 1998, the Congress passed the Freedom From Religious Persecution Act, which mandated a special State Department office, an annual review, and mandatory sanctions. The Administration managed to soften the sanction provisions, but China was the number one "country of concern" to become the target of the law.

Much of the recent China legislation requires the Executive Branch to provide annual reviews or reports on China's human rights abuses, proliferation behavior, or military build-up. Almost every week, one of these reviews or reports comes out with a flurry of negative publicity about China (even the classified reports are soon leaked).

Sometimes the Secretary of State decides to act preemptively to avoid impending legislation. For example, Secretary Albright in October 1997 designated a Special Coordinator for Tibetan issues so as to avoid passage of legislation, which had been on the table since 1994, that would create an ambassadorial rank special envoy for Tibet (an ambassador for Tibet would have implied that we see Tibet as an independent country instead of as part of China). Because of a deadline set by a member of Senator Jesse Helms' staff, the Administration had to announce the Tibet coordinator at the same time as President Jiang Zemin was visiting the US.

Hearings are another device for influencing foreign policy. The more subcommittees there are, the more initiatives to hold hearings. In the 105th and 106th Congresses, the House International Relations Asia Subcommittee Chair Douglas Bereuter and Human Rights Subcommittee Chair Chris Smith, two politicians from different wings of the Republican Party, frequently competed to hold hearings on China.

Requests for documents from the State Department and other executive agencies are another device by which individual members, even if they are not committee chairs, can constrain policy. In recent years, the size and frequency of these requests related to China have become so onerous that they actively interfere with the other work of the State Department.

Consensus On Taiwan

Running counter to the prevailing trend of individualization and fractionalization is the Congressional consensus in favor of support for Taiwan. Everyone in Congress, Republicans and Democrats alike, admires Taiwan, especially now that the small island has become a vibrant democracy. The struggle between democratic Taiwan and communist China has a dramatic "David and Goliath" quality that inspires positive emotion. Many members of Congress do not accept the complex framework of previous U.S. policy toward the PRC and Taiwan, consisting of the three joint communiqués with the PRC (1972, 1979, and 1982) and the Taiwan Relations Act (1997). Regardless of past commitments, in their view Taiwan is a de facto independent country that would be a de jure independent country were it not for the bullying of Beijing.

Taiwan also has one of the best-funded, most effective lobbies in Washington. The 1995 vote to urge the President to invite Taiwan's president, Lee Teng-hui, to the United States was 396-0 in the House and 97-1 in the Senate. Beijing viewed the visit as a serious step toward Taiwan independence and expressed its displeasure in massive military exercises and missile tests close to Taiwan harbors; the United States responded by sending two carrier battle groups to the vicinity of the Taiwan Strait.

Even after this near-confrontation between the U.S. and China over Taiwan, Congress continued to press for incremental improvement in the treatment of Taiwan by the U.S. Government.[18] The issue of arms sales to Taiwan has been a particularly contentious one between the Congress and the Administration. The desire to assist local defense contractors, as well as friendship for Taiwan, led Congress to pressure the Administration to sell more advanced equipment. The 106th Congress passed part of the Taiwan Security

18 Sutter, 78.

Enhancement bill that required the executive branch to consult with Congress about Taiwan's specific arms sales requests before making a decision.

Congressional Leadership And Partisan Effectiveness

A notable exception to the individualism and lack of party discipline that has characterized Congressional action on foreign policy in recent Congresses was when Newt Gingrich was the Speaker of the House of Representatives (1995-98). Gingrich further eviscerated the committees, but strengthened the central authority of the House leadership. He created his own cadre of followers and went around the committees to shape policy through special task forces.

The focus of Gingrich's partisan initiatives in foreign policy was to discredit the Clinton White House. The investigation of President and Mrs. Clinton's alleged improprieties in Arkansas (known as "Whitewater") and the investigation of illegal campaign contributions by Asians to President Clinton were not bearing fruit. The answer, thought Speaker Gingrich, might be to draw a connection between Asian campaign contributions and failure to protect national security. He created a special committee to examine how the Administration had endangered the nation's security by allowing American satellite manufacturers to transfer missile technology through their launches in China, and chose Christopher Cox, an smart and attractive young Representative from California, to chair it. The committee's findings were not compelling until serendipitously an investigation into the Chinese acquisition of nuclear weapon designs at our national laboratories came to fruition with the arrest of Los Alamos scientist Went Ho Lee.

Presidential Leadership And Congressional Action

During the Clinton Administrations, White House successes at leading Congressional action on foreign policy were few and far between. President Clinton faced more resistance from members of his own party, especially on issues related to free trade, than he did from the Republicans. Only with an extraordinary expenditure of effort was President Clinton able to achieve a 237-197 House vote to approve permanent normal trade relations (PNTR, formerly known as MFN) for China once it joined the WTO (the Senate vote was easier to achieve). The labor wing of the Democratic Party was subject to a massive lobbying effort on the part of the AFL-CIO. The Administration's campaign for PNRT, modeled on the successful campaign for the North Atlantic Free Trade Association, required the President and members of the

Cabinet to work on members one-on-one. The Republicans were politically more sympathetic, but they withheld commitments of support until the President demonstrated that he could get key Democrats, like Charles Rangel of New York, on board. The President had to promise to personally campaign in the district of every Democratic member who voted for PNTR, and probably extended other special favors as well. The extremely well organized lobbying effort of the business community was an essential ingredient of the victory. As part of the package, the PNTR bill had to include a new Congressional Commission on China that will substitute for the annual MFN review and give members a vehicle to express their criticisms of China.

Future Congressional Patterns

Because the majorities in the 107th Congress are smaller than ever, we can expect the recent trend of individualism and lack of party discipline to continue; without the annual ritual of MFN/NTR, Congressional actions on China will continue to be fractionalized throughout the year. The interesting question is how a Republican in the White House will affect Congressional dynamics. In the first months of his administration, President George W. Bush has taken a surprisingly confrontational stance toward China that appears to be modeled on the policies of the Reagan administration, and that aligns him with the socially conservative Republicans in the Congress. Bush's Taiwan position seems to be out in front of even the most enthusiastic pro-Taiwan elements in the Congress. Will these positions result in a relatively quiescent Congress or in a new assertiveness on the part of the pro-business, internationalist elements in both parties? The Reagan precedent would suggest that we might see a new Congressional-executive consensus on China policy during the Bush administration.[19] On the other hand, the post-Cold War international situation and the institutional trends in Congress could result in a continuation of the Congressional free-for-all against administration China policies.

---

19 Robert Sutter, "China and the U.S. Congress: Policy Determinants and Constraints," in William T. Tow ed., *Building Sino-American Relations: An Analysis for the 1990s* (New York: Paragon House, 1991), 37.

Part IV
U.S. Leadership in International Institutions and Multilateral Regime-Building

Edward C. Luck

False Choices: Unilateralism, Multilateralism, and U.S. Foreign Policy

For America watchers, 2001 must have been a most perplexing year. But, then again, the decade of the 1990s had also failed to provide a simple and clear-cut picture of the nature and direction of Washington's post-Cold War foreign policy. No doubt especially frustrated were those, found in large numbers in Western Europe, intent on classifying U.S. policies as either unilateralist or multilateralist. Since the U.S. predilection for the former, we are told, could compromise the future of transatlantic relations, it is important to track these supposedly opposing tendencies.[1] For those determined to chart such things, 2001 must have looked like a roller coaster. Prior to the 9/11 terrorist attacks on the United States, the new Bush Administration was regularly chided for its allegedly unilateralist leanings, of which there was ample evidence. Post 9/11, however, even domestic critics credited the Administration with a "policy flip-flop," as it turned to multilateral cooperation as an essential tool in the war on terrorism.[2] By year's end, however, President Bush's decision to rescind the ABM Treaty left many of his NATO partners grumbling about a return to U.S. exceptionalism.[3]

Over the past decade, few questions have divided the United States and its closest allies as starkly or persistently as their divergent appraisals of the proper place for multilateral norms and institutions in global affairs. In an era characterized by globalization, multilateral cooperation, and European inte-

1 In an August 2001 survey of public attitudes in France, Germany, the United Kingdom, and Italy, for example, very large majorities responded that President Bush "makes decisions based entirely on U.S. interests" without taking European concerns into account. Adam Clymer, "Surveys Find European Public Critical of Bush Policies," *New York Times*, August 16, 2001 and Pew Research Center, Online Reports, http://www.people-press.org/bush01rpt.htm

2 Robin Wright and Doyle McManus, "Attacks Redefine Bush Foreign Policy; Presidency: Response Has Reversed Unilateral Stance that Irked Allies,' *Los Angeles Times*, January 7, 2002. Also see Melinda Henneberger, "European Critics of U.S. Find that the War Gives Them Little Ammunition," *New York Times*, December 8, 2001.

3 Steven Erlanger, "Bush's Move on ABM Pact Gives Pause to Europeans," *New York Times*, December 13, 2001.

gration, America's coolness toward the expansion of international institutions and norms has appeared to set it apart, again and again, from its more enthusiastic partners. They, in turn, seem perplexed about the extent to which what they see as Washington's go-it-alone mentality is due to a distinct strategic calculus or to perverse domestic political factors. Either way, the implications for alliance solidarity and for U.S. global leadership would be less than reassuring. As William Wallace has argued, "the rejection by many in Congress of multilateral institutions as vehicles through which to exert U.S. leadership, and the frequent demands by administration officials that allies follow the United States' directions, even when these appear unduly influenced by domestic lobbies, have given impetus to Western European initiatives to increase their autonomy in foreign and defense policy."[4]

Yet it should be asked: 1) had America actually retreated, in any consistent and systematic way, from multilateral commitments and initiatives prior to the 9/11 attacks?; 2) did its subsequent strategy for countering terrorism either reflect or augur a dramatic shift in attitudes toward multilateral cooperation?; 3) are domestic forces inexorably pushing the United States in a unilateralist direction?; and/or 4) have Washington policymakers simply at points interpreted U.S. national interests to be substantively distinct from those of its partners? To these ends, this essay addresses, in broad strokes, the interplay between multilateral processes and U.S. domestic politics, since neither can be properly understood in isolation. It argues that the perception of a wholesale flip-flop following the 9/11 attacks is highly exaggerated, in that neither the rejection nor the embrace of multilateralism was nearly as whole-hearted as has been suggested. The paper concludes, moreover, that, despite the uniting effects of the common struggle against terrorism, over time attitude adjustments will be needed on both sides of the Atlantic to reduce the more dysfunctional aspects of the simmering dissonance among the western democracies. Otherwise, the charge of a wholesale U.S. retreat from international institution building could become a self-fulfilling prophecy.

The paper is divided into five sections. It opens with a brief analysis of the kinds of charges voiced by U.S. partners regarding its alleged penchant for unilateral and exceptional policy choices. It then asks to what extent these caricatures fit the U.S. foreign policy record of recent years. The third section – Dynamic Times, Moving Goalposts – argues that the expansion of international law and institutions has been so rapid over the past decade that, even though the U.S. has largely been supportive of this trend, it has been made to look relatively reluctant compared to its partners across the Atlantic (and the Pacific as well). The fourth section questions whether the events of 9/11 and

4 William Wallace, "U.S. Unilateralism: A European Perspective," in Stewart Patrick and Shepard Forman, eds., *Multilateralism and U.S. Foreign Policy: Ambivalent Engagement* (Boulder, CO: Lynne Rienner for the Center on International Cooperation, 2001), pp. 141-164.

the terrorist challenge will alter these relationships or narrow the differences between the U.S. and European approaches in fundamental ways. Despite these persistent differences, the concluding section offers several suggestions for making the transatlantic debate less divisive and more productive.

The Charges

America's friends have leveled three basic charges against its handling of foreign policy in recent years. The first is that it too often fails to consult with its allies in a timely and effective manner, preferring to follow its own narrowly defined national interests than to build common positions. A second, related, charge is that the U.S. has increasingly been inclined to assert substantive positions in global negotiations that are out-of-step with those of most other countries and then acts to prevent consensus by stubbornly refusing to compromise. Third, critics claim that the U.S. often fails to play by the rules, ignoring international law and the procedures of international institutions when they prove inconvenient.

All three tendencies, it is said, undermine the prospects for building the kinds of international legal and institutional structures that would serve the common interests of western, and other, countries. Yet their effects are likely to be quite different. The first two charges are essentially political, relating to the substance of U.S. positions and the degree to which it is willing to modify them in light of the concerns of others. The U.S., in effect, is alleged to be unilateral in terms of style and exceptional in terms of substance. The third charge, heard often within the halls of the UN and other multilateral bodies, has attracted less publicity and attention from top policymakers. In terms of the implications for international law, however, its effects could well prove to be the most pernicious. For if the most powerful and closely watched state feels it has the option to ignore the rules of the international game, then others may feel that much more tempted to do the same. The fact that its partners also appear to be less concerned about preserving the rules than about gaining U.S. support for their policy goals sends the same message.

For example, before the new administration of George W. Bush was three months old, Prime Minister Lionel Jospin of France had already labeled it "a unilateralist administration" in that "it doesn't seem to think that some of the rules that make the international community work necessarily need to be taken into consideration on certain issues."[5] Yet his ire was provoked not by a U.S. failure to comply with existing law, but by the new President's decision to abandon the ongoing negotiations to complete the Kyoto Protocol

5 "France's Jospin Concerned at U.S. 'Unilateralism,'" Reuters News Service, April 4, 2001.

on global warming. As discussed in more detail below, it is America's caution about expanding international norms – evident well before the advent of the second Bush Administration – that appears to upset its European partners more than any alleged trampling of existing law.

In terms of the third charge, America's once-sterling track record on meeting its obligations to international organizations has slipped badly since the mid-1980s, when Congress began mandating that the U.S. withhold substantial portions of its assessed dues payments from the UN until it got its way on various financial and management reforms within the world body. Commenting on this practice in 1997, John Weston, then the Permanent Representative of the United Kingdom to the United Nations, cautioned that "American exceptionalism cannot mean being the exception to the laws everyone else has to obey."[6] Responding to U.S. withholdings aimed at achieving a reduction in its assessment rate for the regular budget and peacekeeping, Tono Eitel, former German Permanent Representative to the UN, declared in 2000 that "in talking about U.S. arrears, I do not think that Washington should be met half in advance. There should not be any premium on illegal behaviors."[7] True, but years before France, Russia, and China had each made unilateral demands regarding their dues to the UN and received concessions in return.[8]

In terms of this analysis, moreover, it should be asked: how typical are these examples and do they represent broader trends in U.S. foreign policy? Does the unilateralist-multilateralist lens provide a particularly insightful way of viewing U.S. policies and priorities or does it distort a more nuanced reality? As the following section chronicles in more detail, there is ample reason to believe that both unilateralist and multilateralist currents are alive and well in Washington policymaking, that few decisions of importance are taken because of where they would fit on this spectrum, and that in most cases a combination of the two approaches works best. The executive-legislative struggle over UN dues, in fact, was allowed to fester for so many years and to assume

6 "U.S. Debt Called 'Indefensible'; Weston Says It's Catch-22," *Diplomatic World Bulletin*, 28 (April-May 1997), p. 1.

7 Stiftung Wissenschaft und Politik (SWP), *The Security Council and the G8 in the New Millennium: Who Is In Charge of International Peace and Security?*, 5th International Workshop, Berlin, June 30-July 1, 2000, p. 50. For a stinging critique of U.S. policies toward the UN and multilateral issues by a leading developing country representative at the UN, see Singapore's Kishore Mahbubani, "UN: Sunrise or Sunset Organization in the 21st Century?," in Kamalesh Sharma, ed., *Imagining Tomorrow: Rethinking the Global Challenge* (printed by the Merritt Corporation, 2000), pp. 34-44.

8 For a history and political analysis of the various disputes over funding the UN, see Edward C. Luck, *Mixed Messages: American Politics and International Organization, 1919-1999* (Washington, D.C.: Brookings Institution Press, 1999), Chapter 9: "Who Should Pay for the UN," pp. 224-253.

such an ideological character precisely because it was not widely regarded as a matter of high priority.

The governing "ism," if any, on matters deemed important to the United States would appear to be pragmatism. Though American ambivalence about multilateral institutions is as deep-seeded as it is legendary, Washington's willingness to call on existing international bodies or to create new ones as needed remains impressive, as seen so vividly in the post 9/11 war on terrorism. On any given day, the balance between unilateralist and multilateralist tendencies varies markedly from issue to issue. Over time, the balance may shift a bit one-way or the other, as events and politics dictate. But no top policymaker wants to be told that the range of choices open to him or her must conform to some theoretical notion of what the mix of unilateral and multilateral tools should look like.

The United States, moreover, is not the only country to act exceptionally at times in international institutions, though its stance differs in three respects that matter for this analysis.[9] One, as the world's most powerful state, by far, what it says and does about multilateral undertakings carries much more weight, at times threatening to undermine the authority and capacity of particular institutions or initiatives. Two, the U.S. had been the leader in establishing the post-war system of international institutions and in encouraging the development of new dimensions of international law. As a traditional advocate of international law and organization as essential cornerstones for international order, Washington's seeming reversal of course is particularly worrisome to those nations that have shared these values and perspectives.[10] Three, to a remarkable degree, the U.S. seems immune from the criticisms of other countries concerning its behavior in multilateral bodies, for Washington primarily looks to domestic, rather than international, sources for legitimizing its policies and actions.[11] As John Bolton commented, before being tapped to be Under Secretary of State for Arms Control and International Security in the new Bush Administration, "consulting with allies is one thing, but the notion that the Security Council or any other body could actually dilute

9 This author has argued that China, France, and the Soviet Union have also acted at times as exceptional member states of the U.N. See American Exceptionalism and International Organization: Lessons from the 1990s, in Rosemary Foot, Neil MacFarlane, and Michael Mastanduno, eds., *The U.S. and Multilateral Organizations* (Oxford University Press, 2002, forthcoming).

10 For a strategic explanation of why the U.S. turned to the creation of international institutions following victory in World Wars I and II, see G. John Ikenberry, *After Victory: Institutions, Strategic Restraint, and the Rebuilding of Order After Major Wars* (Princeton, NJ: Princeton University Press, 2001), pp. 117-214.

11 For a further exploration of these themes, see Edward C. Luck, The United States, International Organizations, and the Quest for Legitimacy, in Patrick and Forman, op. cit., pp. 47-74.

American decision-making authority is simply not acceptable."[12] This stance has proven disconcerting to others, particularly allies, seeking either to influence U.S. positions within international institutions or to invoke the legitimizing or delegitimizing decisions of those bodies to compel or constrain Washington's use of its unsurpassed power in the real world outside.

The Record

Within multilateral fora, the U.S. has not been shy about going it alone when deemed necessary. Since the mid-1970s, it has not hesitated to oppose the large majority of countries on issues, including many relating to the Middle East and disarmament, on which its interests have been engaged. Some U.S. diplomats even have seemed to relish playing the role of the lonely voice standing up for American values and interests, a stance that often plays well with domestic audiences. While Washington prefers not to cast formal vetoes in the Security Council, it has often done so when its more frequent efforts to forestall initiatives through quiet pre-emptive threats to do so have not been persuasive. Indeed, it has cast far more vetoes than Russia, Britain, France, or China since 1970.[13] And the U.S. stood alone – ultimately successfully – in opposing a second term for UN Secretary-General Boutros Boutros-Ghali. More recently, in September 2001 the United States and Israel were the only member states to walk out of the contentious UN conference on racism in Durban, though many of America's partners shared its dismay over how the proceedings had taken on anti-Israeli and even anti-semitic overtones.[14]

Reflecting strong Congressional pressures since the ill-fated expansion of UN peacekeeping ambitions in the early 1990s, the U.S. also has generally been more cautious than many of its allies about the deployment of new UN peace operations and about keeping down the costs of such missions. The U.S., moreover, has steadfastly refused to put its military units under the command of foreign officers, a position that even Presidents Woodrow Wil-

12 John R. Bolton, "Unilateralism Is Not Isolationism," in Gwyn Prins, ed., *Understanding Unilateralism in American Foreign Relations* (London: The Royal Institute of International Affairs, 2000), p. 74.

13 The U.S. cast the only two vetoes in the Council in 2001, both on the Middle East. On March 27, 2001, the U.S. blocked a move to deploy a UN observer mission in the Israeli-occupied territories. On December 14, 2001, it opposed a resolution calling for the withdrawal of Israeli forces from Palestinian territory. The latter veto was cast even as the U.S. sought to maintain the cohesion of the counter-terrorism coalition.

14 Serge Schmemann, "U.S. Walkout: Was It Repudiated or Justified by the Conference's Accord?," *New York Times*, September 9, 2001 and Rachel L. Swann, "After the Race Conference: Relief, and Doubt Over Whether It Will Matter," *New York Times*, September 10, 2001.

son and Franklin Roosevelt maintained, or to countenance the development of UN stand-by forces under Article 43 of the Charter, even if other member states were to supply the troops. American views on the use of force also depart substantially from the strict provisions of the UN Charter – something that was no doubt reassuring to its allies during the Cold War years but less so with the demise of the Soviet threat. The U.S. maintains the right to use force to protect its interests even without specific Security Council authorization, and it has done so in places as diverse as Grenada, Libya, Panama, Iraq, Kosovo, and Afghanistan. As former Assistant Secretary of State Princeton Lyman has noted, "that is a sore point with many other countries, including America's European allies, who feel much more comfortable with the political cover of a UN mandate even when they agree that force is merited."[15] Despite continued differences, there are some signs of a narrowing of the transatlantic gap. NATO supported the military interventions in Kosovo and Afghanistan, as cases where U.S. military power was employed in the pursuit of alliance-wide security interests. During the first few months after 9/11, the terrorist threat pulled the western alliance together, just as the Soviet threat did during the Cold War. As discussed below, however, the staying power of the newfound cohesion has yet to be tested.

Perhaps the most contentious and public transatlantic disputes, however, have stemmed from the U.S. reluctance to join a series of global norm-building campaigns that have gained strong public and official support not only in allied countries, but in much of the rest of the world as well. In some cases, such as the Ottawa Landmines Convention, the U.S. has neither signed nor ratified. More often, including the Law of the Sea Convention, the Rome Statute for the International Criminal Court, the Kyoto Protocol on global warming, the Comprehensive Test Ban Treaty, the Convention on the Rights of the Child and other human rights agreements, the U.S. signed but the Senate refused to give its consent to ratification. Such inconsistencies between executive branch and Congressional attitudes have simply fuelled the prevalent impression abroad that, because the U.S. is deeply ambivalent about or only superficially committed to a number of international engagements, domestic political considerations are permitted to prevail far too often in Washington. The ire of U.S. partners has also been provoked when a switch in parties in the White House leads to a reversal of course in terms of multilateral commitments and expectations, as happened in 2001 on several fronts. President Bush's announcement that he would not support the Kyoto Protocol, for example, was characterized by *Le Monde* as "a brutal form of unilat-

15 Princeton N. Lyman, "Saving the UN Security Council – A Challenge for the United States," *Max Planck Yearbook of United Nations Law* (vol. 4, 2000), pp. 129-130. The United Kingdom, of course, did not look to the Security Council to endorse its defense of the Malvinas/Falklands in 1982, though it worked hard and successfully to ensure that the Council did not condemn its military intervention.

eralism" and by the French environment minister, Dominique Voynet, as "completely provocative and irresponsible."[16]

As striking as these examples of American exceptionalism appear on the surface, they are not the whole story. Their sensational nature has tended to obscure a much more subtle and differentiated reality. For instance:

- The U.S. supported the creation or expansion of a number of global and regional institutions during the past decade, among them the World Trade Organization (WTO), the North American Free Trade Agreement (NAFTA), the Asia Pacific Economic Cooperation (ASEAN) forum, NATO, and even some UN programs of particular interest.
- On the working level, the U.S. often manages to participate in the operational and substantive activities of multilateral regimes to which it is not a full party. For example, the U.S. has taken the lead on global demining and has curbed its exports of anti-personnel mines, though it still finds the convention to be flawed. The U.S., as well, has been a major supporter of the war crimes tribunals for Rwanda and the Balkans, even as it has balked at ratifying the Rome Statute on the establishment of an International Criminal Court. The same pattern has characterized U.S. human rights policies through the years. The divisions in American society about the wisdom of accepting the legal and binding obligations inherent in such international conventions are of longstanding, but so too are the urges to hold aggressors and tyrants accountable and to promote western values around the world.
- The U.S. has been an active proponent and observer of the essential provisions of the Law of the Sea Convention since its codification in 1982 and has worked with the parties to modify those provisions to which it had objected. It has been little noticed, however, not only that the Clinton Administration submitted the Convention to the Senate for its advice and consent but, more to the point, that the Bush Administration has declared that it, too, "supports accession of the United States to the Convention."[17]
- Likewise, the U.S. withdrawal from UNESCO in 1984 generated enormous publicity, while its gradual warming to the reformed agency has gained little attention or commentary. Though the Bush Administration has not called for re-entry, as President Clinton had, in May 2001 the

16 Quoted in Edmund L. Andrews, "Bush Angers Europe by Eroding Pact on Warming," *New York Times*, April 1, 2001.

17 Statement by Ambassador Sichan Siv, U.S. Representative on the UN Economic and Social Council, to the UN General Assembly, November 27, 2001. U.S.UN Press Release #184(01), December 7, 2001. Also see Marjorie Ann Browne, "IB95010: The Law of the Sea Convention and U.S. Policy," CRS Issue Brief for Congress, February 14, 2001 and Department of State, "The Convention on the Law of the Sea," Oceans Conference, Monterey, California, June 1998, http://www.state.gov/www/global/oes/oceans/980610_los.html.

Republican-led House voted down a move to delete the funds authorized for possible dues payments.[18]

- The U.S. has favored giving the UN a leading role in the struggle against HIV/AIDS, in conflict resolution and nation building in East Timor, the Balkans, Afghanistan, and much of Africa, in monitoring arms in Iraq, and in giving the Security Council sweeping and unprecedented powers for curbing support and financing of terrorism anywhere, anytime.

John Ikenberry goes so far as to argue that the post-Cold War impetus in Washington for institution building paralleled those after World Wars I and II. Though noting some ambiguities and inconsistencies, he concludes that in the 1990s:

> The United States employed institutions as a mechanism to lock in other states to desired policy orientations, and it was willing to exchange some limits on its own autonomy to do so. Other states also seized upon these institutions as ways to gain access to America – either its markets or its policy making.[19]

The U.S. approach to international institutions since the end of the Cold War, however, has lacked the sense of sweeping vision and determined Presidential leadership that so vividly characterized the approaches of Wilson, Roosevelt, and Truman. In an incremental, practical, and economically driven age, the U.S. stance has been highly selective and pragmatic, with fewer pretenses about building a stunningly new or ambitious global architecture. In that sense, multilateral cooperation has moved from being an "-ism" or ideological preference to being an integral part of every day foreign (and even domestic) affairs.

The most dramatic American embrace of multilateralism over the past decade, therefore, has occurred not at the UN but in the sphere of lowering trade barriers. Though less appreciated by those who still see security as the epicenter of high politics, trade is a subject that has traditionally split both major political parties, largely along regional lines, and that has required deft Presidential leadership. In two of its more important foreign policy accomplishments, the Clinton Administration, with the support of key Republicans on Capitol Hill, managed to gain Congressional support for the North American Free Trade Agreement (NAFTA) and the World Trade Organization (WTO) in late 1993 and late 1994, respectively.[20] The latter occurred *after*

18 Jim Lobe, "House Rebuffs Bush on U.N. Payments, UNESCO," Inter Press Service, May 10, 2001. Also see Department of State, "Bush Administration Urged to Seek U.S. Reentry into UNESCO," January 16, 2001, http://usinfo.state.gov/topical/pol/usandun/01011602.htm.

19 Ikenberry, op. cit., p. 234. Though attractive on the strategic level, his analysis takes no account of the substantial influence of domestic political, institutional, and structural factors in helping to shape the American approach.

20 For further information and analysis, see Luck, "American Exceptionalism," op. cit.

the Republicans, with their inward-looking "Contract for America" and unilateralist rhetoric, had won both Houses in the November 1994 mid-term elections.

While from a security perspective it may appear that the U.S. was much more bullish on international institutions in the 1940s than in the 1990s, quite the opposite pattern has characterized the trade sector. In the late 1940s, in fact, a Republican-controlled Congress killed the new International Trade Organization (ITO), which President Harry Truman had regarded as a prime pillar of the post-war system. The WTO's dispute settlement system, in contrast, has far more teeth than the GATT arrangements it replaced in terms of its capacity to authorize national retaliatory action against countries deemed not to have lived up to WTO arbitration judgements concerning trade disputes. True, the U.S. commitment to the WTO rules is just beginning to be severely tested, since the U.S. position usually carried the day during the early years of the new system. Even when it has been on the losing side, however, it has not questioned the legitimacy of these multilateral processes despite domestic complaints.[21] And, arguably, trade is an issue that cuts deeper into the fabric of interstate relations and, certainly, of domestic politics than distant peacekeeping missions or norm-building efforts on topics such as landmines, war crimes, or children's rights.[22]

Even in peacekeeping, the U.S., for all its caution, has permitted a substantial growth in both UN and NATO deployments since the mid-1990s.

---

21 Robert E. Hudec, "The New WTO Dispute Settlement Procedure: An Overview of the First Three Years," *Minnesota Journal of Global Trade*, vol. 8, issue 1 (Winter 1999), pp. 1-53. For an argument that the legalization represented by the WTO favors protectionist forces in domestic politics, see Judith Goldstein and Lisa L. Martin, "Legalization, Trade Liberalization, and Domestic Politics: A Cautionary Note," *International Organization*, vol. 54, no. 3 (Summer 2000), pp. 603-632. For a commentary on the WTO's inability to compel superpowers such as the EU and the U.S., see Benjamin L. Brimeyer, "Bananas, Beef, and Compliance in the World Trade Organization: The Inability of the WTO Dispute Settlement Process to Achieve Compliance from Superpower Nations," *Minnesota Journal of Global Trade*, vol. 10, issue 1 (Winter 2001), pp. 133-168. Also see John Burgess, "U.S. Seeks to Recover From WTO Decision," *The Washington Post*, February 25, 2000; Bob Dole, "3-Strikes Test for the WTO," *The Washington Post*, May 8, 2000; John R. Magnus, "Get the WTO Criticisms Right in the Trade Debate," *Journal of Commerce*, May 3, 2000; and Bruce Stokes, "Preparing to Bypass the WTO," *Financial Times*, March 29, 2000.

22 At the same time, when domestic political impulses do get mixed with trade policy, the unilateralist results can be very displeasing to America's partners. A particularly controversial case has been the extra-territorial provisions of the Helms-Biden Act, which has sought to penalize other countries that invest in or trade with Cuba. As Guillaume Parmentier, an influential French expert on the United States, put it: "l'unilatéralisme auquel s'était ralliée l'Administration Clinton en matière de sanctions secondaires (lois Helms-Burton et Kennedy-D'Amato), a joué un rôle négatif puissant pour l'image des États-Unis. " Préface to Alexandra Novosseloff, *Les États-Unis et l'ONU dans l'Après-Guerre Froide* (Paris : IFRI, 2001), p. 8.

From mid-1999 to November 2001, the number of blue helmets – UN soldiers, military observers, and civilian police – almost quadrupled, from 12,084 to 47,778.[23] With American encouragement and participation, NATO – with over 80,000 troops deployed in the Balkans at the end of 2001 – has been a larger sponsor of peacekeeping than the United Nations.[24] The total of almost 130,000 peacekeepers between NATO and the UN – even before the multinational mission in Afghanistan gets underway – is 64 percent higher than the UN's 1993 peak deployment of 78,744. As these numbers attest, Washington apparently overcame its mid-1990s allergy to peacekeeping well before the terrorist attacks of September 2001. The shift to NATO leadership no doubt reflected declining confidence in the UN's capacity for managing peacekeeping operations, but many other troop contributing countries and UN experts shared that sense of unease.[25] In fact, the most dramatic drop-off in terms of national participation in UN peacekeeping has not been from the U.S., but from more traditional peacekeepers in Western Europe, Canada, and the Nordic countries.[26]

Though the financial stakes are decidedly modest, one of the most divisive multilateral questions between the U.S. and its allies has been how to proportion UN dues assessments. This is not a new issue: even the founding conference in San Francisco could not agree on a burden-sharing formula and Congress has complained about the U.S. share from the world body's earliest days.[27] The first legislation seeking to limit U.S. payments to the UN unilaterally was passed, in fact, in 1953 (though it took the form of a non-binding, sense-of-Congress resolution). In recent years, however, mounting U.S. arrears, which at about $1.6 billion exceeded the UN's annual budget, brought the burden-sharing issue to a boil. Under the terms of the Helms-Biden bill, much of the arrears could be paid, but only if a number of "reforms" were adopted by the UN, including reductions in U.S. regular budget and peacekeeping assessments. As the largest contributors, much of the most difficult tugging and hauling took place among the U.S., its European allies, and

23 For the month-by-month figures, 1993 to 2001, as provided by the UN, see www.globalpolicy.org/security/peacepg/data/pkomctab.htm. Though less than 2 percent of these peacekeepers were Americans, even smaller portions were from the other four permanent members of the Security Council. Of the NATO countries, only Portugal had more troops serving with the UN in November 2001.

24 For further details see www.nato.int/sfor/index.htm and www.nato.int/kosovo/kosovo.htm.

25 Report of the Panel on United Nations Peace Operations, A/55/305, August 21, 2000 (commonly known as the Brahimi Report).

26 Edward C. Luck, "Choosing the Right End of the Telescope: Domestic Politics and International Interventions," paper prepared for the International Commission on Intervention and State Sovereignty, March 2001.

27 For a history of these disputes and of Congress' role in them, see *Mixed Messages*, op. cit., pp. 224-253.

Japan. As the protracted negotiations came to a head in December 2000, the spokesman for the EU, UN Ambassador Jean-David Levitte of France, labeled the Congressional ultimatum as "an absolutely unjustifiable demand" and commented that progress was only being made through "pain, recrimination, screaming."[28] In the end, the U.S. got much of what it wanted, but EU nations did not have to absorb any additional assessments and Japan's share was actually lowered by one percent.[29] The Senate Foreign Relations Committee greeted the result as a great victory and as the start of a new U.S.-UN relationship, though the long history of burden-sharing disputes gives reason for caution, including about the longer-term lessons of seeming to reward such unilateralist tactics.[30]

Dynamic Times, Moving Goalposts

To assess whether the U.S. has been retreating from multilateral norms and institutions entails having a clear notion of where the baseline should be drawn for comparison. Relative to the status quo at the close of the Cold War era, little more than a decade ago, American attitudes and policies over the ensuing years, on the whole, have been progressive. The U.S. has neither been standing still nor regressing. But, internationally, the goal posts or standards of comparison have been moving rapidly down the field in recent years, as far-reaching norms and institutions have been developed or advocated for an ever-widening spectrum of sectors of international, transnational, and domestic activity. In terms of the historical progression of American values and politics, the 1990s appear to be a period of continuity much more than of discontinuity. If there was a retreat in American policy, it was much more from the rising expectations of others than from its own history and domestic roots.

For all of the disputes within international fora about priorities and possible reforms, the growth of both norms and institutions over the past decade has been remarkably rapid, probably even unprecedented. Understandably, the very momentum of this movement has given it an air of inevitability that

---

28 Barbara Crossette, "U.S. and Europe Trade Proposals to End U.N. Dues Deadlock," *New York Times*, December 22, 2000.

29 For the EU refusal to pay more, see Barbara Crossette, "On U.N. Dues, No U.S. Cover from Europe," *New York Times*, December 8, 2000. For the terms of the agreement, see Barbara Crossette, "After Long Fight, U.N. Agrees to Cut Dues Paid by U.S.," *New York Times*, December 23, 2000, and Colum Lynch, "U.S. Dues Cut Gets Support at the U.N.," *Washington Post*, December 23, 2000.

30 For Senate reactions, see Christoper Marquis, "Satisfied with U.N. Reforms, Helms Relents on Back Dues," *New York Times*, January 10, 2001, and Hearing of the Senate Committee on Foreign Relations, *United Nations Reforms*, January 9, 2001.

has spurred countervailing political forces within many countries, not least the United States. The voices of resistance to expanding notions of global governance have traditionally been associated with the Republican Party and are well represented in the new Bush Administration, a point of which America's partners need not be reminded. The ferocity of the resistance to global governance is, in this sense, testimony to the width of its appeal, to the progress that has been made in that direction, and to the perceived threat it poses to traditional notions of sovereignty, even in the strongest countries.[31] Nevertheless, in terms of steps to bolster international law and organization, the United States took the initiative in many cases and in most others was at least broadly supportive. Otherwise, such progress would not have been possible.

Because its assent and cooperation are so often seen as indispensable, however, the cases that generate the most public discussion are those on which the U.S. drags its feet or openly dissents. Congressional prerogatives and the complexity of the process of checks and balances in Washington contribute to a relatively cumbersome decision-making process that compounds the impression of unresponsiveness to the positions and needs of others. Given both its unparalleled power and its wide range of interests, moreover, the U.S. tends to take strong positions on a wider range of negotiating points and issues than do others. In the process, it comes easily to a reputation for being demanding, overly cautious, and/or a reluctant player. As a superpower, the U.S. is likely to approach questions of what constitutes equity in global decision-making and burden-sharing from a different perspective than its partners in any case.

In an era when non-state actors are shaping global events as well as ideas, it should not be forgotten that the American people, through individual and private initiatives, are more engaged with the world than ever before, even if the course of Washington policymaking resembles a roller coaster at times. American internationalists and U.S.-based NGOs, in fact, have been in the forefront of pushing for many of the new multilateral treaties and institutions, which the U.S. government then failed to join. In many cases, the imaginative private philanthropy of major foundations, civil society groups, and private sector leaders like Bill Gates, George Soros, and Ted Turner is helping to fill gaps in U.S. government performance. While the public on the whole remains decidedly internationalist, many Americans, including some who are actively engaged in world affairs, continue to be skeptical of whether government-to-government channels are always the most effective way to get the job done.

---

31 Stephen D. Krasner has suggested that the demands of functional interdependence have served to "undermine domestic sovereignty comprehended simply as control" even if a state's "authoritative decision making" has not been compromised. *Sovereignty: Organized Hypocrisy* (Princeton, N.J: Princeton University Press, 1999), p. 13.

The dynamics of European integration may also complicate the prospects for a convergence of positions across the Atlantic. As the EU works toward a common foreign and security policy, a premium is usually placed on acting in unison in global fora and on maintaining joint positions in the face of alternative proposals from the United States or others. Just as many in Washington seem to feel that their job is largely done when all of the intra-Beltway, inter-agency squabbles have been settled, so too EU representatives to multilateral for a – in their own version of unilateralism – are often reluctant to reopen compromises worked out among their member states. It is understandable, given America's unsurpassed power position, for others to prefer to present a common front to the U.S., something its allies feel far freer to do since the demise of the Soviet Union and the end of the Cold War.

Neither the intra-European nor the domestic U.S. political processes, in other words, are structured in a manner to ease global consensus building. A particularly ugly and damaging illustration of these structural shortcomings came in May 2001, when the U.S. was voted off the UN Commission on Human Rights for the first time since its inception in 1947.[32] Three slots were open to candidates from WEOG – the unfortunately named Western Europe and Others Group – and the three EU candidates – France, Austria, and Sweden – not surprisingly outpolled the U.S. in the vote by ECOSOC members. As a result, nine of the ten slots allocated to WEOG are to be occupied by EU members, leaving Canada as the lone exception. On the one hand, the drive for consensus within the EU made it difficult to press one of its potential candidates to step aside for this round.[33] On the other hand, the result made many in the U.S., and possibly in other WEOG countries, question the equity and priorities of UN procedures. Because several of the states elected from other regions had questionable human rights records, it appeared as if process was once again valued more highly than results. Congress reflexively responded with a unilateral gesture: legislation calling for further withholding of UN dues if the U.S. does not regain its seat in 2002.[34] A vicious cycle has

32 Colum Lynch, "U.S. Loses Seat on U.N. Rights Body; Defeat Laid to Irritation At White House Policies," *Washington Post* May 4, 2001 and Barbara Crossette, "For First Time, U.S. Is Excluded From U.N. Human Rights Panel," *New York Times*, May 4, 2001. This was hardly an isolated incident, since the U.S. had already lost the UN's top development post, as well as its representation on the Advisory Committee on Administrative and Budgetary Questions (ACABQ) and on the International Narcotics Control Board (INCB).

33 According to Guillaume Parmentier, "the U.S. could not have lost its seat without at least some of the Europeans taking revenge for the new administration's unilateralist character" and "EU countries are obliged by EU rules to vote for each other." Quoted in Peter Ford, "Aloof U.S. Loses Clout At the UN," *Christian Science Monitor*, May 7, 2001.

34 See David E. Sanger, "House Threatens to Hold U.N. Dues in Loss of a Seat," *New York Times*, May 9, 2001; Norman Kempster, "House Wants to Withhold Dues to U.N.; Diplomacy: Lawmakers Are Angry That U.S. Was Voted Off Human Rights

long been at work: the tendency to confront the U.S. with bloc positions, whether of the EU, other regional groupings, the G-77, or the non-aligned has, again and again, fueled the doubts of those in the U.S. domestic debate who see multilateral processes as undemocratic, as inadequately reflective of U.S. power in the real world outside, or even as inherently unfriendly to American interests and values.

9/11: A Watershed?

Though headline writers have unabashedly and repeatedly proclaimed that everything has changed since the terrorist attacks of 9/11, history argues for greater modesty in terms of how broad and lasting Washington's new interest in multilateral policy alternatives will turn out to be. For one thing, American attitudes and policies toward multilateral bodies have always been highly targeted and differentiated, depending largely on what the particular organization does, how that relates to national goals, and how well it is believed to be performing. Functional and humanitarian agencies, for example, have usually proven less controversial than political and economic ones. Those bodies, such as the General Assembly, which are perceived to have high symbolic value and low practical or operational utility, have been particularly vulnerable to dismissive critiques and punitive legislation. Partisan disputes between Republicans and Democrats or constitutional struggles between the executive and legislative branches have been played out, again and again, in the realm of multilateral policymaking, where the visibility is often high and the costs to U.S. interests seem relatively low. The domestic sources of American ambivalence toward international institutions, moreover, run very deep. As *Mixed Messages* chronicles, the core themes – the sense of exceptionalism, mistrust of large or distant government, the preference for voluntary or private initiatives, the suspicion of the motives of other peoples and countries, the separation of powers, and a Congressional concern about its prerogatives and about its power of the purse – have remained remarkably consistent over the past century.

In the short run, the need to pull together in the common struggle against terrorism has produced a degree of unity both within the United States and within the alliance that historically has been associated largely with periods of interstate war and of external threats to national and alliance security. Initially, the use of massive U.S. airpower in Afghanistan spurred widespread

---

Panel. Bush Opposes the Punitive Measure," *Los Angeles Times*, May 10, 2001; Juliet Eilperin, "House Votes to Block Payment of U.N. Dues; Anger Grows Over Rights Panel Ouster," *Washington* Post, May 11, 2001; and Susan Milligan, "House Votes to Halt Part of UN Dues," *Boston Globe*, May 11, 2001.

doubts and concerns throughout much of Western Europe about civilian casualties and about possible political repercussions in much of the Islamic world.[35] The second-guessing, however, ebbed rapidly with the military success on the ground, the welcoming of foreign intervention on the part of many Afghanis, and a refocusing on the human rights record of the Taliban regime, especially its repression of women.[36]

Yet there is no assurance that transatlantic differences will not reappear if future stages of the war on terrorism do not proceed as smoothly. In November-December 2001, for example, an elite survey showed sharp differences between American and Western European attitudes about whether "regimes such as Iraq and Somalia" should be attacked by the U.S. and its allies if it turns out that they have supported terrorism.[37] By a 50 to 38 margin, Americans responded affirmatively, while a 37 to 32 percent plurality in Western Europe said that military action should be confined to Afghanistan, with fully 31 percent expressing no opinion. Strikingly, though 70 percent of the Americans felt that the U.S. was "taking into account the interests of its partners" in the war on terrorism, only a third of the Western Europeans agreed, compared to two thirds who responded that the U.S. was "acting mainly on its own interests." As in so many past polls, sharp differences were also found in whether the U.S. "has been too supportive of Israel" as well.

The impact of these distinctions in the two worldviews could well be compounded by two other transatlantic asymmetries that have taken on almost a structural rather than temporal nature: one, the increasing imbalance in military capabilities, and two, the persistent difference in the respective political cultures. In the Persian Gulf War, Kosovo, and now Afghanistan, the U.S. has demonstrated that its edge in conventional military technology over its European allies, as well as the rest of the world, continues to grow over time. The terrorist attacks of 9/11 may have laid bare the vulnerabilities of advanced, open societies, but the apparent success of the U.S. and allied military response in Afghanistan – whether or not it actually crippled the capacity of well-entrenched terrorist cells around the world to strike – may well encourage the American public and policymakers to consider the use of unilateral military power to deter, pre-empt, or respond to future terrorist threats from abroad. Writing before 9/11, William Wallace noted that "an American overemphasis on political and military issues, and in particular a search for new potential enemies, has met a European overemphasis on economics." The result, in his view, had already been divergent threat perceptions and a

---

35 Mary Kaldor went further, suggesting that the U.S. reaction was part of "the new American militarism." In her words, "if September 11 had not happened, the American military-industrial complex might have had to invent it." "Beyond Militarism, Arms Races and Arms Control," Social Science Research Council, After September 11 website, http://www.ssrc.org/sept11/essays/kaldor_text_only.htm.

36 Henneberger, *New York Times*, op. cit.

37 Pew Research Center, Online Reports, http://people-press.org/121901que.htm.

failure "to coordinate the development of NATO and the EU."[38] The war on terrorism, if anything, could well exacerbate these differences. For while many Americans may have been reminded of the value of multilateral cooperation in intelligence sharing, diplomacy, humanitarian assistance, and postwar reconstruction, they have also witnessed another lesson in the utility of the targeted, timely, and decisive application of unilateral military power.

The second transatlantic asymmetry that shows no signs of fading away in the post-9/11 era relates to cultural values and attitudes toward government. While the process of integration has encouraged some convergence of political and cultural values across Europe, the culture wars remain alive and well in the United States. European governments, for instance, have come to common positions on matters, such as the death penalty, family planning, and gun control, that remain highly contentious within the United States. Efforts to codify global standards on such issues are, at best, premature from Washington's perspective. Meanwhile, globalization and the mass marketing of American popular culture have led to a backlash in parts of Europe, where critics tend to caricature the U.S. as weak in values and culture as it is strong in military and economic capacity.

Differences in attitudes toward national government, moreover, are reflected in distinct sets of expectations and preferences concerning the role of multilateral institutions and global governance, with Americans from both the right and left political flanks expressing particularly pointed skepticism of seemingly distant and unaccountable international agencies.[39] Though he, too, was greeted with considerable disdain across the Atlantic initially, President Clinton's mainstream Democratic positions were far more popular in Western Europe than President Bush's more conservative views. In terms of international policies, respondents to an August 2001 survey in the United Kingdom, Italy, Germany, and France gave Clinton a much higher approval rating, by ratios between 3 to 1 and 4 to 1.[40] In Coral Bell's view the Clinton

---

38 William Wallace, "Europe, the Necessary Partner," *Foreign Affairs*, vol. 80, no. 3 (May/June 2001), pp. 17, 26, and 27.

39 Luck, *Mixed Messages*, op. cit., pp. 41-75 and William Wallace, "Living with a Hegemon: European Dilemmas," SSRC website, op. cit., January 2002, p. 4.

40 Pew Research Center, Online Reports, http://www.people-press.org/bush01rpt.htm. Some authors have suggested that these differences are largely among political elites and not the respective publics. Antony J. Blinken, for instance, claims that "the transatlantic strategic split is largely in the minds of Europe's elite, not its people." "The False Crisis Over the Atlantic," *Foreign Affairs*, vol. 80, no. 3 (May/June 2001), p. 43. Yet this conclusion does not take account either of the depth of cross-national public antipathy demonstrated in this survey or of the persistence of such differences in political culture over time. George Joffé contends, moreover, that "the crisis in the Balkans, questions about the future of NATO and the implications of changes within Europe itself for the transatlantic relationship have all highlighted policy areas where the superficial consensus across the Atlantic on occasion conceals growing differences." In Prins, op. cit., p. xi.

Administration should be praised for utilizing existing multilateral institutions and for understanding that "the unipolar world should be run as if it was a concert of powers."[41] To its domestic critics, however, the Clinton Administration, in embracing the notion of "assertive multilateralism," tended to confuse the facade of global processes with the realities of power.

Commentators in Europe seem to find U.S. ambivalence towards multilateral institutions in general and the UN in particular to be especially puzzling. Why, they ask, did many Americans become more disenchanted with the United Nations during the 1990s, just as the world body began to more openly promote western values, such as elections, democratic political processes, human rights, civil society, free trade, and cooperation with the private sector?[42] Paradoxically, without such blatant challenges to western values and interests with the demise of the Soviet Union, the UN and other global bodies may have seemed less essential as places to defend western social and economic tenets. Also, as noted above, the very fact that the diminution of East-West tensions seemed to open new horizons for multilateralism may have fed growing worries about global governance and threats to sovereignty. There may have been, as well, a conscious or subconscious devaluing of the UN and other multilateral security arrangements with the end of the Cold War. Without such acute concerns about the possible escalation of local conflicts in the developing world, the world organization's peace and security role may have seemed less central, at least before the horrific events of 9/11. Significantly, support for the UN, especially among Republicans, men, and conservatives, peaked after the Persian Gulf War and then gradually faded.[43]

Since the terrorist attacks on the United States, there has been a modest expansion of public support for the UN and multilateral cooperation, but – as after the Gulf War – this could well prove transitory. Presidential leadership matters, and it sobering to note that, while President Bush stressed the vital role of the world body in his November 10th speech to the General Assembly, he never mentioned the UN in his eloquent address to a joint session of Congress on September 20th. By a 70 to 24 percent margin, respondents to a November 2001 survey agreed that "the United States should cooperate fully with the United Nations," continuing the positive trend reflected in the March

41 Coral Bell, "American Ascendancy and the Pretense of Concert," *The National Interest*, no. 57 (Fall 1999), p. 60.

42 Perversely, when western positions were most dramatically under siege in the 1970s and early 1980s, Congress did not impose major financial withholdings on the UN.

43 Overall, public support for the UN remains quite high. See Jeffrey M. Jones, "Public Credits United Nations With Doing Good Job of Handling International Problems," Poll Release, March 22, 2001, www.gallup.com/poll/releases/pr010322c.asp. For trends in public opinion, see Steven Kull and I.M. Destler, *Misreading the Public: The Myth of a New Isolationism* (Washington, DC: Brookings Institution Press, 1999), and Luck, *Mixed Messages*, op. cit., pp. 34-40 and 260-268.

1999 results of 65 to 26 and the 59 to 30 margin found in September 1997.[44] Historically, however, these results are lower than those achieved in the 1960s and following the Gulf War in 1991, which hit an all-time high of 77 to 17.[45]

Two surveys by the Pew Research Center for the People and the Press, one conducted just before the World Trade Center attacks and the other a month later in mid-October, confirm a modest growth in internationalist sentiment, but not necessarily in ways that would please European critics of the priorities of the Bush Administration.[46] In the abstract, at least, larger numbers in the post-9/11 poll recognized the need to take the "interests of allies" into account and to make "strengthening the United Nations" a priority. In terms of specific preferences and policies, however, the second survey found a significant surge of support for increased defense spending, for the rapid deployment of "a national missile defense system," and for the Israeli side of its dispute with the Palestinians. Among global problems, on the other hand, there was decreased enthusiasm for promoting democracy, for reducing the spread of AIDS and other infectious diseases, for improving living standards in developing nations, for combating international drug trafficking, for dealing with world hunger, or for addressing global warming. None of this suggests that a more internationalist America will necessarily be any closer to accepting the European worldview in terms of substance and priorities. As this author has noted before, asking an increasingly self-assured U.S. to lead from behind may not be the most promising formula for building a firm foundation for transatlantic cooperation.[47]

Refashioning the Transatlantic Dialogue

In a number of ways, Americans and Europeans do tend to see the world differently. Given all of the distinct strategic, historical, and cultural factors noted above, that is to be expected. A hearty and vigorous debate across the Atlantic about things that matter should be encouraged. But it should be, first and foremost, about strategic questions of alliance-wide significance and about core policy choices. Theological disputes about the relative merits of multilateralism or unilateralism usually raise temperatures much more than

44 Public Opinion Online, Roper Center at the University of Connecticut, accession numbers 0392423, 0326277, and 0285517, respectively. The surveys were sponsored by the Program on International Policy Attitudes (PIPA), University of Maryland (2001) and the Pew Research Center (1999 and 1997).

45 Luck, *Mixed Messages*, op. cit. p. 262.

46 "America's New Internationalist Point of View," October 24, 2001, Pew Research Center for the People and the Press, http://www.people-press.org/102401rpt.htm.

47 Luck, *Mixed Messages*, op. cit., pp. 291-298.

they do understanding. More often than not, it appears that the real issue in contention in such cases is whether the U.S. is willing to consult its allies in a timely, full, and operationally relevant manner. That is an important matter, but questions of intra-alliance decision-making should not be confused with issues of global governance, law, and institutions. It is quite possible for the U.S. to be forthcoming about the former and reticent about the latter at the same time.

Global institutions and agendas have a way of bringing out the worst in terms of transatlantic divisions. On the seemingly endless multilateral agenda, therefore, it is essential to draw distinctions between the issues of greater or lesser importance to the West. Presumably those relating to terrorism, the proliferation of weapons of mass destruction, trade, HIV/AIDS, poverty, fundamental human rights, and the management of local conflict are more central, or at least more urgent, to western countries than some of the more divisive normative questions. Unless the U.S. and its partners can agree at least on the fundamentals of these core issues, then they will be poorly positioned to address the needs and demands of the developing world and will be more vulnerable to the splitting tactics of others, such as Russia and China. At this point, with a new President and party in the White House, the transatlantic agenda should come first, for it is in danger of fraying in the face of rapidly changing conditions, leaving less political capacity for tackling global problems. There is an increasing danger of the tail wagging the dog, in this case of having differences on more distant issues undermine alliance solidarity on more immediate and central matters.

Americans certainly have a responsibility, as well as an interest, in ironing out some of these internal inconsistencies in policymaking and in seeking a less partisan and more sustainable basis for their country's participation in multilateral processes. They should recognize that others are tired of hearing U.S. representatives blame the rigidities of their negotiating positions on purportedly inexorable domestic forces, particularly when others – who have their own domestic constituencies to deal with – believe that these bargaining tactics also serve to give the U.S. unfair advantages. U.S. policymakers and legislators should display greater discipline in refraining from making a great fuss over rather small things that carry greater symbolic than substantive value. Moisés Naim, for example, argues that, in the context of building a global coalition against terrorism, American leaders should "think about the effect that the U.S. reluctance to pay its UN dues had on global public opinion. Is the ill will generated by such behavior worth it?"[48] Washington could also make a greater effort to cast its policies and actions in terms that are more likely to curry the kind of broad-based international support that will enhance their chance of success. Even superpowers – perhaps especially su-

48 "Anti-Americanisms: A Guide to Hating Uncle Sam," *Foreign Policy*, vol. 128 (January/February 2002), p. 103.

perpowers – should work on selling their goals and strategies to global as well as domestic constituencies. As William Wallace has phrased it:

> A central difficulty for the U.S.A's European partners, in responding to the current re-establishment of American military and economic dominance, is that the rhetorical justification for this dominant position is more often couched in Realist than in Liberal terms: with reference to U.S. national interests rather than to shared global values and concerns, with self-conscious unilateralism rather than U.S.-orchestrated multilateralism.[49]

None of these steps would require any sacrifice of national sovereignty or objectives, but they would do a good deal to cool opposition and to facilitate active support among Europeans for U.S. initiatives and policies. Since, as argued above, the U.S. has already accepted much of the substance of the drive for multilateral cooperation, it mostly has to work on its style points.

Much the same could be said of our friends in Europe. They recognize the realities, and to a lesser extent the benefits, of America's unsurpassed power. Testifying to this acceptance is the fact that, other than in the economic and diplomatic realms, the Europeans have done relatively little to try to counterbalance U.S. power. Yet they appear as ambivalent about America's global influence as the U.S. is about multilateral institutions. Rather than celebrating the strength of their leader, they often appear to resent it, in the process posing multilateralism as a way to contain rather than project U.S. influence. Are U.S. domestic practices, such as capital punishment, so abhorrent as to disqualify it for western leadership? The hysteria of some European critics makes it sound that way. America's partners, moreover, should take greater care to distinguish the substance from the style of American foreign policy and to focus on the former. As annoying as the latter may be at times, it obviously matters more whether the transatlantic (and transpacific) bond of shared values and interests remains intact and whether there is some common conception of policy goals and strategies for forwarding them.

Three trends need to be closely monitored because of their potential for exacerbating these transatlantic differences. One, on subject after subject, transnational advocacy groups with a singular focus have made greater progress in shaping international agendas and in spurring global norm-setting than they have in influencing national policies and parliaments. This imbalance is particularly visible in the United States, where liberal internationalist NGOs (non-governmental organizations) tend to flock to international meetings of the like-minded, while more conservative or unilateralist groups find more friendly and fertile soil in Washington, DC, especially on Capitol Hill. With competing advocacy groups pushing multilateral processes in one direction and Washington policymaking in another, it should come as no surprise that the U.S. often seems to be marching to a different drummer. It would be

49 "Living with the Hegemon," op. cit., p. 4.

helpful, of course, if transnational advocacy groups and international secretariats would take fuller account of national interests, domestic politics, and possible trade-offs among issue areas in developing their messages and strategies. That may be a lot to expect of independent, civil society-based organizations. At the very least, however, western governments considering joining single-issue coalitions of like-minded governments and NGOs should give equal consideration to ways of bringing Washington on board, even if that would entail some delays and compromises.

Two, with the end of the Cold War, the political controversies within multilateral bodies have, to a significant degree, shifted from core substantive issues to questions of power, payments, patronage, and priorities within the institutions themselves. As a result, within the UN West-West tensions have largely replaced East-West ones. While North-South issues continue to occupy much of the attention of multilateral institutions, the question of how to respond has sparked further debate among the western developed countries. In recent years, some of the sharpest differences among western member states in the UN have revolved around assessment scales, committee seats, Security Council composition, the choice of Secretary-General, and management reform. All of these somewhat arcane matters, in turn, have attracted the critical attention of legislators not only in the U.S., but in several allied countries as well.

Three, as relative U.S. power has grown through the years, most markedly in military capacity, it has become increasingly difficult to accommodate the resulting asymmetries in multilateral decision-making rules and procedures. American domestic critics regularly charge, with some justification, that the U.S. is far more influential outside of international bodies than within them. For their part, America's partners at times seem eager to grasp within multilateral institutions whatever recognition and glory escaped their reach in the real world outside. Their hesitation at times to protect U.S. flanks within these bodies encourages the tendency among skeptics in America to believe that others favor globalism and multilateralism, in part, as a way of circumventing U.S. dominance of alliance machinery and of constraining the exercise of its power.

Each of these concerns argues for a reassessment of the relationships among domestic, intra-EU, and multilateral processes, on both the political and constitutional levels. It is certainly fair to insist, as America's partners are prone to do, that the United States play by the rules. That principle – not the insistence that the U.S. share the substantive views of its allies (or vice versa) – is essential for allowing the multilateral system to function properly. At the same time, however, it should be recognized that the rules themselves may be due for an overhaul, for it increasingly appears that they are not uniformly understood on both sides of the Atlantic (or Pacific) and that they may not adequately reflect the implications either of European integration or of evolving West-West and North-South power relationships. At the working level, multilateral cooperation is a broadly accepted as the natural way to do business on issue after issue. But on higher political levels, the formal rules and procedures appear increasingly anachronistic, compelling choices at times between observing the rules and achieving results. Until this mismatch is rectified, through deep institutional and structural reform, the tendency will be for Europe to talk about rules and the U.S. results. They will continue to talk past each other, substituting competing caricatures for serious dialogue. Getting serious about what is serious would be a good place to start.[50] In this regard, the social and political cultures of Europe and of the United States are sufficiently distinct to cause frictions over tactics even when the strategic goals are shared.

50 William Wallace, (op. cit., pp. 8-9) attributes "the gap between increasing multilateral cooperation at the working level and increasing mutual irritation at the political and public level" to, among other factors, the failure of leaders on both sides of the Atlantic to educate "domestic audiences about the need for multilateral cooperation on international issues, while many opposition politicians have sought political advantage by attacking those in office for devoting too much time to compromising with foreigners." Taking the opposite tack, George Joffé has cautioned that "the crisis in the Balkans, questions about the future of NATO and the implications of changes within Europe itself for the transatlantic relationship have all highlighted policy areas where the superficial consensus across the Atlantic on occasion conceals growing differences." In Prins, op. cit., p. xi.

Petra Holtrup

The Lack of U.S. leadership in Climate Change Diplomacy

The Sudden Death of the Kyoto Protocol or: the U.S. Administration Pulled the Emergency Brake

The Kyoto Protocol is dead. This was the international reaction after the new U.S. administration under George W. Bush announced on March 13, 2001 its manifested unwillingness to ratify the Kyoto Protocol. The world had placed all its hopes on the Protocol as the only available tool to prevent imminent climate collapse[1] and the U.S. decision destroyed almost all hopes that this could be averted. Without the U.S., whose 4% of the population emits 25% of global Greenhouse gases (GHG) and the last world superpower with considerable political influence and financial resources to address climate change effectively on the global scale, one of the most important passengers had left the "negotiation train." This could be an invitation for other reluctant states to refuse action on climate change protection, as well. Climate change diplomacy seemed to arrive at a dead end.[2] Although the international press presented the U.S. announcement of the final death of the Kyoto Protocol as a deep surprise and shocking event to the world public, scholars of climate change diplomacy were not too surprised at all.[3] They were always aware of the great difficulties in agreeing on a binding agreement on GHG quantitative reduction targets. But nevertheless, even though the negotiation process had

1 At the beginning of the year 2001, the International Panel on Climate Change (IPPC) released its *Third Assessment Report on Global Warming*. The report draws a scenario of the potential impacts of unrestricted global warming that was worse than expected. According to IPCC, global warming will most likely cause a global temperature increase between 1.5 and 6.0 degrees Celsius, mainly due to human activities. Moreover, the global temperature is rising faster and is higher than in any time during the last 10,000 years, more than during the complete period of human civilization. See www.ippc.ch and James Barry, "Warming of earth raises new alarm", *International Herald Tribune* (*IHT*), January 23, 2001.

2 For a detailed overview of the climate change negotiation process, see www.unfccc.org

3 See for example David G. Victor, *The Collapse of the Kyoto Protocol and the Struggle to Slow Global Warming* (Princeton, 2001).

been always difficult, the main actor to blame for the current failure seemed to be easy to identify – the United States of America.

But this reflects only part of the American climate change action and is concentrated on its obvious blocking role in international climate change negotiations.[4] The USA has never led the negotiation on implementing the Kyoto Protocol. While at the first glance it appears to be justifiable to complain about the lack of American leadership, a more distant look shows that the Kyoto Protocol was always and still is far away from its political goal – the effective reduction of GHG. It is common sense that the reduction targets envisioned in Kyoto are too low to have a real effect on man made climate change. Not 5.2% but around an 80% reduction of GHG are needed by the end of this century to reverse global warming. The real push on GHG reduction is envisaged for the second phase of the Kyoto Protocol after 2012. But all signatory states already have major problems in fulfilling their commitments and the prognosis shows a growing energy demand related to higher GHG emission trends at least until 2020.[5] Data show that even Germany has, after years of reduction, rising emission trends since 2000 and needs to start major policy initiatives to fulfill its commitments.[6] In case Germany cannot fulfill its targets, the whole EU concept could fail. When 5% seems to be unachievable, then, how could 80% be realized? By focusing on the implementation of the Protocol, some scholars, especially in the US, criticize that useful time is wasted under the premise of more flexibility.[7] One could wonder, if the U.S. administration was finally brave enough to declare, what every other single government already thought, but was not willing to announce in public – the impracticality of the Kyoto Protocol for the USA and the international community.

Criticizing the USA for lacking leadership must take into account the role of domestic factors. It has to consider the characteristics of the political system, the political philosophy of the Constitution, and the inherent structures of political bargaining. U.S. leadership in climate change was mainly blocked by domestic factors, leading to a lack of political consensus at

---

4 From the American perspective, this evaluation is also true of the EU position.

5 The international energy agency provides several studies on this topic. See IEA, *World Energy Outlook 2000* (Paris 2000); Lee Schipper, Fridtjof Unander, and Céline Marie-Lilliu, "The IEA Energy Indicators: Analyzing Emissions on the Road from Kyoto," www.iea.org/envissu/cop6/eneins.pdf.

6 See Hans-Joachim Ziesing, "Höhere CO2 Emissionen im Jahre 2000," in *DIW-Wochenbericht* 6/01, www.diw.de/deutsch/publikationen/wochenberichte/jahrgang01/.

7 See for example David Victor, "Piety at Kyoto didn't cool the planet," *New York Times*, March 23, 2001; Frank N. Liard, "Just say no to greenhouse gas emissions targets," *Science and Technology Online*, Winter 2000; Daniel Sarewitz and Roger A. Pielke, Jr., *Prediction: Science, Decision Making and the Future of Nature*, (Washington D.C., 2000).

home.[8] After all, one conclusion seems to be clear. Kyoto, as interpreted by the EU, as a tool with a strong regulatory approach, limits and timetables, and reduced flexibility, was never meant to work for the USA, regardless of the changing political majority.[9]

The International Negotiation Train from Rio to The Hague

To understand the behavior of the U.S. administration, attention should be drawn to the general difficulties of climate change diplomacy so far. The climate change negotiation train has always been an uncomfortable journey. The international diplomatic efforts to address the danger of climate change are dealing with the most complex and demanding problem of international environmental policy ever. Climate change protection demands action in all branches of human life. As Hermann Ott puts it, this "issue involves nothing less than a technological and social revolution within the next 100 years."[10]

For a new topic, global warming surprisingly managed to start the international diplomacy train quite quickly and soon led to international negotiations on the prevention of climate change. In May 1992, almost 150 states signed the United Nations Framework Convention on Climate Change in Rio de Janeiro (Rio Convention), which came into force on March 21, 1994. It was the starting point for the follow-up diplomatic process. Whereas the Rio Convention was meant to be a very general political agreement on international action for climate change, the follow-up conferences tried to set up legally binding GHG reduction targets and timetables, as well as policies and measures for the effective implementation of climate change action.

Already during the preparation of the Rio Convention, the delegations' perspectives differed considerably on questions such as how the global warming process might affect nature and human beings, how far GHG limi-

8 Robert Paarlburg provides one of the few studies on domestic factors of US climate change leadership. See Robert Paarlburg, "Earth in Abeyance: Explaining Weak Leadership in the US International Environmental Policy," in *Eagle Adrift: American Foreign Policy at the End of the Century*, Robert J. Lieber, ed., 137-59 (New York, 1997). See also Paul G. Harris, "International Environmental Affairs and US Foreign Policy," in, *The Environment, International Relations and US Foreign Policy*, Paul G. Harris, ed., 3-44 (Washington D.C., 2001); Stephen Hopgood, *American Foreign Environmental Policy and the Power of State* (Oxford, 1998); and Walter Rosenbaum, *Environmental Politics and Policies* (Washington, 1998).

9 The following analysis will focus on the Bill Clinton and George W. Bush Administrations from 1993 until 2001. For analysis on the previous George Bush Administration and the U.S. climate strategy from the beginning see Hopgood, *American Foreign Environmental Policy and the Power of State*.

10 Ibid.

tations should go, and what policy strategies and measures would most likely invoke a reaction. Moreover, the whole debate was framed by the general question, whether a scientifically proven anthropogenic global warming effect exists at all.[11] Article 2 of the Rio Convention finally set the targets for the following years: "The ultimate objective of this Convention and any related legal instruments that the Conference of the Parties may adopt is to achieve, in accordance with the relevant provisions of the Convention, stabilization of greenhouse gas concentrations in the atmosphere at a level that would prevent dangerous anthropogenic interference with the climate system. Such a level should be achieved within a time-frame sufficient to allow ecosystems to adapt naturally to climate change, to ensure that food production is not threatened and to enable economic development to proceed in a sustainable manner."[12]

With this non-binding and flexible formulation, the Rio-Convention declared its process-oriented character. It also reflected the different national opinions and strategies, which became obvious in the duties outlined in Article 4. All signatory states must periodically publish national communications about their GHG emissions and their policies and measures. The developed countries and other countries listed in Annex I[13] should adopt policies and take measures on the mitigation of climate change by limiting their anthropogenic emissions of greenhouse gases and protecting and enhancing their greenhouse gas sinks and reservoirs on the basis of the year 1990. Developed countries were to take the lead in modifying longer-term trends in anthropogenic emissions consistent with the objective of the Convention and annually report their progress. The developed country Parties and other developed Parties included in Annex II[14] should provide new and additional financial resources to meet the agreed full costs incurred by developing country Parties in complying with their obligations. The formulation remained rather vague and left considerable potential for individual interpretation by the signatory Parties. Industrialized states were supposed to follow the target of GHG emission reduction; developing countries instead simply needed to report on GHG emissions, but only in case of support by OECD countries. Shortly after Rio, it became obvious that stronger and more specific regulations on GHG

---

11 Even though the Second and Third IPPC reports concluded that there is evidence of discernible human influence on global change, the international debate about the reliance of climate change models and the role of anthropogenic impact are still mistrusted, especially by some scientists and politicians in the USA. For the scientific and political reaction towards the Third IPPC report results see Philip P. Pan, "Scientists issue dire predictions on warming," *Washington Post*, January, 23, 2001.

12 For the full text of the UNFCCC see www.unfccc.int/text/resource/conv/conv_004.html.

13 Annex I countries are states, which were members of the OECD in 1992, as well as countries in transition.

14 Annex II countries are states of the OECD as well as the European Community.

emissions were needed. The international diplomacy train set off for new negotiations.

The diplomatic follow-up journey is structured by seven conferences of the parties (COP): in Berlin (1995), Geneva (1996), Kyoto (1997), Buenos Aires (1998), Bonn (1999), The Hague (2000) and Bonn (2001), and finally Marrakech (2001). While the Berlin and Geneva COPs were meant to be breakpoints for the next intermediate climate protection steps, with the Kyoto Protocol, the climate change negotiation train arrived at a new station.[15] For the first time, legally binding emission targets for Annex I countries for the post-2000 period had been developed. They committed themselves to reduce their GHG emissions of six different gases by 5.2% between 2008 and 2012 based on the reference year of 1990. Considering that most countries still show rising GHG emissions of around 25% until 2010, the actual reduction need is much higher, around 30% in average.[16] The individual emission cuts vary between nations and nation groups (like the EU). The national delegations not only agreed on specific timetables and reduction targets, but they also developed a broad catalog of policy strategies for implementation.

After long negotiations and several "almost" deadlocks, the main political key to international agreement on the Kyoto Protocol was finally found in the establishment of flexibility. Under the premise of flexibility, the contracting parties agreed on strategies of international emission trading, allowing industrialized countries to buy and sell emissions credits among themselves. They would also be able to acquire emission reduction units by financing certain projects in other states (Joint implementation, JI). Moreover the Kyoto Protocol established a so-called clean development mechanism (CDM), which enables industrialized countries to finance emissions-reduction projects in developing countries and take the credit for this on their own reduction account. Furthermore, the improvement of energy efficiency, the reform of the energy and transportation sector, and, especially important from the U.S. and Russian point of view, the role of forests and agricultural land as carbon sinks was intensively discussed. To come into force, the Kyoto Protocol required a double majority, which meant at least 55 signatory states, as well as the inclusion of developed countries responsible for at least 55% of the total 1990 carbon dioxide emissions. Considering that the USA alone is responsible for almost 25% of the global GHG emissions, the participation of the USA in the Kyoto Protocol was of great importance.

Although flexibility seemed a tempting way out of the diplomatic gridlock, it became the new stumbling block for the continuing negotiations.

---

15 See the following for the most detailed and best analyses about the Kyoto Protocol. Herman Ott and Sebastian Oberthuer, *The Kyoto Protocol: International Climate Change for the 21st Century* (Berlin, 1999); David R. Victor, *The Collapse of the Kyoto Protocol*.

16 See www.unfccc.org.

Even though flexibility offered every state a reasonable amount of freedom to set national climate change policy in respect to its specific needs and conditions, the diplomatic follow-up process would show that every actor interpreted the limits of the use of flexibility to a different degree. The controversy broke out over two major Kyoto mechanisms. First, it concentrated on the more technical questions about the institutional organization, monitoring, implementation control, verification and enforcement mechanisms, and the reliance and effectiveness of certain mechanisms, especially the credit of sinks (like forests and land use measures) for national GHG reduction budgets. Second, the debate centered on the question to what extent each state could use the Kyoto mechanisms to reduce its own emissions account.[17]

Since COP 4 in Buenos Aires (November 1998), the international debate concentrated on the implementation of the Kyoto Protocol and the narrow versus wider interpretation of the use of the Kyoto mechanisms. At COP 6 in The Hague, the parties should have adopted specific rules for all mechanisms, but all hopes were finally destroyed. Despite intense diplomatic consultations and exhausting multilateral and bilateral talks, Jan Pronk, the conference chairman and Environmental Minister of the Netherlands, finally declared the failure of COP 6 on November 25, 2000. The final disappointment came with the announcement by President George W. Bush not to ratify the Kyoto Protocol. Because of the importance of the U.S. for combating global warming, the Bush Administration calculated that with its rejection, the rest of the world would follow. But this calculation did not work out. The European Union, for the first time in a strong and united leadership role, pushed the follow-up process forward and left the USA internationally isolated. With the follow-up conferences in Bonn (COP 6-2) and Marrakech (COP 7), the delegations agreed on most critical questions surrounding operational details and on strengthening implementation and control. The U.S. government still stood firm on its resolve to abandon the Protocol. Although a U.S. delegation participated in each conference, it was not directly involved in the negotiation process.

Despite this mid-term success it remains to be seen whether Bonn and Marrakech will provide the beginning of an effective international response to global warming or whether Bush was right in criticizing the protocol as "fatally flawed." Environmentalists had already criticized the Protocol as weak. With the final agreement, the emission reductions have been watered down to less than 1.8%, according to the World Wide Fund for Nature (WWF), instead of the envisaged 5.2%.[18]

---

17 For information on the very complicated debate about the Kyoto mechanisms, see Ott and Oberthuer.

18 See *Earth Negotiation Bulletin*, vol. 12, no. 189; Miranda A. Schreurs, "Bonn 2001: Saving Kyoto, " *German-American Relations and the Presidency of George W. Bush*, Topics AICGS, Germany 2001.

The USA – The "Bad Guy" of Climate Change Diplomacy?

During the entire time, the U.S. negotiation strategy remained remarkably stable. Economic and industrial interests and the need to consider the domestic discussion, primarily set by Congress, mainly drove its position and political options. Despite all the goodwill at the beginning of the Clinton Administration to invent a new period of global leadership in climate change, it soon became clear that the U.S. could not fulfill its commitments to reduce domestic GHG emission by 2000. In fact, in contrast to reducing GHG emission, they are still rising by around 1.5% each year. Driven by strong domestic forces and antagonists, Clinton had to present a more moderate climate policy that tried to consider domestic interests and constraints as much as possible. This led to the loss of leadership internationally.

The U.S. delegation followed its domestically effective environmental practices of a flexible, market orientated policy approach. It referred to three major pillars: environmental integrity, cost-effectiveness, and environmental effectiveness. The first premise aimed to ensure that the claimed reductions really occurred. Reporting on compliances would therefore be very strict. The second premise focused on market mechanisms and the unlimited use of sinks by the Protocol implementation. The third premise stressed the conviction that all mechanisms envisaged under the Protocol must prove their effectiveness for reducing the climate change effect.[19] Flexibility was the key of the U.S. negotiation strategy. It allowed for action without rigid timetables and guaranteed action on the basis of the least cost principle. This included a very broad interpretation of the use of Kyoto mechanisms, which should not be limited to Annex I countries.

The U.S. strategy stands in clear contrast to that of the EU. The European strategy was mainly structured by the use of the precautionary principle and the support of a rigid quantitative reduction target policy. The European position, however, does not earn the reputation of immense credibility because counties in the EU tend to use the flexible policy mechanisms to a great extent. Nevertheless, the EU tried to present itself as an honest ally of the developing countries in insisting that a serious national climate change strategy must follow the principle of first in first out. Applied to global warming, this implies that the one who started global warming is also obliged to be the first to start the "cooling process." This leads to the conviction that at least the major amount of GHG reduction (more than 50%) should be realized within Annex I countries. The EU countries, therefore, wanted to restrict the use of flexibility.[20]

---

19 See "Statement of Frank E. Loy," in: *Sustainable Climate Protection Policies*, Friedemann Mueller and Alexander Ochs, eds., 19-26 (Ebenhausen, 2000).

20 The role of sinks for GHG reduction is still one of the most controversial issues. Whereas the USA demands the intense use of sinks for meeting reduction commit-

The Importance of Domestic Factors

Regardless of the obvious differences in dealing with climate change during the Clinton and the new Bush Administrations, there is a certain continuity manifested mainly in the political and social system of the USA. These conditions framed the U.S. climate change diplomacy over the last decade and continue to today.[21] Looking from outside, the USA has always played the role of the main brakeman, supported by some allies of the so-called JUSSCANZ group, consisting of Japan, the United States, Switzerland, Canada, Australia and New Zealand. And the American government was always rather successful in getting results consistent with its own interests because the other states were keen to keep the biggest single emitter of GHGs on the negotiation train. The central domestic factor of U.S. climate change policy is the structure of the energy system, which is answering higher energy demands by providing inexpensive and reliable energy resources.[22]

The Characteristics of the American Economic System

The unlimited access to cheap energy is strongly related to the structure of the American economic system and the overall transport geography. Most critics of the Protocol fear that its implementation would reduce economic growth or reinforce the economic decline.[23] The perception of the economi-

---

ments, the EU doubts the reliability of sinks and criticizes the lack of compliance control mechanisms. Indeed a study carried out by the International Institute of Applied Research Analysis (IIASA) supports the EU interpretation. See www.iiasa.ac.at/Admin/INF/PR/PR-00.o8.25.html .

21 Information given in this and the following sections are results from numerous interviews with officials from the American government, Congress and NGOs in Washington D.C. and Berlin during 1999 – 2001. They are not personally quoted. A very helpful and brief overview regarding the systematic factors of decision-making in foreign environmental policy of the U.S. is provided by Carrie Anderson, "Cultural and Systematic Differences: Factors that influence Americans and Germans in Environmental Policy Making," in *Sustainable Climate Protection Policies*, Friedemann Mueller and Alexander Ochs, eds. (Ebenhausen, Stifftung Wissenschaft und Politik, 2000), 104-10.

22 This is most obviously shown by the U.S. debate concerning domestic energy shortages in 2001, which were answered by enlarging the market instead of inventing new energy effective technology and launching a restructuring and modernization of the energy market. For further information see www.eia.doe.gov/neic/press/press176.html, ftp://ftp.eia.doe.gov/pub/pdf/international/0484(2001).pdf.

23 As a matter of fact, cheep energy frees capital to be used in investment and employment generation. In contrast to the USA, high energy prices in Europe do make efficiency profitable, but still draw away capacities that could be used productively elsewhere. This is a trade-off that few in the EU are willing to admit.

cally hostile character of the Protocol can be found in various statements and resolutions from Congress, from various representatives of industrial and energy lobby groups, and from administration officials during official Congress hearings and press releases.[24] Even the Clinton Administration tried to invent climate action and programs that would not introduce too harsh a burden on the American economy and the consumer. George W. Bush followed this strategy in his rejection of Kyoto in a most obvious way. In a response to a March 6, 2001 letter from Republican Senators Hagel, Helms, Craig, and Roberts, Bush answered: "At a time when California has already experienced energy shortages, and other Western states are worried about price and availability of energy this summer, we must be very careful not to take actions that could harm consumers. This is especially true given the incomplete state of scientific knowledge of the causes of, and solutions to, global climate change and the lack of commercially available technologies for removing and storing carbon dioxide."[25]

Another factor of major influence is the strong market driven character of the American economic system. Liberal ideas of market forces and natural regulations dominate. They are especially reflected in the American focus on environmental policies, where market mechanisms of emission trading and market based regulations play a major role. This gives another explanation for the strong U.S. interest to introduce as much flexibility as possible into the Kyoto Protocol and to implement the Kyoto mechanisms as often as possible.

Social Framework Conditions – Particular Interests and the NIMBY (Not in My Backyard) Synonym

With the importance of cheap energy supplies, consumption, and the structure of the U.S. energy market, it is not surprising that shareholder and lobby groups in energy interests are presumed to be the most influential players against the climate change negotiations.[26] The open structure of the American political system provides these groups numerous ways of participation and influence on the political agenda setting.

---

24 A good overview and collection of the most important testimonies, committee meetings, and resolutions is provided by the National Council on Sciences and the Environment, *Global Climate Change: Congressional Responses*, http://www.cnie.org/nle/clim-7/ebgcccon.html. See also Congressional Research Service, Report to Congress 98-664: *Global Climate Change: Congressional Concern About "Back Door" Implementation of the 1997 U.N. Kyoto Protocol*, http://www.cnieorg/nle/clim-16.html.

25 See http://www.whitehouse.gov/news/releases/2001/03/20010314.html

26 See in particular the analysis of Robert Falkner, "Business Conflict and US International Environmental Policy: Ozone, Climate, and Biodiversity," in *The Environment*, 157-77.

Even before the climate change protocol was negotiated in Kyoto, the U.S. Senate released the non-binding Byrd (D-WV) - Hagel (R-NB) resolution,[27] named after its two bi-partisan initiators, cosponsored by 60 votes, and passed on July 25, 1997, by a 95-0 vote. This resolution demanded that the USA should not sign any protocol, unless it also included "new specific scheduled commitments to limit or reduce greenhouse gas emissions for Developing Country Parties within the same compliance period," which became known as the meaningful participation of developing countries. William R. Moomaw, of the Fletcher School of Economics, takes it for granted that the U.S. negotiation strategy to insure the meaningful participation of developing countries is the result of a carefully orchestrated campaign by the U.S. energy companies and their allies. From his interpretation, these groups managed to win Congress' support by fostering the perception that the USA will incur a competitive disadvantage from the current regulations, unless the developing countries are not obliged to undertake national policies on GHG reduction or at least stabilization. Moomow does not see this as a fair altruistic argumentation, but rather as a clever strategy of the U.S. energy lobby to avoid painful policy reform of the energy market at home.[28]

The big oil, coal, and manufacturing companies as well as concerned labor unions have been well organized in Washington from the beginning, and try to influence the political decision making process via various political channels and press campaigns. The coal and utility industries are affiliated in organizations like the Global Climate Coalition, a misleading name for a forceful anti-climate policy group, or the National Coal Association. They oppose carbon taxes, flood the White House with letters, undertake an intense communication process with sympathetic supporters in Congress and the Administration, gain access to hearings and working groups committees, and even send representatives to the climate negotiations to prevent the delegation from acting against their interests.[29] The powerful influence of these groups has become very obvious with George W. Bush's latest decision not to introduce CO2 caps on energy power plants, as regulated by the Clean Air Act. This is mostly regarded as a first political gift to the most supportive contributors of Bush's election campaign, the oil and coal industries and the conservative wing of the GOP.[30]

---

27 See http://www.microtech.com.au/daily/byrd.htm

28 See William R. Moomaw, "Why Wait for the Senate?," in *Sustainable Climate Protection Policies*, 51-57.

29 A detailed overview is provided by Paul G. Harris, *Understanding America's Climate Change Policy: Realpolitik, Pluralism, and Ethical Norms*, OCEES Research Paper No. 15, June 1998 or Norman J. Vig, "Presidential leadership and the Environment: from Reagan to Clinton," in *Environmental Policy in the 1990s. Reform or Reaction?*, 3rd ed., 95-118, Norman Vig and Michael E. Kraft, eds. (Washington D.C., 1997).

30 See *Time Magazine*, April 9, 2001, vol. 157, no. 14, Special Report: Global Warming. Others argue that this perception is too simple. The natural gas industry, which stood

Although the environmental counterpart, the green lobby, is equally well organized and tries to use the same ways of influencing the government, it does not gain equal recognition in Congress and the Administration. In contrast to the horror scenario of American economic and social decline in case of the Kyoto Protocol's implementation, environmental groups quote opinion polls that should reflect the opposite public view. According to these surveys, 75% of the American citizens consider global warming a "very serious" or "fairly serious" problem, and 67% demand further action. Unfortunately, these groups often forget to quote the second part of these polls, where it is stated that only 48% are willing to pay 25 cents more for a gallon of gasoline, and around 50% are not willing to spend more money on utility bills or to risk their job. Moreover the reluctance to share the burden of climate change has increased by approximately 15% between 1991 and 2001.[31]

The Political System – The Freedom of the Citizen and the Divided Government

In contrast to the European tradition of social welfare, a regulatory policy approach, and the conviction that the state is responsible for its citizens, the American political tradition is mainly influenced by its revolutionary roots. The framers of the American Constitution regarded the freedom of the citizen as the supreme priority. Therefore, they incorporated a strong element of federalism and separation of powers to protect the citizens against the abuse of power and limitations of personal rights and freedom by a superior government.[32] The government is the servant of its citizens, not the patriarch. As a result, the Congress, as the main representation of state and regional interests, plays a major role in agenda setting and decision-making in foreign environmental policy.[33]

---

to gain most from CO2 caps, gave much more money to the Bush campaign than the oil industry. The current strategy shows more a lack of alternatives and of time. This again reveals deficits of the Clinton presidency, where not enough action on renewing the Energy market was undertaken.

31 Ibid.

32 From the perspective of the early American immigrants, the European governmental systems represented exactly this. The overall visible and sensible governmental oversight and control was for many the main reason to leave Europe and build up a new state system and society in the United States. See Theodore J. Lowi, and Benjamin Ginsberg, *American Government: Freedom and Power*, 4th edition, (New York: W.W. Norton 1996).

33 See Robert Paarlberg, "Earth in Abeyance: Explaining Weak Leadership in the US International Environmental Policy," in *Eagle Adrift: American Foreign Policy at the End of the Century*, Robert J. Lieber, 135-59 (New York, 1997).

The constitutional importance of national and personal concerns leads to the public belief that the state should reduce its influence to a minimum and policy initiatives and implementation should follow a most flexible bottom-up approach. Americans are thus much harder to convince about the need for governmental regulations. The structure of the Kyoto Protocol very strongly represents the European style and supports a top-down approach, which is obviously doomed to earn intense dislike from the American public and its representatives in Congress. This is especially true for regulations, which supercede national sovereignty. Unfortunately, this is generally the U.S. public perception of UN resolutions and treaties. The other side of this coin is that the U.S. prefers bilateral diplomacy, where one legitimate state makes agreements with another, to multilateral diplomacy, where a "legitimacy deficit" is perceived.

In case of climate policy, the U.S. Constitution assigns the Congress decisive responsibility in implementation process of international treaties, especially when it comes to writing and setting environmental legislation, appropriating, tax purposes, and in ratifying international agreements, like the Kyoto Protocol. Especially during the last decade, the interest of the U.S. Congress in foreign and international policy issues has continuously diminished and led to a concentration on domestic policies. At the same time, the perception of the United Nations as an overloaded, money wasting, ineffective and bureaucratic instrument of the developing countries appeared. Considering the growing UN hostility of the U.S. Congress, it becomes clear that the chances to ratify the Kyoto Protocol were never high.

The Congressional elections in 1994 and 1996 brought a major transformation of the political balance and established a divided government. Based on the "Contract with America"[34] announced by new GOP majority leader Newt Gingrich, Congress gained a new self-confidence in foreign policy matters. As a result, climate change policies faced stronger obstacles in Congress. With the release of the Byrd - Hagel resolution in 1997, Congress clearly rejected the 1995 Berlin Mandate, which excluded developing countries from emissions targets and deadlines. The meaningful participation of developing countries appeared to become the major obstacle between the Clinton Administration and Congress on the one hand and the U.S. delegation and the international community on the other. As long as there was no guarantee of meaningful participation, there would not be any ratification by Congress and no agreement by the U.S. delegation to climate action enforcement under the Protocol either. As stated earlier, a reliable judgment on the role of the "meaningful participation argument" in the U.S. climate change policy is not easy to make. Certainly it offered different actors a convenient excuse for non-action. During the international COPs, the U.S. delegation could refer to the hostile position of Congress on this matter and could

34 See http://www.house.gov/house/Contract/CONTRACT.html

explain the delay of ratification by the national political gridlock. Congress continued to insist on the Protocol's resolution as the major precondition of ratification. Both the executive and the legislative branches knew that this strategy was a reliable tool to prevent any agreement within the COP. The dispute about meaningful participation foreshadowed for years the final breakdown of COP6 in The Hague and the opting out of the USA.

Ever since the emergence of divided government, the relationship between the two branches on climate change matters reached a low point. The intergovernmental and informal bipartisan communication and bargaining process worsened. Governmental agencies that were concerned with Kyoto, like EPA, OSTP, the State Department and CEQ, became targets of the Congressional campaign against Clinton and his "allies" as well as Congress' efforts to curtail bureaucratic power.[35] The lack of communication and the growing disinterest in one another's business led to the situation that administration witnesses saw their invitation to hearings not as a chance to convince the Congress of their political strategy and initiate a constructive dialog, but rather as a defendant who must defend his criminal offense. The Republican majority, moreover, structured hearings to reflect its own interest. The hostility of the Republican Congress against Kyoto can be seen by the title of hearings held during the Kyoto negotiation process as well as by invited witnesses. Most witnesses were known for their anti-climate protection position. Congressional hearings were no longer meant to serve as a more or less neutral place for fact-findings, but emerged as a place to support the already manifested opinion. And with intense media attention, hearings could be used as an effective tool for presentation and promotion of this position to the public. Therefor the selection of witnesses and topics became of major importance.[36]

Congressional staffers reported a similar problem in information meetings and luncheons. These more or less casual and informal meetings, which were meant to set up an open exchange of political views and strategies, were more and more dominated by the political polarization between the White House and the Hill as well as between the two parties. The meetings were either exclusively attended by supporters or opponents of climate policy, depending on who was invited and the topic to be discussed. Thus, these meetings only helped to polarize the discussion and to foster particular interests.

Additionally the failure of Madeline Albright's post-election promise to reinvent an open and constructive communication process especially between

35 See Michael E. Kraft, "US Environmental Policy and Politics: From the 1960s to the 1990s," in *Environmental Politics and Policy, 1960s-1990s*, Otis L. Graham Jr., ed, 17-42 (2000).

36 One of the few publications on this topic is provided by Benito Mueller, *Congressional Climate Change Hearings: Comedy or Tragedy?* (Oxford, 2000), http://www.wolfson.ox.ac.uk/~mueller.

the State Department, which was in charge of international climate change negotiation, and the concerned Congressional committees supported the gridlock situation between the Executive and Legislative branches. Those familiar with the intra-governmental communication process also criticized the general leadership in the State Department. Albright was not interested and left the issue to the Under Secretary level, thus further weakening the Administration's ability to deal with Congress.

To blame the divided government in particular for political gridlock and climate change ice-age in Executive – Congressional relations does not completely reflect reality, although it is the main pitfall of U.S. climate change policy. The international climate protection record of the U.S. had been damaged even before 1994. During the election campaign, Clinton and Gore had promised a new era of environmental leadership. During his first days in office, Clinton announced a new global environmental leadership and started to make changes. He abolished the White House Council on Competitiveness under Vice President Dan Quayle, that was established by President George Bush, and introduced the White House Office of Environmental Policy,[37] which would coordinate interagency cooperation on environmental matters. High-level positions throughout the Executive were given to well known former environmental activists, such as Timothy Wirth, the Under Secretary of State for Global Affairs, Bruce Babbit, Secretary of Interior, or Carol Browner, head of EPA. Environmental activists found open ears for their concerns at the White House and direct political channels were established. In 1993, the Clinton Administration announced to the UN that the U.S. would resume leadership in world climate affairs. Clinton promised the reduction of GHGs at the 1990 level by the year 2000. But Congress, which was still ruled by a Democratic majority refused to agree on a broad energy tax proposal. The reduction of taxes was and still is the main issue of public concern, and Clinton and George W. Bush both promised this during their campaigns. Any political initiative that inherits tax rise will be a non-starter in Congress, no matter if there is a divided government or not.[38]

Climate policy is not an issue exclusively structured by party preferences, but is also effected by state and regional concerns of the representatives and their constituencies. In fact the harshest criticism of Clinton's proposal did not come from a Republican but from Senator Robert C. Byrd, a Democrat from West Virginia, a state dominated by coal interests. Still under the impression of the severe economic recession of 1990 – 1992, the new

---

37 During the Clinton presidency, other intergovernmental councils and working groups, such as the Council on Sustainable Development and the Climate Change Task Force, were set up. For a detailed analysis see Norman J. Vig, "Presidential Leadership and the Environment: from Reagan to Clinton."

38 See the statement of Kyle Mulhall, Associate Counsel for House Minority Leader Richard Gebhardt, Democratic Party, in Müller and Ochs, 69-71.

Clinton Administration was forced to prevent any new financial and social burden from the domestic industry and citizens, and changed its strategy to more deregulatory and voluntary action proposals. Without this tax proposal, Clinton was unable to meet its commitments made to the UN. The U.S. lost its leadership in international climate diplomacy before it began.

A U.S. Climate Change Policy – Illusion or Reality?

The analysis so far has shown that climate policy in the U.S. had to face major impediments, especially those caused by a hostile Congress. Nevertheless the Clinton Administration was trying to initiate some action at home without too much involvement of the Congress, which considering its power proved to be quite difficult.[39] A clear sign of the personal concern of Clinton and his Vice President Al Gore for global warming might be found by the fact that both were believed to be the best informed people in government on this issue. They had weekly formal and informal meetings, luncheons, and were knowledgeable about the technical and scientific details about climate change. An intense interagency communication process was set up under the management of a troika, consisting of the Deputy Chairman of the National Security Council, the chair of the Council of Environmental Quality, and the Chair of the National Economic Council.

To promote the intergovernmental coordination, public awareness and information about climate change, Clinton initiated the Climate Change Task Force under the President's Council on Sustainable Development in 1997.[40] Todd Stern, the Clinton Administration's coordinator of climate change policy became the main manager of climate change policy in the U.S. Although the State Department coordinated the international negotiation strategy, the important scientific and technical questions of reduction strategies as well as the real design of policies and measures were under the oversight of the troika and mainly developed out of negotiations between OSTP, DOE and EPA. Numerous meetings were held on different levels within the Executive. The day-to-day discussion took place at the Assistant Secretary level, with different chairs responsible for specific issues. The State Department was in charge of the general cooperation process, whereas DOE dealt more with technical and specific questions.

Although the interagency bargaining process was very intense, it was not free from dispute. The front line ran between the EPA, CEQ and the State Department on the one side and economic agencies like CEA and Treasury

39 The following information is derived from the author's interviews with staff of the executive branch in Washington D.C., Boulder, CO and Berlin during 1999-2000.

40 See http://www2.whitehouse.gov/PCSD/tforce/cctf/index.html.

on the other. While EPA and State were mostly concerned about image and reducing global warming, the opposite side was always interested in social and economic costs. OSTP stood in between as an advocate for the development and implementation of new technologies by following a social and economically low-cost approach. The DOE played an ambivalent role, divided by its internal contrasting interests. Some departments in the DOE were advocates of the Energy industry and therefore not in favor of strong emission reduction strategies, while others were mostly concerned about the environment and the promotion of energy taxes and new technologies.

Especially before the Kyoto negotiations, the conflicting interests between the agencies complicated the development of a sound U.S. policy strategy on climate change. They were forced to balance the interests of economic growth and prosperity and environmental protection at the same time.

Although the Clinton Administration's range of action was very limited during the whole presidency, it launched a number of national initiatives. In October 1993, it announced a U.S. Climate Change Action Plan, which was meant to be the main piece of domestic climate change initiatives. The Action Plan gathered together about fifty existing and new federal programs based on the strategy of voluntary, flexible, and cost-effective partnerships between the U.S. government and businesses. Moreover, the Clinton Administration introduced a win-win program to develop and deploy energy-efficient technologies and to foster the development and broader use of renewable energy. Although the Action Plan has shown some progress in the establishment of public-private partnerships and small-scale policies, it fell short of meeting its goal to reduce GHG emissions. Improvement of the Action Plan did not arise because of its relatively low political priority in comparison to other actions. More resources were invested into the U.S. Global Change Research Program (USGCRP),[41] which mainly focused on the development of a predictive understanding of global change and negotiations to establish a binding international agreement.[42] In comparison to the budget of the Global Change Action Plan, the annual appropriations for USGCRP were

41 The outcomes of the USGCR were also heavily criticized. The main task of the Research Plan was "to gain predictive understanding of the interactive physical, geological, chemical, biological and social processes that regulate the total Earth system and, hence establish the scientific basis for national and international policy formulations and decision." While the program put tremendous scientific work and financial resources into the prediction of global change, it failed to provide any advise for policy makers. A detailed analysis is provided by Roger A. Pielke, *Policy History of the US Global Change Research Program: Part I, Administrative Development* and *Part II, Legislative Process, Submitted to Global Environmental Change*, October 25, 1999, as well as Roger R. Pielke, "Usable Information for Policy: An Appraisal of the US Global Change Research Program," *Policy Sciences* 28, (1995), 39-77.

42 See Ronald D. Brunner and Roberta Klein, "Harvesting Experience: A Reappraisal of the US Climate Action Plan," *Policy Sciences* 32 (1999), 133-161.

ten times higher. And while the budget on USGCRP increased annually, the budget of the Climate Change Action Plan constantly diminished.[43]

In 1998 the Administration started a $6.3 billion program of tax incentives and investment in energy efficiency, called the Climate Change Technology Initiative. Unfortunately, Congress largely rejected this program by its actions on the 1999 fiscal year budget. For fiscal year 2001, Clinton proposed $1.4 billion in investments for efficient and clean energy, which was a 30% increase over fiscal year 2000. This included funding for energy from biomass, which the President promoted at a public event at USDA in August 1999, funding for energy efficient housing, which the President launched at an event in Los Angeles in May 1998, and funding for highly efficient automobiles – the Partnership for a New Generation of Vehicles – which the Administration launched several years ago and is well on the way to producing cars with three times the fuel efficiency and the same comfort, safety, and performance. Additionally, Clinton initiated a 21st Century truck program. These major proposals in biomass, buildings, and cars and trucks are supposed to greatly reduce U.S. emissions and improve air quality and energy security. Finally, in 1999, the President issued an executive order aimed at the largest consumer of energy in the U.S., the government itself. Each federal government agency is required to reduce its GHG emissions by 30% below 1990 levels by the year 2010.[44]

Despite these smooth and still reluctant actions on climate change, Congress still heavily criticized the Administration for trying to implement the Protocol through the "back door." During the follow up process of the Kyoto conference, every single action, which could be connected to climate change action, especially on energy efficiency and energy saving, was attacked by Congress and faced possible rejection.[45] Because of the continuing polarization between the two branches, Kyoto finally became a no-no in Congress. This is even more interesting considering the fact that, despite the hostility of Congress, a growing dynamic on effective climate change action started from the grass-roots level of single national and multinational industries, companies, municipalities and states.[46] This leads to the careful presumption that without using the word "Kyoto Protocol" in connection with environmental action, much more would be possible in Congress.

43 Ibid.

44 For a detailed listing on domestic action on climate change, see www.epa.gov/globalwarming/actions/national/administration/index.html.

45 A good overview of this issue is *Global Climate Change: Congressional Responses.*

46 See Moomaw.

Conclusion – The New Bush Administration and the Journey Ahead

After George W. Bush officially announced his non-support of the Kyoto Protocol, the international community expressed surprise and spoke of a disastrous effect on international action against global warming. This is not justifiable; a less emotional perspective suggests that astonishment and shock was out of place. In terms of the political outcome during the last ten years, nothing essential has really been changed. Even before the Kyoto Protocol had been signed, the discussion centered on questions of flexibility, preventing harm to national economy and social standards, and fairness with regard to other countries obligations. National and regional constituency interests mainly drove Congress, the main actor of the U.S. domestic and foreign climate change policy. The divided government since 1994 has worsened this situation, but has not changed it substantially. The chance of U.S. ratification of the Protocol was always low. Some European insiders of the diplomatic process even accused the U.S. delegation of enlarging the negotiation topics to such an extent and complexity that in the end the whole process was glutted with topics. In overloading the process, the parties were unable to find sound solutions to the problem. Contrarily, U.S. officials accused the European delegation of never listened carefully to the its position and then interpreting the Protocol agreements in its own interest regardless of the concerns expressed by the U.S. delegation.

Nevertheless there are accountable and visible factors to be considered. Summing up what was analyzed before, the Kyoto Protocol never had a real chance to be ratified by the U.S. Congress due to its central role in that matter, the dominance of particular interests and lobbies, and the need for a 2/3 majority in Congress to pass the Protocol. Clinton refused to send it to Congress because he knew that he would never get 66 Senators to vote for it. In the end, George W. Bush only announced in public what had been fact for a long time.

Since George W. Bush has been in office, shifts can be observed, which change the overall picture of the U.S. debate on climate change. Bush presents more loudly his dislike of climate change policy and has introduced several actions to move backwards on this issue. Everyone who had listened carefully to Bush's election campaign should not be surprised either. He always clearly expressed his negative opinion about Kyoto.[47] In addition, after the election, there have been important changes inside the government organization that show that the new administration is obviously much less in-

47 See Douglas Jehl, "US Going Empty Handed to Meeting on Global Warming," *New York Times*, March 29, 2001. Additional reports are found in the *International Herald Tribune* (*IHT*), March 29, 2001, *Christian Science Monitor*, March 29, 2001, and the *Washington Post* (*WP*), March 29, 2001.

terested in climate change than its predecessor. Until recently there had not been any announcement on any revised strategy on climate change. Christine Todd Whitman, head of EPA, was only allowed to state authoritatively that the Administration's position on global warming was being reviewed at the cabinet level. The new administration, after more than four months in office, was still reviewing a new strategy under the coordination of Mr. Edson, who reports to both the NSC under Rice and the NEC under Lindsey. The White House, EPA, State Department, DOE, DOI, and USDA are all involved. Nevertheless, six weeks before the new negotiation in Bonn started in July 2001, there was no U.S. proposal on the table. Besides some announcements on further research and some new programs on technology development, nothing is known about the general direction of the strategy outside Washington. This brings forth a humbling picture on U.S. climate change strategy – currently there does not seem to be any.

All observers are focusing on the role of Whitman. But her position is weakened by two factors. First, she has to face a strong anti-Kyoto coalition in the Cabinet, led by the President and his White House Staff, Vice President Dick Cheney, Energy Secretary Spencer Abraham, and National Security Advisor Condoleezza Rice.[48] Second, she plays a weaker role inside the Cabinet because the EPA still has no Cabinet rank. This goes back even to the Clinton Administration, when, on February 2, 1994, the House, by a vote of 191-227, defeated a motion to consider H.R. 3425, which would have elevated the head of the EPA to Cabinet level status. It failed primarily because of objections that it would not have allowed floor consideration of an amendment requiring the EPA to prepare cost- and risk-benefit analyses of its regulatory actions.[49] Furthermore, the position of Whitman seems to be weakened by non-information and non-bargaining with the White House. Even while Whitman was still presenting the U.S. strategy on Kyoto as existing policy, the Bush cabinet had already opted out.[50]

It is more interesting, however, to observe a slight, but steady change in Congress' position. Under Clinton, the hostile Congress had been the main brake of national performance and therefore also of international negotiations; this role now seems to be changing. Although George W. Bush keeps referring to the people's denial of the Kyoto Protocol and the strong opposi-

48 See Amy Goldstein and Eric Pianin, "Hill Pressure Fueled Bush's Emissions Shift," *WP*, March 15, 2001, and Brad Knickerbocker and Francine Kiefer, "The Costs of Bowing out of the Global-Warming Treaty," *Christian Science Monitor*, March 29, 2001.

49 For a detailed analysis on that topic see http://www.cnie.org/nle/rsk-2.html .

50 The Bush strategy could be also observed in the press. See Eric Pianin, "EPA Chief Lobbied on Warming Before Bush's Emissions Switch," *WP*, March 27, 2001, Douglas Jehl, "U.S: Stance on Warming Puts Whitman in Tense Spot," *New York Times*, March 30, 2001, or Douglas Jehl and Andrew C. Revkin, "President Cancels Clean-Air Vow," *IHT*, March 15, 2001.

tion of Congress, the opposite situation is emerging. The anti-climate change front in Congress is no longer so clearly identifiable. As a matter of fact, a growing number of Representatives are shifting towards a more relaxed position. This shift already appeared during the last year of the Clinton presidency and now there are some actions, which affirm this change.

The positively observed effects of grass-roots level action mostly drive this change. A growing number of industries and companies, as well as municipalities and states have launched a wide variety of actions concerning climate chance. Now they want their investment to pay off, which means that they trust the government to continue to set economic, financial and tax incentive, and to reward climate change action. The coal and energy utility industry remains a financially powerful lobby group, but it has become an increasingly isolated opinion that no longer represents the general public interest. On April 6, 2001, the Senate approved a bipartisan measure sponsored by Senator John F. Kerry (D-MA) and James M. Jeffords (R-VT.) to restore over the coming decade $4.5 billion in funds for climate change programs that the Bush Administration had sought to cut. It also intends to broaden the authority of the State Department to enable the U.S. "to fully engage with the international community in on-going and highly complex negotiations" towards a global warming treaty.[51] A week before, a group of 57 Democrats in the U.S. House of Representative sent a letter to President Bush asking him to reconsider his position on non- CO2 reduction in power plants. And even Clinton has left Bush a nice welcome present. On April 9, 2001, a 150 page report, called *Climate Change Impact on the United States*, published by the Cambridge University Press, presented a concerned scenario of global warming effects on the USA[52] The new Administration will not welcome these results, but it will most likely face a more sensitized American public. This could again foster a more positive attitude towards climate action in Congress.

Still in the aftermath of Bonn conference, Bush announced some moderate programs and action on climate change. The U.S. government put major emphasis on voluntary measures by industries, a new long-term technological initiative, further climate research and again a new U.S. Climate Change Research Initiative to study areas of climate uncertainty and identify areas for investment. With these very moderate actions, Bush tried to please the strong domestic opponents of immediate action on GHG reduction measures as well as critics of the U.S. position regarding action at home.

---

51 See "Senate Budget Vote Rebuffs Bush on Global Warming," *Washington Post,* April 7, 2001.

52 The Assessment report was called for by a 1990 law, and was conducted under the U.S. Global Change Research Program in response to a request from the President's Science Advisor. It is available at http://www.gcrio.org/NationalAssessment. See also Charles Arthur, "Climate Time-bomb Ready to Explode Under Bush," *UK Independent*, April 6, 2001.

During this time, it seemed justifiable to be carefully optimistic about a very moderate, but still slowly moving U.S. position towards more climate protection, especially considering the changing situation in Congress in favor of more action on GHG reduction. The September 11, 2001 terrorist attacks caused a major fall back,[53] as the climate change debate in the U.S. government and in public diminished in priority. Hardly anyone was interested in the results of COP 7 in Marrakech, or even knew that this conference had taken place. It left environmental groups at a loss. Opinion polls prior to September 11 showed a great public dissatisfaction with Bush, his energy policy, his plans of drilling in Alaskan wildlife refuge and his position towards the Kyoto Protocol. After the attacks, the situation changed completely as Bush's popularity rose over 80%, while the public support for environmental topics dropped.

Nevertheless, some time after September 11, politics are slowly returning to normal and again some shifting in U.S. climate change policies has become visible. Like prior to the Bonn conference (COP 6-2), numerous voices have arisen from Congress again, demanding a U.S. response to climate change negotiations, among them John McCain (R-AZ), Joseph Liebermann (D-CT) and James Jeffords (Indep.-VT). Jeffords, the head of Senate Environment and Public works Committee, has been promoting a "four-pollutant" bill that would set limits on industrial emissions of CO2, mercury, sulfur dioxide, and nitrogen oxides.

What conclusion can be drawn from this? The basis for climate change action in the USA is not as bad as perceived, despite all the critics from outside, but it follows specific rules, which are set by domestic factors. The way for a successful cooperation with the USA on climate change is not confrontation, but accepting things as they are. The political system and the habits to deal with problems are very specific characteristics of each society and state. As shown, the American system differs widely in its perceptions of policy rules, appropriate policies and measures, in particular from the European style.[54] One can heavily criticize the American way of problem solving or, depending on the perspective, "not-solving," but it will not help the continuation of the climate change negotiation train. Considering the limited progress of the last ten years, it is time to think over the old strategy. Not only the USA has not signed and is not willing to sign the Protocol in the near future. Other important Annex I countries are still very reluctant to do so. One could even think that nothing better could have happened than

53 See Miranda A. Scheurs, "A View from the United States: COP 7 and the Kyoto Protocol, " in *German Foreign Policy in Dialogue, Newsletter* 2, no. 6 (4th Quarter 2001) (http://www.deutsche-aussenpolitik.de).

54 A very illustrating picture on the differences between the US and European Systems is provided by *The Guardian*, see "The Great Divide," *The Guardian*, April 4, 2001, www.guardianunlimited.co.uk/globalwarming/story/0,7369,463260,00.html.

Bush's announcement. During the whole climate negotiations so far, the partners have been very keen to keep the U.S. on the train. They made numerous concessions and very often the two sides were only able to meet on the lowest common denominator. The EU could then blame the U.S. for its obduracy and ignorance concerning its own responsibility and the need to develop policy. The U.S. could counter by arguing unfairness. This led to the political gridlock in The Hague. The announcement of the French President Chirac that the Kyoto Protocol would represent the first component of an "authentic global governance" was intended as an insult to the U.S. and the final step towards the deathblow of the Protocol for the U.S. Administration and Congress.[55]

With the Administration's rejection of the Protocol, the European community and its allies were under pressure. They have proven, however, that they are really willing to take the next steps and fulfill their commitment. The announcement of the EU to proceed, even without the U.S. participation, was important. It will put pressure on the U.S. Administration and in the long run even have a positive incentive on the U.S. policy. The Bush Administration has already promised to present a new, fairer strategy on climate change. For the road ahead, leadership by the EU will be urgently needed. But to keep the U.S. involved, although it might not be under the frame of the Kyoto Protocol, demands more understanding of the U.S. specific situation. It must allow more use of flexibility. An introduction of pilot projects for more bi- and multilateral action programs on specific climate change policies and measures, Joint Implementation and Clean Development Mechanisms, as well as a stronger support of win-win action and private-public partnership are important strategies. This does not imply it is time to bury the Kyoto Protocol, but it does demand a more transparent and innovative process of cooperation and learning under its frame.[56]

America, as every other state in the world, lives under a growing economic and political interdependency. Sooner or later, the interest of participating in the emerging new world market on green technology, which is already developing with an intense dynamic, will also influence the U.S. to change its position on climate change. The current rejection of economic and energy market reform can only delay the progress. Even without climate change, a new restructured energy system and labor market reforms will be forced upon the U.S. by the growing energy demand and diminishing resources domestically and worldwide. The U.S. government is wasting time by delaying urgent action and is wasting political credibility. If it would react early enough, the U.S. would be able to use the remaining time for undertak-

---

55 See Christopher C. Horner, "Kyoto Cools," *Washington Times*, April 5, 2001.

56 Ott offers some interesting ideas of new policy strategies for the follow-up Kyoto process even in case the U.S. government is not changing its position. See Ott, "Climate Change", 13-16.

ing economically smooth well composed actions to adapt on climate change, without too heavy a burden for the American society. Washington is jeopardizing carelessly its possibility of international leadership in climate negotiations. It has forgotten, that participation is the best guarantee to design political decisions and movements; opting out instead means the loss of design and important influence.

Selected Reading List

Anderson, Terry L. (Ed.): The Greening of U.S. Foreign Policy. The Hoover Institution on War, Revolution and Peace. Stanford/Ca.: Hoover Institution Press, 2000.

Barber, Benjamin R.: Jihad vs. McWorld. How Globalism and Tribalism Are Reshaping the World. New York/N.Y.: Ballantine Books, 1996.

Bergsten, C. Fred: The Primacy of Economics. In: Foreign Policy (Washington/D.C.), (Summer 1992) 87, S. 3-24.

Bergsten, C. Fred; Henning, C. Randall: Global Economic Leadership and the Group of Seven. Washington/D.C.: Institute for International Economics, 1996.

Berman, William C.: From the Center to the Edge. The Politics and Policies of Clinton Presidency. Lanham/Md.: Rowman and Littlefield, 2001.

Bierling, Stephan G.: Wirtschaftshilfe für Moskau. Motive und Strategien der Bundesrepublik Deutschland und der USA von 1990 bis 1996. Paderborn: Schöningh, 1998.

Bierling, Stephan G.: Amerika führt - Europa folgt? Eine Beziehung sucht ihren Zweck. In: Internationale Politik (Bonn), 53 (Februar 1998) 2, S. 9-18.

Bierling, Stephan G.: Partner oder Kontrahenten? Präsident und Kongreß im außenpolitischen Entscheidungsprozeß der USA (1974-1988). Frankfurt/ Basel/ New York: Lang, 1992.

Boren, David L. (Ed.): Preparing America's Foreign Policy for the 21st Century. Norman/Okla.: Univ. of Oklahoma Press, 1999.

Brzezinski, Zbigniew: Die einzige Weltmacht: Amerikas Strategie der Vorherrschaft. Frankfurt/Main: Fischer, 1999.

Brzezinski, Zbigniew: The Grand Chessboard. American Primacy and Its Geostrategic Imperatives. New York/N.Y.: Basic Books, 1997.

Burwell, Frances G.; Daalder, Ivo H. (Eds.):The United States and Europe in the Global Arena. New York/N.Y.: St. Martin's Press, 1999.

Campbell, Colin (Ed.): The Clinton Legacy. New York/N.Y.: Chatham House Publ., 2000.

Calleo, David P.: The United States and the Great Powers. In: World Policy Journal (New York/N.Y.), 16 (Fall 1999) 3, S. 11-19.

Calleo, David P.: Can the United States Afford the New World Order? In: SAIS Review (Washington/D.C.), 12 (Summer-Fall 1992) 2, S. 23-33.

Cox, Michael (Ed.): American Democracy Promotion. Impulses, Strategies, and Impacts. Oxford: Oxford Univ. Press, 2000.

Crabb, Cecil V. (jr.); Antizzo, Glenn J.; Sarieddine, Leila E.: Congress and the Foreign Policy Process. Modes of Legislative Behavior. Baton Rouge/La.: Lousiana State Univ. Press, 2000.

Czempiel, Ernst Otto: Die Versuchung der USA. In: Internationale Politik und Gesellschaft (Bonn), (1997) 2, S. 141-154.

Daalder, Ivo H.: Are the United States and Europe Heading for Divorce? In. International Affairs (London), 77 (July 2001) 3, S. 553-567.

Daalder, Ivo H.; Goldgeier, James M.; Lindsay, James M.: Deploying NMD Not Whether, But How. In: Survival (Oxford), 42 (Spring 2000) 1, S. 6-28.

Dembinski, Matthias; Gerke, Kinka (Hrsg.): Cooperation or Conflict? Transatlantic Relations in Transition. Hessische Stiftung Friedens- und Konfliktforschung. Frankfurt/Main: Campus, 1998.

Dembinski, Matthias; Rudolf, Peter; Wilzewski, Jürgen (Hrsg.): Amerikanische Weltpolitik nach dem Ost-West-Konflikt. Stiftung Wissenschaft und Politik. Baden-Baden: Nomos, 1994.

Dittgen, Herbert: Amerikanische Demokratie und Weltpolitik. Aussenpolitik in den Vereinigten Staaten, Paderborn: Schöningh, 1998.

Dizard, Wilson P. (jr.): Digital Diplomacy. U.S. Foreign Policy in the Information Age. Westport/Connecticut.: Praeger, 2001.

Dobson, Alan P.; Marsh, Steve: US Foreign Policy Since 1945. London: Routledge, 2001.

Foyle, Douglas C.: Counting the Public in: Presidents, Public Opinion, and Foreign Policy. New York/N.Y.: Columbia Univ. Press, 1999.

Haass, Richard N. (Ed.): Transatlantic Tensions. The United States, Europe, and Problem Countries. Washington/D.C.: Brookings Institution Press, 1999.

Hacke, Christian: Zur Weltmacht verdammt. Die amerikanische Außenpolitik von Kennedy bis Clinton. Berlin: Propyläen, 1997.

Haftendorn, Helga: Der gütige Hegemon und die unsichere Mittelmacht. Deutsch-amerikanische Beziehungen im Wandel. In: Aus Politik und Zeitgeschichte (Bonn), (16. Juli 1999) B29-30, S. 3-11.

Halberstam, David: War in a Time of Peace. Bush, Clinton, and the Generals. New York/N.Y.: Scribner, 2001.

Hogan, Michael J. (Ed.): The Ambiguous Legacy. U.S. Foreign Relations in the "American century". Cambridge: Cambridge Univ. Press, 1999.

Hönicke, Michaela: Die verunsicherte Supermacht. Amerikanischer Führungsanspruch zwischen Alleingängen und Kooperation. In: Jahrbuch internationale Politik 1999-2000. / Forschungsinstitut der Deutschen Gesellschaft für Auswärtige Politik. München: Oldenbourg, 2001.

Hubel, Helmut; Kaim, Markus; Lembcke, Oliver (Hrsg.): Pax Americana im Nahen Osten. Eine Studie zur Transformation regionaler Ordnungen. Baden-Baden: Nomos, 2000.

Hunt, Michael H.: American Decline and the Great Debate. A Historical Perspective. In: SAIS Review (Washington/D.C.), 10 (Summer-Fall 1990) 2, S. 27-40.

Huntington, Samuel P.: The Clash of Civilization and the Remaking of the World Order. New York/N.Y.: Simon and Schuster, 1996.

Huntington, Samuel P.: Der Kampf der Kulturen. The Clash of Civilizations; Die Neugestaltung der Weltpolitik im 21. Jahrhundert. (Orig.: The Clash of Civilizations and the Remaking of World Order.). Aus dem Amerikanischen von Holger Fliessbach. 6. Aufl. München: Europa, 1997.

Hutchings, Robert L. (Ed.): At the End of the American Century. Americas's Role in the Post-Cold War World. Washington/D.C.: Woodrow Wilson Center Press, 1998.

Janes, Jackson: Bush und die Europäer. Ein schwieriges Kennenlernen. In: Internationale Politik (Bielefeld), 56 (Juni 2001) 6, S. 10-18.

Johnston, Douglas; Brzezinski, Zbigniew; Hamilton, Lee; Lugar, Richard (Eds.): Foreign policy into the 21st Century. The U.S. Leadership Challenge. Center for Strategic and International Studies. Washington/D.C.: CSIS, 1996.

Kagan, Robert (Ed.): Present Dangers. Crisis and Opportunity in American Foreign and Defense Policy. San Francisco/Ca.: Encounter Books, 2000.

Kagan, Robert: Power and Weakness, in: Policy Review, no. 113, June & July 2002 (http://www.policyreview.org/JUN02/kagan.html).

Kaiser, Karl: Reforming NATO. In: Foreign Policy (Washington/ D.C.), (Summer 1996) 103, S. 128-143.

Kaiser, Karl: Die deutsch- amerikanischen Sicherheitsbeziehungen in Europa nach dem Kalten Krieg. In: Europa- Archiv (Bonn), 47 (10.Januar 1992), 1, S. 7-17.

Kaiser, Karl: Patterns of Partnership. Security Relations: Germany. In: From Occupation to Cooperation. The United States and United Germany in a Changing World Order. Eds: Muller, Steven; Schweigler, Gebhard. New York: Norton, 1992.

Kennedy, Paul: The Rise and Fall of the Great Powers. Economic Change and Military Conflict from 1500 to 2000. New York/N.Y.: Random House, 1987.

Keohane, Robert O. (Ed.): After the Cold War. International Institutions and State Strategies in Europe, 1989-1991. Written under the Auspices of the Center for International Affairs, Harvard University. Cambridge/Mass.: Harvard University Press, 1993.

Kissinger, Henry Alfred: Does America Need a Foreign Policy? Toward a Diplomacy for the 21st Century. New York/N.Y.: Simon and Schuster, 2001.

Krauthammer, Charles: The Unipolar Moment. In: Foreign Affairs (New York/N.Y.), 70 (1991) 1, S. 23-33.

Krugman, Paul R.: The Age of Diminished Expectations. U.S. Economic Policy in the 1990s. Cambridge/Massachusetts: MIT Press, 1990.

Kull, Steven; Destler, I. M.: Misreading the Public. The Myth of a New Isolationism. Washington/D.C.: Brookings Institution, 1999.

Kupchan, Charles A.: After Pax Americana. Benign Power, Regional Integration, and the Sources of a Stable Multipolarity. In: International Security (Cambridge/Mass.), 23 (Fall 1998) 2, S. 40-79.

Lieber, Robert J. (Ed.): Eagle Rules? Foreign Policy and American Primacy in the Twenty-First Century. Publ. in coop. with the Woodrow Wilson International Center for Scholars. Upper Saddle River/N.J.: Prentice Hall, 2002.

Lindsay, James M.: Looking for Leadership. Domestic Politics and Foreign Policy. In: The Brookings Review (Washington/D.C.), 18 (Winter 2000) 1, S. 40-43.

Luttwak, Edward N.: The Endangered American Dream. How to Stop the United States from Becoming a Third World Country and How to Win the Geo-Economic Struggle for Industrial Supremacy. New York/N.Y: Simon and Schuster, 1993.

MacEvoy-Levy, Siobhan: American Exceptionalism and US Foreign Policy. Public Diplomacy at the End of the Cold War. Houndmills: Palgrave, 2001.

McArdle Kelleher, Catherine: Foreign Policy Culture in the United States and Europe. In: The Transatlantic Link. Ed.: Bo Huldt . Stockholm: Swedish National Defense College, 2001, S. 67-78.

May, Bernhard: Demokratisierung statt globaler Eindämmung. Perspektiven der amerikanischen Politik gegenüber der Dritten Welt. In: Amerikanische Weltpolitik nach dem Ost-West-Konflikt. Matthias Dembinski; Peter Rudolf ... (Hrsg.). Baden-Baden: Nomos Verlagsgesellschaft, 1994. - (Internationale Politik und Sicherheit; Bd. 42), S. 243-263 (Kap.9).

May, Bernhard: Globalisation, Democracy and Trade Policy. In: The World Trade Organization Millennium Round: Freer Trade in the Twenty-First Century. Ed. by Klaus Günter Deutsch. London: Routledge, 2001., S. 72-81.

May, Bernhard: New Challenges for Transatlantic Economic Relations. In: The New Transatlantic Agenda. Ed. by Hall Gardner. Aldershot: Ashgate, 2001. (The G8 and Global Governance Series), S. 173-190.

Mead, Walter Russell: The American Foreign Policy Legacy. In: Foreign Affairs (New York/N.Y.), 81 (January-February 2002) 1, S. 163-176.

Mead, Walter Russell:Special Providence. American Foreign Policy and How It Changed the World. New York/N.Y.: Knopf, 2001.
Mead, Walter Russell: The Jacksonian Tradition and American Foreign Policy. In: The National Interest (Washington/D.C.), (Winter 1999-2000) 58, S. 5-29.
Mearsheimer, John J.: The Tragedy of Great Power Politics. New York/N.Y.: Norton, 2001.
Mearsheimer, John J.: The Future of the American Pacifier. In: Foreign Affairs (New York/N.Y.), 80 (September-October 2001) 5, S. 46-61.
Mearsheimer, John J.: Back to the Future. Instability in Europe after the Cold War. In: International Security (Cambridge/Mass.), 15 (Summer 1990) 1, S. 5-56.
Medick-Krakau, Monika (Hrsg.): Wandel in der amerikanischen Außenhandelspolitik. In: Außenpolitischer Wandel in theoretischer und vergleichender Perspektive: Die USA und die Bundesrepublik Deutschland. Baden-Baden: Nomos, 1999.
Miller, Steven E.: The End of Unilateralism or Unilateralism Redux? In: The Washington Quarterly (Washington/D.C.), 25 (Winter 2002) 1, S. 15-29.
Nau, Henry R.: At Home Abroad. Identity and Power in American Foreign Policy. Ithaca, N.Y.: Cornell Univ. Press, 2002 (A Century Foundation Book).
Nau, Henry R.: Why "The Rise and Fall of the Great Powers" Was Wrong. In: Review of International Studies (Cambridge), 27 (October 2001) 4, S. 579-592.
Nau, Henry R.: The Myth of America's Decline. Leading the World Economy into the 1990s. New York/N.Y. u.a.: Oxford University Press, 1990.
Nye, Joseph S. (jr.): The Paradox of American Power. Why the World's Only Superpower Can't Go It Alone. Oxford: Oxford Univ. Press, 2002.
Nye, Joseph S. (jr.): The American National Interest and Global Goods. In: International Affairs (London), 78 (April 2002) 2, S. 233-244.
Nye, Joseph S. (jr.): The US and Europe: Continental Drift? In: International Affairs (London), 76 (January 2000) 1, S. 51-59.
Nye, Joseph S. (jr.): American Strategy after Bipolarity. In: International Affairs (London), 66 (July 1990) 3, S. 513-521.
Nye, Joseph S. (jr.): Bound to Lead. The Changing Nature of American Power. - New York/N.Y.: Basic Books, 1990.
Patrick, Stewart (Ed.): Multilateralism and U.S. Foreign Policy. Ambivalent Engagement. Center on International Cooperation. Boulder/Colorado: Rienner, 2002.
Paulsen, Thomas: Economic Diplomacy. Die Ökonomisierung der amerikanischen Außenpolitik unter Präsident Clinton 1993-1996. Opladen: Leske und Budrich, 1999.
Rielly, John E.: Pragmatischer Internationalismus. Öffentliche Meinung und Außenpolitik in den USA. In: Internationale Politik (Bonn), 50 (März 1995) 3, S. 47-54.
Rielly, John E.: Zurückhaltendes Engagement. Amerikanische Positionen zur Außenpolitik. In: Internationale Politik (Bonn), 54 (April 1999) 4, S. 70-80.
Rielly, John (Ed.): American Public Opinion and U.S. Foreign Policy. Chicago/Ill.: Chicago Counsil on Foreign Relations, 1991,1995,1999.
Ripley, Randall B. (Ed.): U.S. Foreign Policy after the Cold War. Pittsburgh/Pa.: Univ. of Pittsburgh Press, 1997.
Rodman, Peter W.: Drifting Apart? Trends in U.S.-European Relations. Foreword by Robert Ellsworth. Washington/D.C.: The Nixon Center, 1999.
Rodman, Peter W.: Uneasy Giant. The Challenges to American Predominance. Washington/D.C.: The Nixon Center, 2000.
Roloff, Ralf: Europa, Amerika und Asien zwischen Globalisierung und Regionalisierung. Das interregionale Konzert und die ökonomische Dimension internationaler Politik, Paderborn: Schöningh, 2001.
Rosecrance, Richard N.: A New Concert of Powers. In: Foreign Affairs (New York/N.Y.), 71 (Spring 1992) 2, S. 64-82.

Rosecrance, Richard N.: The Rise of the Virtual State. In: Foreign Affairs (New York/N.Y.), 75 (July-August 1996) 4, S. 45-61.

Rudolf, Peter; Wilzewski, Jürgen (Hrsg.):Weltmacht ohne Gegner. Amerikanische Außenpolitik zu Beginn des 21. Jahrhunderts. Stiftung Wissenschaft und Politik. Baden-Baden: Nomos, 2000.

Ryan, David: US Foreign Policy in World History. London: Routledge, 2000.

Schild, Georg: Die bedrohte Supermacht. Amerikanische Aussen- und Sicherheitspolitik vom Ende des Kalten Krieges bis zur Proklamierung der "Achse des Bösen", Berliner Schriften zur Internationalen Politik, Forschungsinstitut der Deutschen Gesellschaft für Auswärtige Politik e.V., Opladen: Leske + Budrich, 2002.

Schweigler, Gebhard L.: Globalisierung und Außenpolitik. Identität und Interdependenz. In: Weltmacht ohne Gegner: Amerikanische Außenpolitik zu Beginn des 21. Jahrhunderts. Peter Rudolf; Jürgen Wilzewski (Hrsg.). Baden-Baden: Nomos, 2000, S. 21-37.

Schweigler, Gebhard L.: "America First"? Die öffentliche Meinung und die amerikanische Außenpolitik. In: Amerikanische Weltpolitik nach dem Ost-West-Konflikt. Matthias Dembinski; Peter Rudolf u.a. (Hrsg.). Baden-Baden: Nomos, 1994, S. 23-67.

Sloan, Stanley; Locke, Mary; Yost, Casimir A.: The Foreign Policy Struggle. Congress and the President in the 1990s and Beyond. Washington/D.C.: Institute for the Study of Diplomacy, 2000.

Stokes, Bruce (Ed.): Future Vision for U.S. Trade Policy. Sponsored by the Counsil on Foreign Relations. New York/N.Y.,1998.

Waltz, Kenneth Neal: Globalization and American Power. In: The National Interest (Shrub Oak/N.Y.), (Spring 2000) 59, S. 46-56.

Wilzewski, Jürgen: Demokratie und Außenpolitik. Friktionen zwischen Präsident und Kongreß. In: Weltmacht ohne Gegner: Amerikanische Außenpolitik zu Beginn des 21. Jahrhunderts. Peter Rudolf; Jürgen Wilzewski (Hrsg.). Baden-Baden: Nomos, 2000 S. 38-61.

Wittkopf, Eugene R. (Ed.): The Domestic Sources of American Foreign Policy. Insights and Evidence. 3rd ed. Lanham/Md.: Rowman and Littlefield, 1999.

Wittkopf, Eugene R. (Ed.):The Future of American Foreign Policy. 2nd ed. New York/N.Y.: St. Martin's Press, 1994.